For Poincy and John,
companions in the long
journey through the parish
of Academe

Alec

16 January 1978.

JANSENISM IN SEVENTEENTH-CENTURY FRANCE

Voices from the Wilderness

Jansenism in Seventeenth-Century France

Voices from the Wilderness

Alexander Sedgwick

Charlottesville
University Press of Virginia

THE UNIVERSITY PRESS OF VIRGINIA
Copyright © 1977 by the Rector and Visitors
of the University of Virginia

First published 1977

Library of Congress Cataloging in Publication Data

Sedgwick, Alexander, 1930–
    Jansenism in seventeenth-century France.

    Bibliography: p.
    Includes index.
    1. Jansenists.   I. Title
BX4722.S43   274.4   77-2812
ISBN 0-8139-0702-0

Printed in the United States of America

To Sarah Cabot Sedgwick

Contents

Preface

Many interpretations of French Jansenism have appeared since the seventeenth century. Often contradictory, these interpretations in many instances reflect the prejudices and ideals of particular eras. They make any attempt to define the movement more difficult. In the eighteenth century, Voltaire, Diderot, and other philosophes regarded Jansenism as antithetical to the secular principles of the Enlightenment. They deplored the misanthropic focus of the Jansenists and ridiculed their inconsequential theological speculations.[1] After the French Revolution, however, conservative writers such as Joseph de Maistre maintained that the rebellious attitude of the Jansenists toward the authority of Church and state contributed substantially to the Enlightenment and the destruction of the old regime.[2] On the other hand, liberal writers— including the abbé Grégoire, Victor Cousin, and Ernest Renan— admired these same Jansenists for their heroic resistance to the oppressive policies of Louis XIV.[3]

This admiration for the valiant behavior of the Jansenists was conditioned in part by the Romantic fascination with the hero who, true to himself, stands his ground against overwhelming odds and with little or no chance of success. A work reflecting the influence of Romanticism is Sainte-Beuve's monumental *Port-Royal*, published between 1840 and 1859. "The moral austerity" of the Port-royalists appealed to Sainte-Beuve, who believed that quality to be lacking in his own time. He extolled "the Christian heroism of that race of Port Royal, that singular virtue, which was no doubt an anachronism, but which tended to fortify the soul, and which the French character is incapable of sustaining."[4] In the isolation of the valley of the Chevreuse, the nuns and *solitaires* participated in the "far-off springtime of mysticity and of grace." For Sainte-Beuve, the religion of Port Royal, "this idyllic and pastoral christianity,"[5] was almost pantheistic, in that the natural and the spiritual were joined together in the wilderness. But this religious spirit, molded in solitude and introspection, was responsible for the perseverence that sustained its adherents. Port Royal's mission, according to Sainte-Beuve, was to rekindle faith (after a century of incredulity) by its exemplary piety, in order to prevent Christendom from being overwhelmed by the rising tide of secularism. The Jansenists seemed almost to foresee the Enlightenment, with its emphasis on human, rather than divine, capabilities, and they warned their contemporaries that the heavenly city was in danger, but ironically, instead of strengthening its foundations, Bishop Jansen and his supporters unwittingly opened the gates of the city to the philosophes. The indifference to Christian ideals that was characteristic of the Enlightenment was caused, at least in part, by the frightening predestinarian doctrine and the forbidding ethics associated with Jansenism. Sainte-Beuve's *Port-Royal* is a representative work of French Romanticism in its emphasis on the heroic, in its identification of piety with rustic simplicity, in its rejection of the facile optimism that many regarded as the chief characteristic of the Enlightenment, and in its respect for Christian ethics. More than this, however, the work's significance lies in the fact that it presented for the first time a comprehensive account of the history of Port Royal and Jansenism.

Another prominent literary historian, Ferdinand Brunetière, writing at the turn of the century, agreed with Sainte-Beuve that Jansenism resisted those currents of seventeenth-century thought that culminated in the Enlightenment. In an essay entitled "Jansénistes et Cartésiens," which appeared in 1911, Brunetière asserted that Christian idealism was undermined on the one hand by libertinism, which attempted to weaken religious controls over human behavior, and on the other hand by Cartesian philosophy, which boasted the omnipotence of reason at the expense of faith. Whereas Sainte-Beuve had contended that Jansenism facilitated secularism because of its austere theology, Brunetière maintained that the Jansenists, with their strict penitential ethic and their distrust of reason, were able to ward off, at least for a while, the rising tide of secularism by means of inspirational writings such as Saint-Cyran's published correspondence and Pascal's *Provincial Letters*. The wanton destruction of Port Royal in 1711 had a detrimental effect on French culture. Cartesianism and libertinism, hitherto stifled by the severe Jansenist ethic, revived as a result of Louis XIV's tyrannical action. The Enlightenment emerged phoenix-like from the ruins of Port Royal, and French culture as a whole was dangerously corrupted by the facile optimism of the philosophes and by their naive faith in the powers of reason and science. Like so many intellectuals of his generation who were in revolt against the prevailing ethos of positivism, Brunetière deplored the continuing influence of the Enlightenment, the source of positivism.[6]

Sainte-Beuve and Brunetière believed that Jansenism was, on the whole, a constructive element in seventeenth-century culture; the historian Henri Brémond emphasized its destructive elements, however. A modernist, Brémond hoped that the Church would be able to accommodate itself to the twentieth century by recovering the mystical vitality and humanistic commitment that it had lost three hundred years earlier. In his massive *Histoire littéraire du sentiment religieux en France*, published in twelve volumes between 1915 and 1932, Brémond argued that one of the great achievements of the Counter Reformation had been the blending of Catholic doctrine with Renaissance humanism. Saint François de Sales and other Christian humanists emphasized the beauty of man's nature and the sanctity of his work. Their religious belief was both optimistic in terms of man's potential for good and compassionate in terms of his weaknesses. From their point of view, Christian idealism ought to encourage rather than to agitate the human spirit. By refusing to repudiate the homocentric focus of the Renaissance, the Christian humanists hoped that the Church would benefit from the human energies that were shaping the modern world. The Counter Reformation also produced a strong mystical current. The spirituality of Cardinal Bérulle, among others, was conditioned to some extent by a darker view of human nature. By means of prayer, the Christian was to abandon himself to the will of Christ. But prayerful contemplation, the essence of Berullian mysticism, was a joyful experience culminating in a triumphant union of man and God. What made the Counter Reformation in France so dynamic, in Brémond's opinion, was the dual impulse of humanism, with its positive view of man's capabilities, and of mysticism, with its emphasis on divine inspiration. The tragic achievement of Jansenism was that it effectively counteracted both. The Jansenists made original sin the focal point of Christian belief. By stressing the difficulty of salvation, they sowed the seeds of despair rather than of hope in the hearts and minds of the faithful. While Brémond admitted that there were mystical elements in Jansenist spirituality, he insisted that it was ultimately perverted by the refusal of Jansen and his disciples to look beyond man's corrupt nature to Christ's redemptive powers. Instead of looking within themselves to find God, the Jansenists found only themselves. Ironically, while appearing to repudiate self-interest in order to serve God's purpose, the Jansenists, in effect, asserted the interests of self to the exclusion of God. This anarchic egotism was destructive not only to mysticism but to belief as well. Thus did Jansenism sap the energy and progressive spirit of the Counter Reformation.[7]

An influential twentieth-century champion of Jansenism was Augustin Gazier, a professor of philosophy at the Sorbonne whose family had deep Jansenist roots. Gazier wrote a number of books and articles on Jansenism, including his *Histoire générale du mouvement janséniste*, published in 1923. He contended that Jansenism was a heresy invented by the Jesuits to mask their own insidious efforts to cripple the Church. (So strong indeed was Gazier's own aversion to the Jesuits that he refused them admission to the manuscript collection housed at the Bibliothèque de la Société de Port-Royal, of which he was the custodian.) In his opinion, the theology of the so-called Jansenists was entirely orthodox. Bishop Jansen and his followers had done their best to resist the dangerous innovations of the Jesuits, who tried to weaken penitential discipline, and of the papacy, which sought to impose an illegal authority over the Church as a whole.[8]

In our own time, a Marxist interpretation of Jansenism has emerged to complement the liberal and conservative interpretations that appeared during the nineteenth century. The proponent of this interpretation was Lucien Goldmann, who argued that the Jansenists adopted a tragic vision embodying a pessimistic view of human nature, a rejection of the world, and a conception of a "hidden God"—a God not readily accessible.[9] Such a perspective reflected the declining fortunes of a prominent social group—the nobility of the robe—which contained a significant number of Jansenist writers. This group, whose wealth and prestige depended on the monarchy, found in the middle of the seventeenth century that its wealth was adversely affected by a fluctuating economy and that the loss of its political influence was the result of the crown's increasing reliance on other officials. Its worldly position threatened, the nobility of the robe inclined toward an unworldly, even an antiworldly, ethos that conditioned the attitude the Jansenists were to take toward earthly authority in the era of the Fronde. Unlike liberal and Romantic interpreters of Jansenism, who regarded the movement as a manifestation of heroic individualism, Goldmann viewed it as a form of social protest.

Since the Second World War, a number of other works pertaining to Jansenism have appeared in addition to those of Goldmann. Critical editions of the writings of leading Jansenists such as the abbé de Saint-Cyran, Barcos, Le Maistre de Sacy, and Pascal have also been published. Jean Orcibal, Louis Cognet, and Bruno Neveu, the most distinguished scholars of seventeenth-century Jansenism today, have not as yet attempted extensive histories of the movement as a whole, but have devoted their energies to biographical works as well as to studies of certain aspects of Jansenism. These historians stress the psychological, spiritual, and political complexity of the movement, which makes it difficult to define, and they insist on the differences rather than the similarities within Jansenist thought. The spirituality of Saint-Cyran, for example, ought not to be confused with the Gallicanism of Pasquier Quesnel. Orcibal's extensive work on Saint-Cyran has shown that the abbé was the spiritual heir of Cardinal Bérulle and that early Jansenism was a part of, rather than a perversion of, the spirituality of the Counter Reformation. Saint-Cyran's desire to revive the penitential discipline of the early Church ran afoul of the political exigencies of Cardinal Richelieu. Contrary to Brémond, Orcibal and Cognet have stressed the intense piety of Saint-Cyran and Angélique Arnauld, both of whom, they maintain, were magnificent examples of French religious sentiment.

My own study of Jansenism was undertaken, in part, because there are no recent works on the subject in English that take into account the great mass of materials relating to the movement that have appeared in the last thirty years. More importantly, it was begun in order to satisfy my own curiosity about those aspects of Jansenism that particularly antagonized the authorities of Church and state. Were the Jansenists the innocent victims of the despotic policies of the French government and of the papacy, as the abbé Grégoire, Augustin Gazier, and Paule Jansen would have us believe? Or were there characteristics inherent in Jansenism that appeared to these authorities as a genuine threat to the social order. Like others before me who have written on the subject, I was interested in determining the degree to which Jansenist attitudes toward authority resembled those of the philosophes a century later. In order to answer these questions, I have studied the writings of the most influential Jansenists—including Saint-Cyran, Antoine Arnauld, Nicole, Pascal, Quesnel, and Duguet—as well as the memoirs and correspondence of the nuns of Port Royal. I have taken into consideration not only their religious beliefs but their philosophical views and political opinions as well. This research has convinced me that the Jansenists' emphasis on the spiritual and intellectual integrity of the individual, their rejection of worldly values, and their willingness to suffer persecution in behalf of the truth as they understood it brought them inevitably into conflict with the absolutist pretentions of crown and papacy. Their preoccupation with the nature and limitations of authority caused the Jansenists to adopt a rebellious attitude of a unique sort, which became apparent during the era of the Fronde in the middle of the century. Furthermore, their ideas about the structure of the Church, as well as about the rights and responsibilities of clergy and laity, ran counter to the dominant trends in Church and state. Finally, the political opinions and personal associations of the Jansenists were not favorably regarded by influential political and ecclesiastical officials.

As Orcibal and Cognet have suggested, there were differences of opinion and attitudes among the Jansenists. Some believed in the need to defend their beliefs publicly, while others were persuaded that one must suffer in silence. Some were drawn to Cartesian philosophy, others toward Pyrrhonism. The opinions of some with respect to the structure of the Church were more radical than those of others. Nevertheless, there are certain common characteristics that enable the historian to speak of "Jansenist thought" in the same way that historians have always spoken of "Enlightenment thought." The religious ideals expressed in the writings of the most influential Jansenists—the abbé de Saint-Cyran (in 1643), Pascal and Nicole (in 1656), Antoine Arnauld (in 1679), and Quesnel and Duguet (in 1713)—reflect certain common concerns: a profound commitment to the doctrine of efficacious grace and to a rigorous penitential ethic; a respect for the integrity of the individual Christian, both priest and layman; and finally a conviction that politics ought to serve the interests of the Church.

The common characteristics inherent in Jansenist thought also reflect character traits and experiences shared by many Jansenists. Their personalities, to be sure, were different. Antoine Arnauld and Pascal were more gregarious and less austere than Saint-Cyran, Singlin, and Barcos. Nicole found disputation distasteful, whereas Arnauld and Le Roy found it exhilerating. These differences affected the ways in which Jansenists defended their beliefs. Yet there were striking similarities among Jansenists, in terms of their social status and their native ability. Saint-Cyran, the Arnaulds, and Pascal were members of prominent families with social connections that greatly facilitated successful careers. Highly intelligent, articulate, well-educated, and extremely ambitious, these persons seemed destined to achieve distinguished positions of one sort or another. Nevertheless, they eventually espoused a form of religious belief that repudiated worldly honors. Their writings, including Saint-Cyran's letters from prison and Pascal's *Pensées*, bear witness to a continuous struggle within themselves between their spirituality on the one hand and their worldly ambitions on the other. Thus, when Jansenists insisted that even the genuinely repentant sinner was in constant danger of falling from grace, they spoke from personal experience as well as from conviction.

This study is primarily concerned with those Jansenists who were associated in one way or another with Port Royal, the focal point of the movement. I have therefore used the terms "Jansenist" and "Port-royalist" interchangeably. Saint-Cyran was the spiritual director of the convent even during his imprisonment. His protégé, Antoine Arnauld, youngest brother of its reforming abbess Angélique, maintained close ties with Port Royal throughout his life, as did Nicole and Pascal. Quesnel and' Duguet, though less closely identified with the convent, were nonetheless protégés of Arnauld and were the direct spiritual descendants of Saint-Cyran, two generations removed. Many of the most important works associated with Jansenism were written in or around Port-Royal-des-Champs, situated in the wilderness not ten miles from Versailles—where the Sun King was to immortalize his reign in the pomp and splendor of the chateau and its gardens, and which was the antithesis of every value cherished by the Jansenists.

This study would not have been possible without a six-month leave of absence given to me by the University of Virginia in 1967, and a year's leave in 1970–71. This time away from my teaching obligations enabled me to do essential research in France and to write a part of the book. A grant-in-aid from the American Council of Learned Societies in 1967, a grant-in-aid from the American Philosophical Society in 1971, and summer fellowships awarded by the University of Virginia in 1965, 1966, 1968, 1969, and 1971 provided me with indispensable financial support to complete the project. I am indeed grateful to all these institutitons.

I wish to express my appreciation to Richard Golden of Clemson University, Albert N. Hamscher of Kansas State University, Robert Isherwood of Vanderbilt University, H. C. Erik Midelfort of the University of Virginia, and J. H. M. Salmon of Bryn Mawr College, all of whom took time out from busy schedules to read earlier drafts of the work. Their criticisms and suggestions for improvement were extremely helpful to me, as were those of Eleanor P. Abbot and of my wife, Charlene M. Sedgwick. I am also indebted to René Pintard and Hubert Carrier of the University of Paris, who read a portion of the work and who provided me with useful information. Others who provided me with information and suggestions to whom I am also grateful are the late Stanley Loomis and Harry Paul of the University of Florida. I want to take this opportunity to thank the many librarians in France and in this country, particularly at the Houghton Library of Harvard University and at the Alderman Library of the University of Virginia, whose efforts facilitated my research. I could not have done without the forty volumes of Antoine Arnauld's collected works obtained for me by the Alderman Library or without the kindness shown to me by M. André Gazier, who introduced me to the important Jansenist collection housed in the Bibliothèque de la Société de Port-Royal in Paris. I also wish to thank Ella Wood and Lottie McCauley, who spent a good part of three summers typing various drafts of my manuscript, and the Committee on Research of the University of Virginia for financial assistance in the preparation of the manuscript.

Alexander Sedgwick

Stockbridge, Mass.
June 1976

JANSENISM IN SEVENTEENTH-CENTURY FRANCE

Voices from the Wilderness

I. *Introduction*

The roots of the Jansenist movement are to be found in the Counter Reformation, or, as some historians prefer to call it, the Catholic Reformation. Begun in the sixteenth century, the Counter Reformation affected both ecclesiastical and political institutions and generated a revived piety and spirituality throughout Catholic Europe. Its high-water mark was the Council of Trent (1545–63), at which Catholic dignitaries from all over Europe attempted to redefine the doctrine of the Church and to establish principles relating to institutional reform as well. The Catholic reform movement, however, did not significantly affect France until the beginning of the seventeenth century. Protestantism had attracted adherents from all classes of society in that kingdom during the previous century, but because the crown, together with a majority of its subjects, remained loyal to Catholicism, a violent civil war (the Wars of Religion, 1562–95) broke out, sapping the religious and political energies of the country. Churches and monasteries were destroyed, priests and monks vanished, and Catholic communities in many parts of France became vulnerable to Protestantism, superstition, or disillusionment. When Henry IV became king in 1588, there were bishops who had never visited their dioceses and priests who had never taken up residence in their parishes. Many prelates preferred the role of courtier or warrior to that of spiritual guide. There were Catholic parishes, particularly in the countryside, that were without vicars or were attended by ignorant, uneducated priests incapable of sustaining religious life. A significant element within the lower clergy did not know how to say the Mass, to baptize children, or to absolve sinners. Even in Paris, which was so loyal to the Church that Henry IV had difficulty gaining political control of the city, priests were discovered erecting altars to Beelzebub.[1]

Religious life began to revive in France during the reign of the first Bourbon king, Henry IV, who managed to restore some degree

of order and stability after the ravages of civil war. Old churches
and abbeys, including Port Royal in the valley of the Chevreuse,
were rebuilt, and new ones were constructed. Between 1600 and
1650 thirty convents were built in the archdiocese of Autun
alone.[2] Seminaries were established, and secular orders were organ-
ized to inspire parish priests with a greater sense of spiritual
mission. Old orders such as the Benedictines and Capuchins were
reformed, and new ones such as the Ursulines, the Oratory, and
the Daughters of Calvary were founded. However, the most influential order, both in France and throughout Catholic Europe, was
the Society of Jesus, which had founded colleges in all corners of
the kingdom and was responsible for the education of many noble
and bourgeois subjects of the crown. Jesuits were confessors of
prominent political figures, including the first three Bourbon kings,
and even Cardinal Richelieu recognized their usefulness as spiritual
directors, while at the same time deploring their political influence.
Because of the order's important role in the religious life of the
kingdom, Protestants, and some Catholics as well, looked upon
the Jesuits with a certain amount of suspicion and distrust, believing that they had too much political influence or that they were
instruments of papal policy, as opposed to French policy. Jesuit
colleges were the object of jealousy on the part of older educational institutions. The faculty of the Sorbonne and the Parlement
of Paris looked with disfavor on the College of Clermont, founded
in the capital city by the Society in 1564, and efforts were occasionally made to revoke its charter. In 1594, at the conclusion of
the Wars of Religion, the faculty of the Sorbonne moved to expel
the Jesuits from the university. In the same year the parlement,
together with other sovereign courts, issued decrees expelling the
society from the kingdom entirely, because of allegedly subversive
activities. Prominent in the proceedings against the Jesuits at the
Sorbonne and at the Palace of Justice was the lawyer Antoine
Arnauld, whose children were later to become deeply involved in
the Jansenist movement. Henry IV eventually permitted the order
to return to France in 1603 and took as his confessor the Jesuit,
Pierre Coton, who also served Louis XIII in the same capacity
until that king's death in 1626. The Society of Jesus flourished in
France during the seventeenth century, although it continued to

inspire envy, suspicion, and contempt within and outside of the Catholic community because of its prestige.

During the reigns of Henry IV and Louis XIII, religious orders founded hospitals and other charitable institutions; they also founded schools for boys and girls, in the hope that increased literacy would improve the quality of devotional life and would strengthen resistance to Protestantism. The great figures of the French Counter Reformation—Saint François de Sales, Saint Vincent de Paul, and Cardinal Bérulle—devoted much of their efforts to improving the quality of the priesthood. Requirements for admission were tightened, the number of seminaries was increased, and scholarships were established for the relief of candidates with insufficient income. The net result of these reforms, at least in Paris and the surrounding area, was a corps of priests who were better disciplined, better educated, and imbued with a greater commitment to serve the Church. Other manifestations of religious zeal in this period included the founding in 1630 of the Company of the Holy Sacrament to promote charitable works and to eradicate blasphemy and heresy. But even as it was improving the quality of religious life in France, the Counter Reformation encountered obstacles that were ultimately to prove detrimental to its effectiveness. Theological disputations prompted by religious zeal troubled public opinion and aroused the suspicions of ecclesiastical and political authorities, who feared that acrimonious debates over doctrinal issues might encourage heresy and undermine social order and stability. Furthermore, institutional reforms within the Church threatened vested interests, which in many instances were protected by the authorities of Church or state.[3]

A major problem for French Catholics was the continued existence of a prosperous and influential Protestant minority in the country. In his effort to restore peace to his kingdom, Henry IV had promulgated the Edict of Nantes (1598), by which the Huguenots were given certain rights and privileges enabling them to maintain their cult. This arrangement, however, was unacceptable to many statesmen and prelates—for political, as well as for religious, reasons. The existence of a Protestant "state within a state," some argued, threatened the security of France. The clergy, its commitment to the spiritual mission of the Church strengthened by the Counter Reformation, asserted that the Edict of Nantes fostered heresy, and influential members of the First Estate never lost an opportunity to urge its revocation. When Louis XIII and Richelieu waged war against the Huguenots in the 1620s in order to reduce Protestant military power, they were able to rely on substantial contributions from the Church. Clergymen. including Richelieu, unable to extirpate Protestantism by the sword, undertook to do so by the pen. Although the steady flow of religious polemics written by Catholics and Huguenots throughout the seventeenth century probably caused only a small number of conversions, the endless reassertions of tedious theological arguments contained in these treatises undoubtedly promoted skepticism and libertinage by the end of the century.

Catholics were troubled not only by the doctrinal differences that separated them from Protestants but also by the theological disagreements that existed among themselves. Some Catholics were influenced by the humanist currents of the Renaissance, which continued to affect French thought during the seventeenth century. Montaigne's disciples, whose opinions were conditioned by classical philosophy and by a growing awareness of non-Christian cultures, tended to view morality in natural terms, arguing that men shape their thought and belief through their experience, independent of any dogma. In 1641, La Mothe Le Vayer, an admirer of Montaigne, published a book entitled *De la vertu des payens*, in which he contended that nature provided the means by which men might lead virtuous lives regardless of whether they were Christian or not. La Mothe's critics, including the Jansenist Antoine Arnauld and the philosopher Descartes, retorted that such opinions minimized the necessity of becoming a Christian. If the forces of nature were capable of producing meritorious acts in men who had never heard the gospels preached, what need was there for revelation, and what was the point of sending missionaries throughout the world to instruct pagans in the teachings of Christ? La Mothe Le Vayer and other contemporary humanists including Gabriel Naudé and Guy Patin may well have been good Catholics, but to their critics their writings appeared to be dangerously unorthodox free thought.[4]

Although no Catholic writer of the seventeenth century

approved of libertinism, some Catholics were more favorably disposed towards man's natural capacity for good than were others. Saint François de Sales, inspired by the great Christian humanist Erasmus, wrote that "we have an inclination to love God above all things,"[5] as well as a natural power to know God and those things that please him. Socrates, Plato, Aristotle, Seneca, and Epictetus knew God, and their ethical precepts were of value to the Christian.[6] The Jesuits, whose theological opinions were influenced by humanism, encouraged in their pupils an interest in the culture of antiquity, and they were sympathetic to the writings of some of the philosophers of Greece and Rome. The favorable disposition toward man's natural ability to do good, combined with a benign attitude toward pagan culture on the part of some Catholics, left them vulnerable to the criticism by other Catholics that they encouraged free thought.[7]

While some Catholics may be described as having a comparatively optimistic view of human nature, others, influenced by Augustinian theology, were more pessimistic about man's natural inclinations. In his later years, Saint Augustine had vigorously attacked what he perceived to be the heretical convictions of Pelagius and his followers. Influenced by the ethical principles of Stoicism as well as of Christianity, the Pelagians emphasized the human potential for good, at the expense of original sin. Augustine, on the other hand, insisted that man's nature had been seriously impaired by original sin, for which reason man on his own had no potential for good. Only by means of God's healing grace was man able to achieve salvation. "For what ought to be more attractive to us sick men, than grace," wrote Augustine, "grace by which we are healed; for us lazy men, than grace, grace by which we are stirred up; for us men, longing to act, than grace, by which we are healed?"[8] Pelagius was excommunicated in 418 and his views declared heretical by the Church, but Pelagianism was never entirely destroyed. Semi-Pelagianism, a modified version of the heresy, appeared in the fourth and fifth centuries and, in the opinion of some theologians, again in the sixteenth and seventeenth centuries in the form of Christian humanism. What Perry Miller has called "the Augustinian strain of piety,"[9] with its emphasis on the helplessness of the human condition and the

overwhelming power of divine grace, continued to combat the
Pelagian strain throughout the long history of the Church. The
Augustinian strain contributed to the Reformation, and it continued to influence some Catholics after the Protestant break with
Rome. Among the more prominent French theologians of this
school was Cardinal Bérulle, founder of the Oratory in France.
Bérulle contended that man's greatness lies in his ability to realize
by means of prayerful introspection that he is nothing and that
God is everything. Man is unique among the creatures of God,
according to Bérulle, because of his ability to understand his absolute dependence upon God's mercy. Adam's fall had altered the
divine plan by which man was linked to God and had, in effect,
condemned mankind to death. "We are born children of the wrath
of God," wrote Bérulle, "and slaves to sin and to the devil. Our
mind, corrupted by original sin and filled with self-love, has no
power."[10] But God restored the link between the divine and the
human through Christ, who provided the means by which man
might be redeemed. The Christian must rid himself of pride, which
had been encouraged by pagan philosophers and humanists, and
must approach God with humility and a prayerful heart, recognizing that man's salvation is God's work alone.[11]

These conflicting opinions concerning man's propensity for
good brought to the fore once again a doctrinal question that had
plagued theologians since the days of Saint Augustine: the relationship between man's freedom to act for good or for evil and the
efficacy of God's grace. In his writings against the Pelagians, Saint
Augustine argued that God had predetermined those from among
all mankind who would be redeemed, and that the elect were to
be redeemed by means of divine grace. But this free gift of grace
in no way undermined human freedom, which cooperated with
divine necessity. Saint Thomas Aquinas also insisted that divine
grace in no way negated human freedom.[12] No theologian was
prepared to argue that man was capable of achieving redemption
entirely on his own, nor were there any who entirely rejected the
Christian concept of freedom. With the Protestant Reformation,
this complex doctrinal issue became explosive because of the
Protestant insistence upon human corruption and the overwhelming power of God's grace. At the Council of Trent, Catholics

rejected what they regarded as the Protestant repudiation of human freedom, but this was done in such general terms that further debate on the issue was inevitable, given the differences that existed within Catholic thought with respect to human nature.

While the Council of Trent was in session, a professor at the University of Louvain, Michel de Bay, or Baius, undertook to explain the doctrine of grace in terms of early Christian theology. He was accused in Rome of favoring Protestantism, and in 1567, Pius V promulgated an encyclical condemning seventy-six propositions attributed to the Flemish scholar. But the doctrine of grace continued to attract scholars at Louvain, where Jansenius and his friend Saint-Cyran were later to enroll as students of theology. The Jesuits, however, were wary of any doctrine inclined toward Protestantism, tending instead to emphasize man's free will. The order was therefore instrumental in the condemnation of Baius's propositions. (Jesuit scholars at Catholic universities were continually engaged in quarrels over the issue.) In 1588 there appeared on the scene an important book entitled *De Concordia Liberii Arbitrii cum Divinae Gratiae Donis*, written by a Spanish Jesuit, Molina. The author's thesis was that, although grace was necessary in order for the Christian to achieve salvation, the Christian was nevertheless free to accept or reject God's grace. Grace was not efficacious unless it was freely accepted. Some Catholic theologians, especially the Dominicans—who were the chief rivals of the Jesuits at many universities—were appalled by what they regarded as Molina's attempt to subordinate grace to human freedom, and the ensuing debate over what some scholars regarded as a clear reassertion of the Pelagian heresy grew so acrimonious that Pope Clement VIII, fearing a further weakening of the Church in the face of the Protestant menace, decided to intervene. Jesuits and Dominicans were invited to develop their arguments at hearings that opened at Rome in 1598. Despite the fact that many of the theologians of the curia were opposed to the Jesuit position, Loyola's order was so important to the advancement of the interests of the Church throughout the world that the Vatican was unwilling to censure Molina's work. Instead, in 1611 and again in 1625, the papacy issued decrees prohibiting further debate on matters pertaining to grace. Given the continuing quarrels with the Protestants and the divergent views of human nature within Catholicism, silence on this most perplexing question proved to be impossible. Those Catholics whose views were similar to Molina's were vulnerable to the charge of reviving the Pelagian heresy, while those who emphasized the efficacy of divine grace were vulnerable to the accusation that they were crypto-Protestants. Fear of heresy within the Church, which might encourage Protestantism or free thought, caused the papacy and the crown to take a particular interest in these disputes and to try to assert greater control over Catholic thought.[13]

Another problem troubling Catholic thinkers during the first half of the seventeenth century was the value to religious thought of what has been called Christian Pyrrhonism. Interest in this philosophical tradition was a product of Renaissance humanism. Pyrrhonism, the suspension of judgment "on all questions on which there seemed to be conflicting evidence, including the question whether or not something could be known,"[14] was regarded by some Catholics as an effective weapon against what they believed to be a cardinal Protestant principle, that scriptural interpretation rested on personal judgment. Who was to say whether one man's judgment was better than another's? —in which case, scriptural interpretation reinforced by theological tradition was far more likely to be valid than any particular construction. Montaigne, in fact, used Pyrrhonist arguments to challenge not only Protestant certitude but also philosophical dogmatism. Pyrrhonism was a useful means by which to humble pride in human reason. Some Catholics with a relatively pessimistic view of human nature maintained that Christians were incapable of knowing God other than through faith. Pierre Charron (1541–1603), a friend of Montaigne, asserted that a man had only to look inside himself to discover that he was constantly being misled by his senses and by his reason. Having rid himself of all illusions about his natural capabilities, the repentant sinner stood naked before God, ready to be illuminated by faith. Charron's views had a considerable impact in some Catholic circles, both as a weapon to be used against the Protestants and as a means of inspiring the essential penitential attitude of humility. Charron's beliefs, and those of Montaigne, were also influential in devout circles because they emphasized the importance of introspection, by means of which the individual came to know himself and his limitations. But other Catholic theologians regarded Christian Pyrrhonism as dangerous to the faith as well as to rational argument because Pyrrhonists were critical of Scholastic definitions and demonstrations, upon which much of Catholic tradition was based. Charron's views came to be regarded by some critics as a subtle form of libertinism.[15]

Seventeenth-century Catholic thought was a major cause of the intellectual crisis that damaged traditional values and ultimately contributed to the Enlightenment. Roland Mousnier attributes the crisis in part to the destruction of the traditional conception of man and the universe embodied in the Scholastic synthesis.[16] This dissatisfaction with Scholasticism is to be found among seventeenth-century philosophers, as well as among Protestant[17] and Catholic theologians. The Scholastic tradition, so vital to religious belief during the late Middle Ages, appeared impractical to theologians of the Counter Reformation such as the abbé de Saint-Cyran because it did not seem to encourage the Christian in his penitential obligations, distracting him instead with metaphysical speculations.[18] Furthermore, in the minds of some Catholic writers, Scholasticism relied upon outdated Aristotelian concepts and definitions that served no useful purpose in terms of understanding the natural world. This conclusion encouraged Pyrrhonism among some Catholics. Other Catholics, however, fearful of Pyrrhonism and Protestantism, searched for a theological-philosophical system capable of providing some degree of certainty with respect to faith and reason. Jansenism came into being partly as a result of the intellectual crisis that caused some religious thinkers to adopt a sympathetic attitude toward Pyrrhonism and others to espouse Cartesian principles in order more effectively to defend Catholic truth against heretics and libertines.

The Catholic reform movement had not only to contend with complex theological and philosophical questions but also with the institutional requirements of Church and state. Nowhere was this more in evidence than in France. One obstacle to religious reform was jurisdictional conflict within the Church. Bishops bent upon establishing greater control over their dioceses often found themselves in conflict with religious orders, including the Jesuits, who claimed immunity from episcopal authority. Thus, for example, if a bishop attempted to inaugurate certain reforms in his diocese, he might find his orders contravened by a religious order or even by canons of the local cathedral chapter, who were able to take a position independent from that of their bishop because they owed their benefices to some other political or ecclesiastical official. Jurisdictional disputes were often the cause of bitter disputes between university faculties and the Jesuits, who appeared to be encroaching on the rights and privileges of the older teaching orders. At the parish level as well, curés, jealous of their own rights and immunities, resented the expanding influence of the Society of Jesus, a resentment which contributed to the rebelliousness of many Parisian curés during the era of the Fronde.

Another contentious issue within the Church at this time was papal infallibility. The Vatican's assertion that the pope was the final authority in matters pertaining to doctrine was intended to increase Rome's power over the Church and to prevent quarrels from further weakening the Church after the shattering impact of the Reformation. Opposition to papal infallibility was also based on jurisdictional principles. Bishops resisted infallibility by claiming that they owed their offices to God and the apostolic succession rather than to the pope, and that therefore they had the right and the obligation to define doctrine in their own dioceses and to participate in the formulation of doctrine for the Church as a whole by means of a general council. This point of view—derived from the tradition of the early Church as well as from the conciliar movement of the late Middle Ages, which had also emphasized the primacy of a general council in matters pertaining to doctrine—was known in France as episcopal Gallicanism, and prelates adopted it to prevent papal or temporal authority from encroaching on their rights. Episcopal Gallicanism made it especially difficult to establish doctrinal unity within the Church, because any bishop might reject any outside attempt to force his diocese to accept a theological principle with which he did not agree.[19]

A vigorous defender of Gallican liberties was Edmond Richer, chosen syndic of the faculty of theology at the Sorbonne in 1608. His outspoken criticism of papal infallibility eventually led to his dismissal from that office. Nevertheless, Richer continued to develop his ideas concerning the governance of the Church—which Christ had bestowed, he believed, upon the entire priesthood, including the lower orders, and not upon the pope alone or even upon the corps of bishops. The Vatican and most bishops rejected this radical view of ecclesiastical government, but what became known as Richerism continued to influence certain segments of the lower clergy, which, revitalized by the spiritual currents of the Counter Reformation, sought a more responsible role in the affairs of the Church.[20]

Another obstacle to reform was the crown, which during the seventeenth century succeeded in weakening, though not in destroying, resistance to its authority. Since the Middle Ages, the French monarchy had extended its control over the Church to the point where rejection of papal authority altogether, as in the case of England, was unnecessary. The King of France, *fils aîné de l'église* ("oldest son of the Church") controlled most important ecclesiastical appointments, his highest courts of law retained appellate jurisdiction over everything pertaining to the Church that he regarded as affecting his sovereignty, and he and his courts were also able to reject papal decrees that might be interpreted as undermining his authority. The decrees emanating from the Council of Trent were never formally accepted in France because they appeared to challenge Gallican liberties. Royal Gallicanism, as distinct from episcopal Gallicanism, consisted of a set of principles by which the state resisted encroachments of ecclesiastical authority on what it regarded as its own area of jurisdictional competence. Occasionally there were differences of opinion between the crown and the sovereign courts about what constituted such an encroachment. The courts were jealous of their role as guardians of French laws and customs and opposed anything that might appear as an ultramontane threat, whereas the crown, for political reasons, often found it expedient to come to terms with the papacy on a given issue, despite the objections of the magistracy or, for that matter, of the Sorbonne. Neither Henry IV nor Louis XIII was as adamantly opposed to receiving the decrees of the Council of Trent as was the Parlement of Paris.

The kings of France were bound to resist any serious effort to weaken their control over ecclesiastical appointments, which provided the government with a system of patronage. A lucrative benefice was a source of income for a noble family and a means by which the crown was able to retain the loyalty of influential subjects. Richelieu and Louis XIV were able to secure the support of the vast majority of the higher clergy for government policies through the careful manipulation of benefices. The assemblies of the clergy during the seventeenth century provide another example of the crown's tendency to use the clergy as an instrument of policy. These assemblies met every five years to vote a subsidy to the crown. Made up of leading dignitaries of the First Estate, the assemblies sought assurance from the government that it would respect the theoretical immunity of the Church from taxation, in return for which they voted a free gift (*don gratuit*) to the crown. Richelieu, Mazarin, and Louis XIV were not only able to increase the size of the free gift but also to involve the assemblies in matters of doctrine and politics. Although the assemblies occasionally re-sisted the pressures of the crown, the crown was able to rely on the loyalty of the assemblies in matters pertaining to domestic and foreign policy.[21] Given the power of ecclesiastical appointment in the king's hands and his ability to manipulate the assemblies of the clergy and even the Sorbonne, it was not easy for the Catholic reform movement to advocate changes inimical to the interests of the crown.

The intensity of the reform movement as it developed in France during the first half of the seventeenth century constituted a challenge to the authority of Church and state in a number of ways. Institutional reform threatened vested interests. The Church was wary of doctrinal disputes that might lead to further schism, and the state often regarded such disputes as potentially subver-sive. Dissatisfaction with the traditional structure of thought and belief caused some Catholics to consider new philosophic concepts that undermined certain premises upon which both spiritual and temporal authority rested. A renewed piety and reforming zeal made some Catholics increasingly critical of ecclesiastical officials who appeared less pious and less zealous, and in some instances they questioned policies of the state on the grounds that these policies were insufficiently motivated by Catholic ideals. Some of the king's critics, who became known as *dévots*, disapproved of royal policy at home and abroad because it seemed not to serve the interests of Catholicism or not to take into account the spiritual and material well-being of the king's subjects. *Dévot* political ideals were reminiscent of the ideals of the Catholic League during the Wars of Religion. Just as the League had attempted to align France with Catholic Spain against the Protestant powers during the latter half of the sixteenth century, so too during the following century did some Catholic statesmen object to the hostile relations between the two Catholic kingdoms as well as to the French inclination to seek alliances with Protestant states in its struggle with Spain. *Dévot* opposition to government policies was regarded as disloyal by the king and his ministers who—not forgetting the difficulties that the Catholic League had caused the state—attempted to silence that opposition, particularly during periods when France and Spain were at war.[22]

Jansenism was to a great extent caused by these problems encountered by the French Counter Reformation. Spiritual need and religious conviction in the face of what appeared to be conflicting requirements of Church and state forced certain devout persons to confront an issue that was already familiar to many Protestant reformers and that was to become increasingly familiar to others during the two centuries preceding the French Revolution: the rights and obligations of the individual weighed against spiritual and temporal authority.

II. *Mère Angélique, the Abbé de Saint-Cyran, and the Origins of French Jansenism*

The term *Jansenism* is usually applied to a movement that derived its name from Cornelis Jansen, or Cornelius Jansenius, bishop of Ypres in the Spanish Netherlands, from whose book *Augustinus* several propositions were extracted and judged to be heretical by the Church. Those who defended Jansenius's theology became known as Jansenists, despite their objection that they were orthodox Catholics. The term used in this sense, therefore, could not be applied to any person or development before 1640, when the *Augustinus* was published. Yet the term used in this sense implies that Jansenism was primarily concerned with theological problems, which it was not. It also implies that Jansenius began the Jansenist movement, which he did not. The two most important influences on the French movement were Angélique Arnauld and Abbé de Saint-Cyran. A history of French Jansenism must begin, then, with Angélique's "conversion" and her efforts to reform the convent of Port Royal.

In the year 1602, Jacqueline Arnauld, eldest daughter of Antoine and Catherine Arnauld, became abbess of the convent of Port Royal of the Cistercian Order situated in the valley of the Chevreuse, not far from Versailles. Two years earlier, the eleven-year-old child had taken the religious name of Angélique de Sainte-Madeleine. She had acquired her position as abbess (which, according to the dictates of canon law, she ought not to have obtained until she was seventeen years old) as the result of her family's political connections and a special papal dispensation. The Arnauld family was part of what came to be known as the nobility of the robe and was closely affiliated with the Parlement of Paris. Angélique's mother's family was also of the *noblesse de robe*, and it was primarily through her maternal grandfather Simon Marion's influence with Henry IV that Angélique became an abbess. A younger sister, Jeanne, was appointed abbess of Saint-Cyr at the age of five. Antoine and Catherine Arnauld had twenty children, of whom ten survived infancy. All the daughters—including Jeanne, the future Mother Agnès—were to become nuns at Port Royal, and their mother took up residence in the convent after her husband's death. Angélique's three brothers, Robert Arnauld d'Andilly, Henri, and Antoine, *fils*, were to play crucial roles in the Jansenist movement.

A vivacious child, Angélique had no desire whatsoever to enter a convent, but as was so often the case, family interests rather than personal conviction dictated the choice that was imposed upon her. The family was not well-off, and there were many daughters to support. After a year at another convent by way of preparation, Angélique entered Port Royal in 1601 as coadjutant abbess, succeeding to the highest rank a year later, when the former abbess died. Conditions at the convent were poor, owing to the impact of the civil wars. The buildings were in disrepair, and the agricultural potential of the surrounding fields was somewhat diminished. The dowry of the nuns was not large, and their servants were often dishonest. Not wanting his daughter to live in such conditions, Antoine Arnauld took a proprietal interest in the convent, which he and his wife often visited. But Angélique was not happy. She loved all the worldly appurtenances from which she was to be forever cut off, and she toyed with the idea of escape. She even considered converting to Protestantism in order to repudiate her vows. Then in 1608, during Lent, a Capuchin monk preached at Port Royal on the subject of Christ's incarnation. The sermon so moved Angélique that she became suddenly "converted" to God's purpose. According to her niece, to whom she described the event many years later, she was literally seized by divine grace. "God moved her so strongly that the seeds that produced all her future virtues were then implanted."[1] From that moment on, Angélique regarded herself as a creature of God. At first, concerned primarily with her own spiritual needs, the abbess considered renouncing her position in order to become a simple nun, but she was soon persuaded that she must reform the abbey as well as herself. When she announced her intention of implementing the monastic rules laid down by Saint Benedict, she encountered serious opposition from some of the nuns, whose life of comparative ease was threatened by a return to austerity. Her

father, having learned of her intentions, was also opposed to innovations that he believed might injure his daughter's health.
Weakened by fasting and discouraged by opposition from the nuns
and from her family, Angélique was at the point of renouncing
her reforming intentions. But another sermon, based on the
Gospel according to Saint Matthew ("Blessed are they who are
persecuted for righteousness' sake," 5:10), revived her will. She
began to institute changes at Port Royal, such as enclosing the
convent from the outside world, abolishing private property, and
admitting to the order only those novitiates who were genuinely
committed to a religious life, whether they had a sufficient dowry
or not.

The quarrel between Angélique and her family over the abbess's
desire to reform the convent came to a head on 25 September
1609, when Antoine Arnauld, his wife, and his eldest son—Robert
Arnauld d'Andilly, who was himself to abandon the world one
day for the solitude of the valley of the Chevreuse—paid a visit to
the convent. When they arrived, they found the great gate closed
and only a small window open, from which Angélique invited her
family into a small adjoining parlor—the only room in the abbey
to which visitors were admitted after the reestablishment of the
Benedictine rule of enclosure. Infuriated by what he regarded as
filial ingratitude, Monsieur Arnauld demanded admittance to the
building proper. When one of the nuns who witnessed the confrontation suggested that it was a shame to keep her father out,
Angélique retorted: "My parents did not consult me when they
made me a nun. Why should I consult them when I wish to live
like a nun."[2] Confronted with such sincere intransigence, Arnauld's rage subsided, and he agreed to respect his daughter's
wishes. The abbess, suddenly filled with remorse at having upset
her father, fainted. An arrangement was finally made whereby the
family agreed not to enter the convent proper, but Antoine Arnauld retained the right to supervise the maintenance of buildings
and grounds. The significance of the confrontation lay not only
in the conflict between Angélique's familial and spiritual obligations but also in her definitive rejection of the world and its values.

Angélique eventually reached the conclusion that the convent
of Port Royal was incapable of accommodating the increasing

number of nuns who sought to enter it. Furthermore, because the buildings were situated at the bottom of a valley, surrounded by pestilent swamps, epidemics took their toll among the sisters. Fifteen died within the space of two years. With her mother's help, the abbess managed to find suitable and unpretentious quarters in the Faubourg Saint-Jacques in Paris, and in 1626 the nuns left what became known as Port-Royal-des-Champs for the new Port-Royal-de-Paris. The dowager queen, Marie de Médicis, became a patroness of the new convent, in recognition of the reforming zeal of its abbess. In 1627, with papal approval, Louis XIII renounced his right to designate the abbess (a decision his son Louis XIV would later regret), and Port Royal returned to the ancient monastic custom whereby the nuns elected their abbess every three years.

While instituting her reforms at Port Royal, Angélique Arnauld was able to rely on the vital support of the abbot of Cîteaux and general of the order, Dom Boucherat, who died in 1625. His successor was far less committed to monastic reform, for which reason Angélique decided to remove Port Royal from the jurisdiction of the Cistercian Order and to place it under the direction of the bishop of Langres, Sébastien Zamet. Zamet's father, a rich Italian banker, had provided Henry IV with financial support, in return for which his son was rewarded with a bishopric. Having acquired the reputation of being among the more worldly courtier-bishops of his day, Zamet experienced a spiritual conversion after a serious illness and became strongly committed to religious reform. He had been introduced to Mère Angélique in 1622, and she found him to be "a man full of zeal, of mortification and devotion."[3] In order to obtain jurisdiction over Port Royal, the bishop of Langres needed permission from Rome, which he hoped to obtain by establishing a new order, the Institute of the Holy Sacrament, with Port Royal as its nucleus. The new order was to be placed under secular jurisdiction, but because its proposed center was to be Paris, further jurisdictional complications arose. Paris was a separate diocese, and its bishop was understandably jealous of his episcopal rights. In 1627 the Vatican removed Port Royal from the jurisdiction of the Cistercians and put it under the direction of three prelates, the bishop of Langres and the archbishops of Paris and Sens. The archbishop of Paris withheld his approval of this change for three years, bestowing it only after he had been designated "principal superior" by the pope. The king gave his approval to the Institute in 1629. Zamet had new and more magnificent quarters constructed near the Louvre, and in order to cover construction costs, a dowry of ten thousand pounds was required of entering nuns—in violation of Angélique's principle that no dowry was necessary for admission.

Zamet wanted special prayers drawn up for the nuns, expressing the religious ideals of the order, and Angélique's sister Agnès, the former Jeanne Arnauld, who had entered Port Royal some time earlier and was at that moment abbess of the Institute, wrote a *Chapelet du Saint-Sacrement* under the supervision of Zamet's friend Condren, Cardinal Bérulle's successor as head of the Oratory. The archbishop of Sens, who had been critical of what he regarded as Zamet's excessive influence over the Institute, denounced the *Chapelet* to the Sorbonne in 1633 as containing heretical notions. Eight theologians—including Nicolas Cornet, who was later to discover heretical doctrine in Jansenius's *Augustinus*—agreed with the archbishop that the *Chapelet* contained a mystical element that appeared to obliterate the distinction between the divine and the human. Zamet, alarmed by these accusations, invited a learned and devout theologian, Abbé de Saint-Cyran, to defend the *Chapelet*. Saint-Cyran responded with an *Apologie du chapelet*, stressing the orthodox Bérullian meaning of the work. The good works of man, who is nothing, he argued, are produced by Christ, who is everything. Such was the effect of Saint-Cyran's effort that it managed to prevent the *Chapelet* from condemnation. It also earned the abbé the gratitude of Zamet, who desirous of spending some time in his diocese of Langres, left Saint-Cyran in charge of the spiritual needs of the Institute. The affair of the *Chapelet* constitutes an important event in the history of Jansenism both because it marked the beginning of Saint-Cyran's association with Port Royal and because for the first time Port Royal came under suspicion of harboring heretical beliefs.[4]

Not only did Abbé de Saint-Cyran respond to the needs of the Institute by warding off the charge of heresy, he also satisfied the personal spiritual needs of Angélique Arnauld, who had always experienced difficulty in finding a suitable confessor. Many of the priests whom she encountered were either too young or insufficiently committed to religious reform, although for a while she was able to obtain spiritual satisfaction from François de Sales. "I had always wanted to meet him," she later wrote, "and the sight of him increased my desire to unburden my conscience to him, because God was truly visible in him, and I had never yet seen in any person what I saw in him, even though I had met many priests with the reputation of being devout."[5] Angélique began to correspond with de Sales, and having complete confidence in him, she was able to submit herself to his spiritual guidance. He, in turn, though impressed with her piety, was concerned about her intolerance toward the vast majority of Catholics who, from her point of view, lacked adequate commitment and devotion. He once said to her: "My daughter, isn't it better to catch many fish than simply to catch a few big fish?"[6] The question implied two distinct points of view that were characteristic of the religious reform movement and that were to be at the heart of the Jansenist controversy. François de Sales believed that God was so generous with his grace that even weak sinners might take comfort in his mercy. Such an opinion facilitated the missionary efforts of the Church. Angélique, on the other hand, was convinced that salvation was possible for only a relatively few hardy souls who were worthy of God's grace. This austere opinion appeared too harsh and discouraging to many Catholics.

The saintly bishop of Geneva died in 1622, and for a long time Angélique was unable to find spiritual solace in another confessor. What made her especially unhappy was her fear that her growing reputation as a reformer would destroy her humility. At one time, Saint-Cyran cautioned her about abbesses who had reformed their convents but not their persons.[7] Angélique had met the abbé, a family friend, for the first time in 1625, but it was only in 1635, when Saint-Cyran had temporarily taken over the position of spiritual director of the Institute, that their close personal relationship began. He caused her to entirely subjugate her will to the will of God and to remain detached from the world and its values. Long after his death, Angélique wrote of Saint-Cyran: "It should be said that this holy man did not awaken a proper penitential attitude in people by force or constraint, nor did he recommend

an undue amount of mortifications or austerities. But by God's
grace he spoke the truth so clearly that he was able to inspire in
human hearts love of and respect for God, together with a sense
of remorse at having offended him. . . . His exactitude was in no
way painful to the soul, but on the contrary, because he was
motivated by a spirit of charity and righteousness and not by a
severe and scrupulous attitude, he was able to provide comfort for
the soul and to cause it to believe . . . that God would heal it."[8]
Angélique's spiritual needs corresponded perfectly with Saint-
Cyran's conviction that a confessor ought to become deeply
involved in the devotional life of the sinner.

The new spiritual director of Port Royal, Jean Duvergier de
Hauranne, future Abbé de Saint-Cyran, was born at Bayonne in
1581 into a prosperous family of merchants and civic leaders. His
father, a member of the municipal council, had remained loyal to
the French crown in the face of pressures from the Catholic League
during the Wars of Religion, and the family was therefore able to
rely on a certain amount of influence with the king when the wars
were over. One of thirteen children, Jean was intended for the
Church at an early age. He began his studies at the Jesuit college
at Agen, and then moved on to the Sorbonne. After receiving his
M.A. in 1600, the young scholar decided to continue his studies
at the Jesuit college affiliated with the University of Louvain in
the Spanish Netherlands. There he undertook an intensive study
of the writings of the early Church fathers before returning again
to Paris to examine the scholastic tradition. In 1606, Duvergier
de Hauranne returned to Bayonne, where he was provided with a
benefice that enabled him to pursue his studies with a measure of
financial independence. Between 1609 and 1616, Duvergier and a
fellow student from Louvain, Cornelius Jansenius, undertook an
intensive analysis of scripture as well as of scriptural commentaries
at Bayonne, and at Paris. Both scholars appeared to be more
interested at this time in biblical studies than in the theological
controversies of the day. The intellectual abilities of Duvergier
de Hauranne, together with his family connections—which included
the bishop of Bayonne, grand almoner to Henry IV—seemed to
assure a brilliant future in the Church and at court. With this in
mind, the ambitious young scholar published his first work, *La*

Question Royale (1609), in which he examined the casuistical question of whether one might commit suicide, despite the prohibition of the Church, if the intention behind the act was to save the king's life. The problem was known to have intrigued Henry IV. Duvergier argued that, given the circumstances, the suicidal act was not sinful, because it was motivated by a desire to save the king rather than to destroy the self. In his second work, *Apologie pour M. de Poiters* (1615), Duvergier again dealt with a complex ethical question. The work was intended to resolve a problem that concerned the warrior bishop of Poitiers: whether a prelate had the right to bear arms if necessary. Anxious to please one whose influence might prove beneficial, the author contended that a bishop might indeed take up the sword in a just cause. Duvergier de Hauranne was ordained in 1618, and two years later his services to the bishop of Poitiers earned him the lucrative abbacy of the Benedictine monastery of Saint-Cyran.

Although Abbé de Saint-Cyran took up residence in Paris and accepted another advantageous benefice in 1621 (honorary almoner to the Queen Mother, Marie de Médicis), he refused a number of other positions that would have enabled him to play an increasingly influential role in the political life of the kingdom. Ironically, these positions were made available to him through his friendship with Robert Arnauld d'Andilly, brother of Angélique and then a prominent figure at court. Saint-Cyran's decision to devote more time to study, prayer, and meditation was the result of the growing influence of another friend whose acquaintance he had made at this time, Cardinal Bérulle. The cardinal's devotional principles stressed the need for humility and self-abasement as an essential first step in the process of redemption. Saint-Cyran often spent six or seven hours a day in the company of the founder of the French Oratory, and his religious beliefs were formed as a result of this crucial friendship to a far greater extent than by his association with Jansenius.

In 1626 Saint-Cyran became involved in a literary quarrel with a Jesuit scholar, Garasse, who had undertaken to attack libertinage in all its forms, including the theological arguments of Pierre Charron, and to assert traditional Catholic principles in a four-volumed *Somme théologique.* Upon discovering that Garasse's synthesis was filled with countless doctrinal and philosophical errors, Saint-Cyran published a refutation of the work entitled *Somme des fautes et faussetez principales contenues en la somme théologique du Père Garasse.* Dedicated to Cardinal Richelieu, whom he had met through the bishop of Poitiers, the *Somme des fautes* effectively refuted the arguments of Garasse and also defended Charron from the Jesuit's charges of atheism. Charron had stressed the efficacy of Pyrrhonism as a means of understanding man's weakness and his need of God's redemptive powers. By downgrading man's rational powers, Charron had attempted to show the necessity of faith, by which God made himself known to man. Garasse deplored Charron's Pyrrhonism as dangerous to Catholic truths that were dependent to some extent upon rational arguments. Saint-Cyran, in turn, argued that Charron was right to emphasize human ineptitude. Not only was reason incapable of comprehending the divine, but it was also unable to learn much about nature. "The essential features of even the least things in nature . . . escape the mind and intelligence of the greatest philosophers," wrote the abbé, and almost as if he were anticipating the metaphysical speculations of seventeenth-century philosophy, he warned against human efforts to probe into the secrets of God.[9] Saint-Cyran's distrust of reason, which was to become an important element in Jansenist thought, may well have been a reaction against his own early writings, influenced as they were by humanist ideals.[10] His conviction that reason as well as all other human faculties were naturally inclined toward evil increased this distrust. The senses drew men down to the level of beasts, but reason was worse than the senses because it inspired vanity and distracted the mind from its Christian responsibilities.[11] Only through faith did one become wise. Faith was the reverse of human reason, and those who were regarded as wise in this world were taken for fools in heaven, whereas those who were taken for fools on earth were regarded as sages in the hereafter.[12]

Saint-Cyran's quarrel with Garasse was part of a larger quarrel between the Society of Jesus and the Oratory. Established to improve the quality of the secular clergy, the Oratory was bound to protect its rights against the jurisdictional encroachments of regular orders. The quarrel was the result of a disagreement between an

Oratorian missionary in England and the Jesuits, who were also active in that Protestant kingdom. Saint-Cyran came to the defense of the Oratorian's rights in two works written in Latin under the pseudonym Petrus Aurelius and published in 1632. Inspired in part by the influence of Bérulle and in part by a growing distrust of the Jesuits, the abbé upheld the jurisdictional authority of the episcopal hierarchy over the activities of the regular orders in the diocese. Furthermore, he exalted the role of the secular clergy, emphasizing the point that priests and bishops were divine instruments. By idealizing the role of the secular clergy, Saint-Cyran hoped to provide further incentive for clerical reforms. His efforts were commended by several assemblies of the clergy, always jealous of episcopal rights, but his attacks on the Jesuits—who, in his opinion, constituted a threat not only to the episcopacy but to the universities and the crown as well[13]—earned him the enmity of that prestigious order.

The Petrus Aurelius writings appeared shortly before Abbé de Saint-Cyran was asked by the bishop of Langres to defend his Institute against charges of heresy. Successful in the endeavor, the abbé was invited by Zamet to become spiritual director of the Institute during his absence. However, when he eventually returned to Paris after an extended sojourn in his diocese, the bishop of Langres was disturbed by the strong spiritual influence that Saint-Cyran had begun to exert over Angélique Arnauld and some of the nuns. A rivalry had clearly developed within the Institute between supporters of the abbé and supporters of the bishop. Some nuns, including Agnès Arnauld, had difficulty deciding between the two directors. In September 1636, Angélique, always the dominant figure within the convent, wrote a letter to Zamet, asking him to disassociate himself from the Institute. At the same time she sought the protection of the archbishop of Paris who, only too delighted to obtain complete jurisdiction over the convent, closed the Institute of the Holy Sacrament and sent the nuns back to their old quarters in the Faubourg Saint-Jacques. Zamet, infuriated by these proceedings, appealed to Richelieu to take action against his former friend who had frustrated his attempts to found a new order.

Shortly after his quarrel with the bishop of Langres, Saint-Cyran became associated with a group of men who came to be known as the *solitaires* of Port Royal. The first *solitaire* was Antoine Le Maistre, a young nephew of Angélique Arnauld. During the 1630s Le Maistre rapidly acquired a reputation as one of the best lawyers in Paris, but he decided to abandon his career for a life of seclusion and prayerful meditation. Fearful that his worldly ambitions might not be pleasing in the sight of God, Le Maistre consulted with Saint-Cyran, who advised him not to act precipitately but to give careful thought to such a momentous decision. The lawyer remained at the bar for several months, but in 1637 he notified his father and the chancellor, Pierre Séguier, that he would no longer continue as a barrister. To Séguier he wrote:

. . . I renounce once and for all my claims to ecclesiastical as well as to civil offices; I am not merely changing my ambition. I have none at all. I am even less inclined to enter into holy office than I am to renounce my present career, and I would regard myself as unworthy of God's mercy if after so many infidelities that I have committed against him I were to imitate a rebellious subject who, instead of kneeling before his prince in tearful submission, was presumptuous enough to expect to attain the highest offices of the kingdom. . . .
Whatever happens, my Lord, I ask of God no other favor than to live and die in His service, and to have no further commerce either orally or in writing with the world, which will think me lost, and [I desire] to pass the rest of my life in solitude, as if in a monastery.[14]

Instead of retiring to a monastery, however, Le Maistre took up residence in a little house in the Faubourg Saint-Jacques near Port-Royal-de-Paris. He was soon joined by others who had come into contact with Saint-Cyran, including Le Maistre's younger brother, Le Maistre de Sacy, and Claude Lancelot and Antoine Singlin. Other *solitaires* were to include Arnauld d'Andilly, Jean Hamon, Antoine Arnauld, Pierre Nicole, and Nicolas Fontaine, some of whom remained laymen. Singlin and Le Maistre de Sacy were ordained priests and became confessors to the nuns of Port Royal. The number of *solitaires* was never very great, twenty-five at most, counting only those who renounced the world entirely for a secluded life around Port-Royal-de-Paris, and later, after the arrest of Abbé de Saint-Cyran, around Port-Royal-des-Champs.[15]

They gave their worldly goods to the convent in exchange for a subsistence pension, and they performed manual tasks usually despised by the upper levels of society. Jean Racine, a student at the Little Schools of Port Royal, later wrote of the *solitaires*: "But theirs was not an idle penitence. While some took charge of the temporal affairs of the convent, others were not above cultivating the soil like simple day laborers. They even repaired a part of the walls that had fallen into ruins, and raised up others that were too low. Thus they made habitation in this wilderness more healthy and more comfortable."[16] The *solitaires* spent much of their time reading the Bible and patristic theology. Some of them translated devotional works into French. Arnauld d'Andilly translated the *Confessions* of Saint Augustine, and Le Maistre, the life of Saint John Chrysostom, the reforming patriarch of Constantinople who was martyred for his efforts to root out corruption in the Church. A most important project undertaken by the *solitaires* was the establishment of the Little Schools under the auspices of Abbé de Saint-Cyran, who believed that the purpose of a good education was to preserve the baptismal innocence of the child until he was old enough to be responsible for his own actions.

After his own conversion, begun under the tutelage of Bérulle during the 1620s, Abbé de Saint-Cyran had made a number of enemies, including the Jesuits and the well-connected bishop of Langres. He had angered Father Joseph, Richelieu's *eminence grise*, because of conflicting opinions about monastic reform, and he had annoyed Chancellor Séguier because of his influence on the chancellor's protégé, Antoine Le Maistre. Cardinal Richelieu himself was coming to regard his old friend as a menace to Church and state, among other reasons because of the abbé's political associations and opinions.

An important source of opposition to Richelieu's policies at home and abroad came from a loosely knit group known as the *dévots*. Among the more prominent members of the group were Cardinal Bérulle (until his death in 1629); Michel de Marillac—who was for a time, keeper of the seals; and Abbé de Saint-Cyran. Maintaining that politics should be based on religious principles, the *dévots* disapproved of the growing antagonism between France and Spain during the 1620s. War against the Hapsburg powers, in their opinion, was not in the interests of the Catholic Church or of the king's subjects, upon whom the burden of war would weigh heavily. As Marillac wrote to Richelieu in February 1629: "The management of affairs obliges me to point out to you that we are doing a number of things that cause great affliction among the people. . . . It seems to me that the glory of good government is to consider the relief of its subjects as well as the proper regulation of the state."[17] Richelieu, on the other hand, argued that the security of France depended upon an aggressive anti-Hapsburg foreign policy, and he saw no reason why the king's subjects, particularly the lower classes, should not suffer greater hardships in the interests of the state. "The aversion of the lower classes toward war does not deserve consideration as a reason for making . . . peace," he wrote in a memoir to the king in 1630.[18]

The quarrel between Richelieu and the *dévots* over the direction of royal policy came to a head in 1630. Trying to turn the waning prestige of the Queen Mother and regent, Marie de Médicis, to their advantage, the *dévots* attempted to persuade the king through his mother to dismiss Richelieu and to reject his policies. So confident were Marie de Médicis and Marillac of success that they promised their supporters rewards and offices after the downfall of the cardinal-minister. Saint-Cyran accepted the offer of a bishopric. But on November 10, 1630, the Day of Dupes, Louis XIII refused to heed his mother's entreaties and remained steadfast in his support of Richelieu. Marillac was subsequently imprisoned and the Queen Mother, humiliated, was soon compelled to leave the country. Saint-Cyran remained free after the Day of Dupes, but his activities as a leader of the *dévot* faction were known to Richelieu, and the abbé further antagonized the minister when he opposed the government's efforts to have the marriage of the king's brother, Gaston d'Orléans, to Marguerite of Lorraine annulled for political reasons. While other influential members of the clergy supported the king on the issue, Saint-Cyran refused to endorse it, on the grounds that marriage was a sacrament that could not be violated.

In 1635 France became involved in a war with Spain that was to last for twenty-four years. In the same year, Jansenius, bishop of Ypres, published a pamphlet entitled *Mars Gallicus*, which reasserted *dévot* political principles in extreme terms. Spain, according to the bishop, represented the interests of Catholicism against the heretical Swedes and Dutch, for which reason the Thirty Years' War was essentially a religious war. By allying himself with Protestant powers, the king of France was, in effect, pursuing policies injurious to the faith. Louis XIII ought therefore to dismiss those whose advice was so disastrous and to heed the counsel of men who were more respectful of the will of God. Soldiers who fought for the French king against Catholic Spain endangered their immortal souls.[19] When a French translation of *Mars Gallicus* began to circulate throughout the kingdom in 1637, Richelieu, who was particularly sensitive to *dévot* opposition in time of war, became increasingly suspicious of Jansenius's close friend Saint-Cyran, previously implicated in the Day of Dupes.

Saint-Cyran's writings include little of a specifically political nature, but he was nevertheless opposed to Richelieu's alliances with Protestant powers,[20] and he was well aware of the plight of the poor, particularly during time of war. "God ends war and achieves peace," he wrote, "because of the poor, who are the most afflicted by war and who feel its effects worse than anyone else in their persons and in their possessions."[21] In 1638 the abbé completed a commentary on the life of Abraham. This work, only recently published, contains what may be regarded as veiled references to contemporary politics as well as general political maxims that were characteristic of the *dévot* group and were inspired by the ideals of the Counter Reformation. There are several references in the commentary to the sanctity of marriage, undoubtedly relating to Gaston d'Orléans's marriage problems,[22] and statements about political alliances, such as "the just should seek alliances with the just, knowing full well that there is nothing more formidable than a virtuous man, because God fights on his side and is the enemy of his enemies." The *Vie d'Abraham* includes a discussion of the just war: "it does not suffice to have a reason to make war, but it must be necessary to have justice on one's side as well. It is not just to bear arms against those who ought not to be engaged in war or against religion or sacred objects or sacred persons, nor should a city or a chateau or a family in the service of God be seized without running the risk of having victory snatched from the victorious and of making new enemies." A significant theme in the commentary is the need for princes to seek the advice and counsel of wise and virtuous men. Princes are inclined not to seek such counsel, wrote Saint-Cyran, unless it coincides with their own passions and interests. "We must learn to respect the opinions of people devoted to God who are wise, knowledgeable, and disinterested, and who give us advice for our own good even if it seems a bit harsh."[23] This emphasis on the necessity for Christian counsel was very much a part of the *dévots's* program—who were convinced that Richelieu's service to Louis XIII was not in the interests of God or the faith—and it was reiterated throughout the century by those opposed to royal policy on the grounds that it was not inspired by Christian ideals.

But political matters alone did not cause the rift between Saint-Cyran and the cardinal-minister. There was also a significant disagreement between them over a theological issue relating to penitential discipline, an issue of the utmost importance in the era of the Counter Reformation. Richelieu agreed with many of the ideals of the Counter Reformation and as bishop of Luçon had introduced reforms into his diocese. He also prided himself on being a theologian of ability and was the author of several theological and devotional treatises. At issue was the penitential attitude of the sinner at the time when he sought absolution from a priest for his sins. Saint-Cyran believed that a man must have *contrition* before he could be absolved of his sins, that is to say that a man's love of God had to be such that he was deeply penitent and fully resolved to change his life in order that he might more easily avoid sin. Genuine repentance, according to the abbé, should emanate from a love of God and not from *attrition*, or fear of God's punishment. Reasserting an argument set forth by both Saint François de Sales and Cardinal Bérulle, Saint-Cyran insisted that attrition was based upon love of self, and that he who was motivated by attrition to confess his sins was acting in his own interests and was therefore not worthy of redemption. The key to the abbé's religious beliefs was the process of "conversion," by which God transformed man's love of self into love of God. A "converted" sinner was by definition contrite and therefore worthy of redemption, whereas a man acting in terms of his own interests had no right to receive absolution.[24]

Cardinal Richelieu, on the other hand, argued that contrition was very rare, a quality usually to be found in saints. If a man were genuinely contrite, then he was automatically absolved of his sin by God without having to confess to a priest; for the ordinary mortal, attrition was sufficient as long as he confessed his sin to the priest, at which time he must have the intention of performing the penance set by the priest. If he failed to perform the penance, then he was guilty of yet another sin, and he had to submit to the process of confession and absolution a second time.[25] Obviously the doctrine of attrition was much easier on the sinner than the doctrine of contrition, but Richelieu and many other Catholic theologians who endorsed it were convinced that the mystical power of the Church was such that it could automatically reconcile self-interest with God's first commandment to love him. "This sorrow [at having sinned] is motivated by fear of punishment in hell, by the deprivation of heaven as well as by the shamefulness of one's sin. And even if the principal motive of a man in these circumstances is self-interest, yet is he also inspired in part by a love of God. And the deprivation of heaven means that he will not enjoy God's presence, which is the source of eternal happiness."[26]

The contritionist controversy touches on the crucial issue of individual responsibility in the process of salvation. Saint-Cyran and his followers believed that the priest's power of absolution had no effect on the sinner who had been unable to overcome self-interest and to mend his ways. Redemption, in the eyes of Saint-Cyran—as well as of Angélique Arnauld—was accessible only to a few hardy souls. Placing greater emphasis on the redemptive powers of the Church, Richelieu and the attritionists believed that less resolute sinners might also benefit from God's mercy.[27] The argument was of concern not only to theologians but to laymen as well. Louis XIII, whose conscience was especially sensitive, was much disturbed by a book entitled *De la sainte virginité*, written in 1638 by an Oratorian priest by the name of Séguenot. The book, which was an exaggerated statement of the contritionist position, contradicted the more lenient penitential views of Richelieu and the king's Jesuit confessor. There were many at court, including Richelieu, who believed that Séguenot had received his ideas from Abbé de Saint-Cyran.

Thus during the 1630s, Saint-Cyran's religious principles had involved him in a number of quarrels. He managed to antagonize the Jesuits, influential prelates, the chancellor of France, the cardinal-minister, and the king himself. At the outset of the war with Spain, France was faced with a dangerous military situation. Mounting social unrest and tensions within the kingdom had been brought about by depressed economic conditions, by increased taxes, and by other wartime burdens. Richelieu, whose position as the king's chief minister was never entirely secure, found it difficult to tolerate what appeared to him to be the growing influence of one of the leaders of the *dévot* party opposed to the war effort and to policies that increased social tensions.[28] Nor was Richelieu inclined to look with favor upon what he regarded as dangerous theological innovations that might lead to another schism. He was of the opinion that had the Emperor Charles V made a greater effort to arrest Martin Luther, the Reformation might never have taken place.[29] On May 14, 1638, therefore, soldiers acting under the orders of the cardinal-minister arrested Saint-Cyran at his lodgings in Paris and conducted him to the prison at Vincennes. Richelieu is said to have remarked to a prince of the blood that the spiritual director of Port Royal was more dangerous than six armies.[30] To Hardouin de Beaumont de Péréfixe—future archbishop of Paris, who was to play a crucial role in the Jansenist controversy a quarter of a century later—he said: "I had the abbé de Saint-Cyran arrested this morning by order of the King. . . . No matter what anyone may say to me . . . I am certain that both Church and state will thank me for what I have done, for I have done both a great service. I have it on excellent authority that the abbé holds strange and dangerous opinions that might upset the public and trouble the Church someday. It is one of my maxims that religious controversy is harmful to the state."[31]

The charge brought against Abbé de Saint-Cyran was that he was a heretic who taught a penitential theology contrary to the principles of the Council of Trent. Indeed, the bishop of Langres accused him of belittling the Council. Although Saint-Cyran's papers were seized and eminent churchmen such as Vincent de Paul were interrogated about his activities, nothing to justify the charge of heresy was discovered by the investigators. Nevertheless, Saint-Cyran was kept in prison despite his innocence before the charges and the pressure brought to bear on Richelieu by bishops, magistrates, and other prominent officials.

If his initial reaction to prison was one of terror, and if in his dark, uncomfortable cell he experienced doubts about his religious convictions to the point of stating publicly that attritionism was an acceptable doctrine, the abbé gradually recovered his composure and came to the realization that imprisonment afforded him the opportunity to strengthen his belief. He learned that persecution was a means by which God tested his faith, and in the confines of his cell (he later was moved to more comfortable quarters) his conversion to God's purpose and his rejection of the world became complete. There he found the solitude necessary for introspection and meditation. Saint-Cyran remained the spiritual director of Port Royal, and in letters smuggled out of Vincennes by visitors, he was able to offer religious advice not only to the nuns but to a large number of people who learned of his reputation as a confessor. His published correspondence includes letters to the saintly Madame de Chantal, to the princesse de Guéménée, and to the Comtesse de Brienne, as well as to magistrates of the robe such as Bignon and Barillon—letters that provided solace to many others after Saint-Cyran's death. Those, like Pascal, who never knew Saint-Cyran personally, found in the writings from prison a source of inspiration, and within the convent of Port Royal they served to sustain what became a cult of Saint-Cyran.[32] Widely circulated, these letters established the Jansenist position on penitential discipline.

The penitential theology of the abbé, as reflected in his prison writings, emphasized the crippling effect of original sin upon humanity as a whole. In order to dramatize man's dependence on God's mercy, Saint-Cyran contrasted Adam's condition before the Fall with his condition after he had disobeyed God of his own free will in the Garden of Eden. At the time of his creation, Adam had more power than any king or emperor was to have because, whereas even the greatest potentate has been disobeyed, "man in his first innocence was endowed with such absolute power that no creature was able to oppose him, and all the movements of his body and soul depended upon his will to the extent that he could not feel any joy or sorrow or have any thought that he had not willed. And whereas kings govern over only a part of the earth, man [in his innocence] had dominion over the entire world."[33] Adam was at liberty to do good or ill according to the dictates of his will, and he was, therefore, responsible for his actions. After the Fall, Adam and his children no longer had the power to choose between good and evil, because the human will had become so corrupt that it was capable on its own of choosing only between different kinds of evil.[34] Adam's choice of evil resulted in the condemnation of all mankind to eternal damnation, and only because of Christ's redemptive powers were the gates of heaven open to a small number of Adam's descendants.[35] Saint-Cyran and his followers were at pains to emphasize that human corruption was caused by man's free will and not by any immutable decree of God before the creation of the world. Man alone was responsible for his predicament, and God alone was responsible for the salvation of the elect, whose ultimate disposition he had predetermined. Although he adhered to a doctrine of predestination, Saint-Cyran contended that such a doctrine was not indicative of divine cruelty or intransigence, but rather of God's mercy and justice. Jansenists, in fact, argued that it was the Protestant doctrine of predestination that was cruel and unjust, because God appeared to save some and damn the rest even before Adam's fall. The Protestants attributed damnation to God's will, whereas the Jansenists attributed it to Adam's sin, which subsequently tainted all mankind.[36] "Predestination is nothing but the eternal love that God bears for certain of Adam's children after having seen all of them condemned by the sin of their father. The rest [of Adam's children] are consigned to the hell that they have merited. As the sun causes good and bad days, so God causes some men to be redeemed and others to be damned even though God is not the cause of their damnation, but rather the sin that they have committed in Adam, and the resulting infection that has tainted them at their birth combined with the criminal and dissolute lives that they have led."[37]

These theological opinions were intended to make clear to the penitent sinner his helpless condition and his need for divine grace to achieve good. An awareness of the debilitating effects of original sin inspired humility, "it being impossible to be genuinely pious without humility, or to become humble without knowing the miserable condition to which we have been reduced by Adam's fall as well as the need we have to be sustained at each moment by grace in order not to falter."[38] In the mind of Saint-Cyran, the true importance of theology was not to provoke debate among scholars but to encourage the Christian to undertake spiritual exercises that might eventually lead to his conversion to God's purpose. The letters and devotional tracts written in the prison of Vincennes are primarily concerned with practical advice about spiritual exercises suitable to the needs of a particular correspondent. To a lady seeking spiritual solace Saint-Cyran wrote, "You must understand, Madame, that the desire to perform charitable acts obliges us to purify ourselves by means of all sorts of pious exercises so that we may render ourselves worthy of the diverse gifts of God, in order then to spread them among those who need them without losing our plentitude, even adding more [to it] by the effusion of our charity."[39]

Prayer and introspection were essential to the sinner seeking to purify himself. Self-knowledge, according to Saint-Cyran, made one aware of those "hidden sins," the greatest obstacles to conversion,[40] and it provided the individual with a clearer understanding of the effect of original sin upon him. With keen psychological insight, the abbé, and subsequently his disciples, stressed the pain involved in introspection. Writing many years after Saint-Cyran's death, the Jansenist moralist Jacques-Joseph Duguet asserted that the cruelest result of introspection was the destruction of one's illusions.

In vain does one dissimulate, in vain does one try to protect oneself; the veil is ripped off as life and its cupidity vanish, and one becomes convinced that one must lead a new life when one is no longer permitted to live [according to the dictates of the world]. One must begin with the sincere desire to see oneself as one is seen by his Judge. This view is shattering, even to persons who profess themselves to be opposed to disguise, because [self-examination]

rids us of our good qualities and the esteem that we have acquired
by them. One becomes aware that one has been living a life of
vanity and illusion, that one has nourished oneself on sweetmeats,
that one has regarded virtue in terms of dress and adornment, and
that one has neglected the essential. What is essential is to relate
everything to God and to salvation and to mistrust oneself in every
way, not by a wiser vanity or a more enlightened pride, but by an
awareness of one's own injustice and misery.[41]

In the *Pensées*, permeated with the devotional ideas of Saint-Cyran,
Pascal pointed out that by means of introspection one became
aware of the paradoxes inherent in the human condition. "Let
man now judge his own worth, let him love himself, for there is
within him a nature capable of good; but that is no reason to love
the vileness within himself. Let him despise himself because this
capacity remains unfilled; but that is no reason to despise this
natural capacity. Let him both hate and love himself; he has within
him the capacity for knowing truth and being happy, but he
possesses no truth which is either abiding or satisfactory."[42] But
the sinner, according to Pascal, prefers illusion to reality and therefore does all in his power to avoid introspection, " . . . for nothing
could be more wretched than to be intolerably depressed as soon
as one is reduced to introspection with no means of diversion."
But realization of one's own vileness leads also to an awareness
that God unites himself with man in the depths of his soul.[43]

Saint-Cyran and his disciples invariably sounded this hopeful
note. Angélique Arnauld wrote to a nun of Port Royal in 1637,
"Do not imagine that it is impossible to rid yourself of your
afflictions, because it is a diabolical illusion to feel that way. The
abyss of our weakness and our misery ought not to frighten us,
because the abyss of God's mercy passes it infinitely."[44] In a
letter of reassurance to one of his correspondents discomforted
by self-analysis, the prisoner of Vincennes wrote, "The pain that
you feel and that makes you troublesome to yourself . . . is the
first stage of humility, and it is the cornerstone on which the Holy
Spirit builds his dwelling place in you."[45] Introspection, then, was
the means whereby the sinner became aware not only of his imperfections but also of the stirring within him of God's grace,
which provided him with the capacity for good. By means of
efficacious grace, the penitent experienced a "conversion" to

God's purpose that enabled him to repudiate his own interests. All Jansenists, including Saint-Cyran and Angélique Arnauld, underwent conversion, not as a result of a sudden, extraordinary transformation brought about by the miraculous intervention of God, but as the result of hard work. The miraculous intervention did, of course, occur to Jansenists, most notably in the case of Pascal's "night of fire," but also in the case of Angélique Arnauld when she heard the Lenten sermon preached at Port Royal in 1608. But if the seeds of future good works were sown by the blinding flash of divine inspiration, they could only be cultivated by the sustained effort of the sinner, who was always in danger of falling once again from grace. Antoine Le Maistre defined the nature of conversion in a letter written to his uncle Arnauld d'Andilly, when the latter was about to renounce a distinguished political career for the solitude of Port-Royal-des-Champs: "And when [the soul] wishes to detach itself from its old habits, to rid itself of all its passions in order to consecrate itself entirely to God, . . . it becomes, as Saint Paul said, a new creature."[46] Once having subordinated his own self-interest to the will of God, the sinner experienced genuine contrition for his sins.

In order to undertake intensive introspection and, hopefully, to experience conversion, the penitent was required to seek solitude in order to isolate himself from the world. Throughout the prison correspondence, Abbé de Saint-Cyran insisted on the need for solitude, if only for a few hours each week. If a person was unable to go away on a retreat, he should remain alone in his room whenever possible. "I do not know of any better advice in order to merit an increasing amount of God's grace," he wrote to a young lady in 1642, "than to accustom yourself to spending as much time with [God] during the day in the solitude of your bedchamber or study as should not prevent you from performing those obligations required by your social position."[47] To another acquaintance about to take a journey, Saint-Cyran wrote:

I advise you to eschew any discourse with the world or any news of the day. It is better to sleep or to read from a sacred book. When you arrive at a hostelry, if it is not too late at night, you should go straight to church in order to salute the son of God. . . . I go to church whenever I go on a journey, no matter how far away it is. Having chosen your room, you should leave it whenever the maids come in, and you should have nothing to do with dissolute men. Leave them instantly as you would the maids, making the excuse that you have to visit the stables, and stay in the street while waiting for supper. The best thing would be to close yourself in a room in order to pray to God for an hour. . . . In this way your voyage will provide you with an excellent opportunity to find solitude.[48]

Solitude enabled one to withdraw from the world. According to Saint-Cyran and his followers, this meant the repudiation of worldly values and the avoidance of worldly temptations. Saint-Cyran often counseled his correspondents to fast a certain amount each week, to give up wine entirely, to avoid balls, gaming tables, and the theater, and "to shun novels"[49]; other Jansenist moralists denounced drama and fiction because they aroused such passions as pride, ambition, jealousy, and vengeance. In his *Traité de la comédie*, Pierre Nicole wrote that, because they were modelled on the theater of antiquity, contemporary plays inevitably inspired pagan virtues. The illusions stimulated by the theater were hardly conducive to a proper understanding of the human condition.[50] According to Pascal, poetry, music, dancing, and the theater consisted, for the most part, of fantasies created by men to avoid introspection.

For Catholics a confessor is crucial to the sinner in his efforts to renew his life through Christ. One of the first obligations of the repentant sinner is to find a spiritual director. "You can do nothing at the outset of your retreat, at which time you will be building the foundations of your future life," wrote the abbé de Saint-Cyran to a young nobleman in 1641, "without the advice of a good confessor. The true liberty of a man consists in submitting himself with a good heart, without reservations, and with complete confidence to [a priest] through whom, as through his living oracle, God will make his desires known for the present as well as for the future."[51] Angélique Arnauld's difficulties in finding a spiritual guide at the time of her conversion and intermittently throughout her life illustrates her and Saint-Cyran's belief that it was the responsibility of the penitent to seek out a conscientious and capable confessor. This responsibility was matched by the confessor's responsibility to arrive at an understanding of the penitent in terms of his spiritual strengths and weaknesses, and to offer counsel suitable to that particular individual. Saint-Cyran wrote: "Each person has his gift from God, according to Saint Paul, and one should not serve [God] with someone else's gift rather than his own. He who is unable to fast should seek solitude, and he who is unable to seek solitude should mortify himself. And he who is unable to mortify the flesh may be able to mortify the spirit, and even in the midst of a group of people to make secret signs to God in order to please him."[52]

The withdrawal from the world so ardently recommended by Saint-Cyran did not necessarily mean a refusal to participate in social activity but rather a refusal to be governed by the world's standards. Having determined after intensive introspection that his vocation came from God, the Christian was then obliged to fulfill those responsibilities connected with his social function. Such responsibilities were ascertained in the light of charity and not of self-interest, and the proper performance of one's duties was a means by which the Christian was able to learn whether his actions were indeed a manifestation of God's grace working within him. "No one estate has a special privilege in terms of perfection," said the prisoner of Vincennes. "A man may be redeemed in the humblest profession if he obeys God's commands."[53] In his opinion, there were four obstacles to Christian virtue: social prominence, wealth, high office, and physical and intellectual prowess. All four encouraged self-destructive pride and ambition. Nobles who asserted the rights and privileges of their order above all else, those who sought political office for the purpose of satisfying ambition, merchants who put personal profit ahead of public good, soldiers who sought personal glory on the battlefield, and scholars whose intellects were employed for the purpose of self-aggrandizement— all such persons were unlikely to win God's favor.[54] Those Christians from the higher orders of society, where the obstacles to salvation were great, had a special obligation to perform charitable services. A person of wealth was required to give generously to the poor. Wrote the *solitaire* Le Maistre de Sacy to a nobleman: "it is good that you consider what the late Monsieur de Saint-Cyran used to say, that in order to dispose properly of one's wealth, it does not suffice merely to give what is superfluous [to one's needs] to the poor. One has to give more than what is superfluous in order to satisfy fully that which Christian, rather than human, justice, honesty, liberality, and generosity require."[55] Saint-Cyran maintained that the poor existed as a visible sign of the poverty and misery of humanity, and as a means whereby the rich obtained salvation through charitable actions. The rich were given their wealth by God for the sole purpose of distributing it to others.[56] All social functions were intended by God to improve the earthly conditions of mankind as a whole and not for the satisfaction of personal ambition. The social ethics of Saint-Cyran and his disciples manifested themselves to some extent in the policies of the *dévot* faction, in that those policies sought to encourage rulers to concern themselves with the welfare of their subjects and to discourage their attempts at self-aggrandizement.

By emphasizing the need for solitude in order to obtain divine justification for any action and by stressing the corrupting influence of worldly associations, Saint-Cyran and subsequent Jansenist moralists created a tension in the minds of their adherents between the spiritual needs of the individual and his social responsibilities. Christian life began with solitude and introspection, and only after the individual had made the necessary commitment to God was he then able to go forth into the world in order to improve it. As Le Maistre de Sacy wrote to a friend: "It is always right to love solitude, but it is not always right to be in solitude. For his own sacred reasons, God obliges us to mingle with our fellow men. Under these circumstances, we must be sustained by our love of solitude."[57] Another *solitaire*, Antoine Singlin, admonished a penitent: "You do not take time enough to pray to God before undertaking anything."[58] Such opinions were not likely to encourage confident social action. Furthermore, these views indicated that, in the Jansenist mind, the Christian's primary concern must be his own spiritual well-being. In a society favorably disposed toward the devout activities of the committed Christian, there would not be much likelihood of a conflict between the individual's personal responsibilities and his social obligations. But in a hostile society, the dedicated Christian might well be forced to choose between active resistance to worldly ethics or complete withdrawal into the self.

This tension between the personal needs of the individual and the demands of society distinguished Jansenists—some more than others—from other Catholics, who were more confident that their good works were acceptable to God. Saint Vincent de Paul, members of the Company of the Holy Sacrament, and non-Jansenist *dévots* were less hesitant about becoming actively involved in worldly affairs than were Saint-Cyran and his followers. Richelieu, who never doubted his own commitment to God's purpose, was highly critical of the inclination to withdraw from the world. He may well have had the *solitaires* in mind when he wrote at the end of his life: "It is an opinion shared by many that a man cannot commit himself to God if he does not withdraw from the world and its affairs. The concern that my position in life requires me to have for the public good of Church and state causes me to reject this opinion and to argue instead that one cannot do better than to labor in the vineyard, where much needs to be done, when God so commands one. There are those who say that complete repose enables men to dedicate their thoughts to God. I say that, ordinarily, the less leisure one has, the better off one is, because leisure degenerates into idleness."[59] Continuous solitude and contemplation, thought Richelieu, hampered activity in behalf of the public good. Introspection was more likely to be inspired by self-love than by a charitable concern for one's fellow man. "Action is more meritorious than contemplation. It is better to love God than to spend one's time wondering whether he loves God or not. It is impossible to keep God continually in mind without a special grace. He who is inclined to do so loses more than he gains in terms of his salvation, because he misses numerous opportunities to do good. God's presence, which is so important to us, is less a presence of mind than of heart, which is felt through certain actions by which we consecrate ourselves to God."[60]

Saint-Cyran's letters from prison and his other writings reflect a particular concern with the priesthood in terms of both the spiritual qualifications of the clergy and its social functions. This interest was common among the leaders of the Counter Reformation, including Cardinal Bérulle, and it was to become a fundamental characteristic of Jansenism. Religious reformers had always stressed the importance of a true vocation—without which no man or woman had any right to hold any position in the

Church—in the face of a prevailing tendency to satisfy personal ambition through the acquisition of one or more benefices. "If no member of the Church can accomplish the slightest good work without receiving a vocation and an internal application of the Spirit of Jesus Christ, who communicates only to a very small number of the faithful whenever it pleases him," wrote Saint-Cyran, "how can one become involved in the consecration of His body and blood and in the governing of souls if one is not called or solicited by God in a voice so sensible and audible that one cannot doubt it?"[61]

Saint-Cyran's attitude toward recruiting young men suitable for the priesthood is illustrated by his attempts to persuade the *solitaire* Antoine Singlin to succeed him as confessor to the nuns of Port Royal. Singlin, the son of a wine merchant, was born in Paris in 1607. While an apprentice in his father's business, Singlin decided that his true calling was to the clergy, and to that end he sought out Vincent de Paul, who placed him in a seminary. After taking orders, Singlin became a confessor at the Hôpital de la Pitié in Paris, where he soon came into contact with Abbé de Saint-Cyran. Dissatisfied with the administration of the hospital and increasingly influenced by Saint-Cyran, Singlin became a *solitaire* in 1637. For a while he abandoned his clerical functions in order to undergo the introspection necessary for spiritual regeneration. Because Singlin was aware of the awesome responsibilities of the priesthood as well as of his own inadequacies, Saint-Cyran selected him to become confessor and preacher at Port Royal while the abbé was in prison. When the abbé was released from Vincennes in 1643, Singlin informed him of his intention to withdraw entirely from his priestly functions. Saint-Cyran replied that this decision was based upon self-interest and not upon God's will. When asked by Singlin how he was able to recognize God's intentions, the abbé replied that on the basis of Singlin's spiritual agonies, which he knew about as his confessor, he believed that the former wine merchant's apprentice was admirably suited to the office of priest and spiritual director. "Our ministry must involve perpetual prayer and perpetual fear and trembling, but this does not mean that we should forsake it."[62] A true ministerial vocation, according to Saint-Cyran, required both a sense of unworthiness and a sense of compassion for others. They could only be discerned by experienced and competent confessors, and those who fulfilled such requirements were hard to find. Only one in ten thousand priests had the qualifications necessary for the spiritual guidance of penitent souls, Saint-Cyran contended,[63] and Singlin, whose sermons in the chapel of Port Royal were to become famous throughout Paris, was one of those rare creatures because of his abilities as a confessor and as a preacher.

Saint-Cyran made a distinction between the person of the priest on the one hand and the dignity of his office on the other. The essential characteristic of the person of the priest was, of course, humility, but the office itself was exalted above all other earthly functions. The priest was, in a sense, a king, anointed by God and endowed with the mystical power to "produce the body and blood of Christ in the sacrament."[64] The priest was a "prince of souls," whose power exceeded all others on earth because it was communicated directly to him by God.[65] Because of the divine authority by which he administered the sacraments and because of his powers of absolution, which made him the earthly executor of God's mercy, the power of the priest was above even that of the angels.[66] Because the priest held the keys to the kingdom of heaven—a privilege not granted even to kings—according to Saint-Cyran, God had no higher office to bestow upon a Christian than the priesthood, and no greater punishment to mete out than to the false Christian who had become ordained under false pretenses.[67]

A spiritual director himself, it was this aspect of the priesthood that most concerned Saint-Cyran. Because an inept confessor prevented the sinner from understanding his Christian responsibilities, the priest was required to adhere to the rules of sound penitential discipline and needed a great deal of experience with penitents in order to be able to recognize a genuinely contrite soul. If the penitent was incapable of changing his ways and rededicating his life, the confessor was left with no choice but to abandon him. "It is perfectly clear to me that I can no longer serve her in the condition that she is in," wrote Singlin in a letter to Angélique Arnauld, referring to a repentant woman. "Sooner or later she will have to leave me, or I will have to return her to the world."[68] The confessor's responsibilities were so burdensome, in Saint-Cyran's mind, that he was strongly averse to the curing of souls, primarily because he rarely encountered a true penitent. Those with whom he usually had to cope required cajolery and demanded an accommodating attitude on the part of the confessor.[69] Such reluctance on the part of the devout pastor again illustrates the tension that existed between the spiritual demands of the individual and his social function. Continued association with hardened sinners might jeopardize the ultimate redemption of the priest.

Saint-Cyran and his followers favored an enlightened clergy capable of differentiating between ecclesiastical tradition and dangerous innovation. Scholasticism was objectionable to them for a number of reasons, among them the belief that it obscured Christian truth and encouraged heresy and libertinage. Wrote the abbé:

One must say in truth that in these last centuries the Schoolmen have been primarily responsible for the undermining of ancient ecclesiastical discipline that has adversely affected the Church, and that their influence has increased during these last three hundred years because of ignorance. Because Scholasticism, although useful in some respects, is so complex, it has raised some very ticklish questions that one cannot comprehend unless one has studied philosophy for a long time and has read a great number of theological treatises, most of which are incapable of making priests any more able to maintain the discipline of the Church and to govern souls. From these treatises one must move on to a study of casuistry, which is confusing unless one is virtuous and enlightened. Most priests today content themselves with these [Scholastic works] instead of reading scripture and the works of the holy fathers, as if they were irrelevant to Christian doctrine.[70]

In order to become properly educated, a priest ought to go to the sources of Catholic belief, as Saint-Cyran and Jansenius had done as young men at the Camp-de-Prat, rather than to rely on late medieval commentaries, whose subtleties were often misleading and dangerous to the faith. The priest was the defender of Catholic doctrine and discipline, and his powers of absolution were essential to salvation. Saint-Cyran wrote: "One of the Church fathers was right in saying that a sinner in the clutches of his sin must not approach Jesus Christ by himself, but must simply touch his garment if he is able to, that is to say, if he is able to cast his eye on some priest who is humble and who believes himself to be the lowliest creature in the Church, the garment of Christ. Such a priest is the fringe attached to the garment. . . . The theologian says that a touch of the fringe is capable of curing the sinner by means of either humble prayer or sincere confession."[71] The abbé's views on the priesthood were important to the structure of penitential discipline that was of such significance to Jansenist belief, and they were particularly important to the morale and sense of mission of the lower clergy, which had suffered for a long time from lack of discipline and from neglect. Jansenism, with its exalted concept of the priesthood derived from the convictions of Saint-Cyran, was to become particularly attractive to the lower order of the French clergy later in the seventeenth century and throughout the eighteenth century.

During the period of Saint-Cyran's imprisonment, the link between the first and second generations of French Jansenists was formed by the close friendship established between the abbé and the youngest child of Antoine and Catherine Arnauld. Antoine Arnauld, *fils*, known to his contemporaries as *le grand Arnauld* despite his diminutive physical stature, was born in 1612. After his father died in 1619, the boy was brought up by his mother and by his older sister, Catherine Le Maistre, the mother of the first *solitaire*. A brilliant student at the Sorbonne, Arnauld decided to satisfy his worldly ambition by pursuing a successful career in the Church. He had begun to work toward his doctorate at the Sorbonne when his cousin and close friend Antoine Le Maistre announced his intention of withdrawing from the world. This event profoundly affected young Antoine and caused him to turn to his family's spiritual director, the abbé de Saint-Cyran, by then incarcerated in Vincennes. The abbé urged him to continue his studies, which culminated in Antoine's receipt of the doctorate in 1641. Renouncing his ambitions—as well as the offer of a lucrative ecclesiastical benefice made available to him by a cousin—Arnauld, with the firm support of Saint-Cyran, decided to utilize his intellectual energies in support of the religious ideals advocated by the prisoner. Arnauld became a frequent visitor at Vincennes, where he received encouragement from Saint-Cyran to defend the doctrine of contritionism. One of Arnauld's earliest works (1641) was an attack on a book written by the Jesuit theologian Sirmond, a staunch attritionist. Saint-Cyran also encouraged his protégé to denounce La Mothe Le Vayer's work, *De la vertu des payens*. A skilled and enthusiastic polemicist throughout his life, *le grand Arnauld* believed that he was using his intellectual gifts in defense of the ideals of the imprisoned abbé, who had suffered for the truth.[72]

Cardinal Richelieu died in December 1642, and in the following February, Saint-Cyran was released from the prison where he had been incarcerated for over four years. When he visited Port Royal shortly after his release, all the nuns were assembled in the parlor to receive his blessings. The abbé told the nuns that it was his intention "to work in the defense of that divine virtue [charity] against those who had undertaken to destroy it in this century." If he lived long enough, the abbé resolved to write on this important matter and to establish the doctrine of contrition.[73] But his poor health, which had caused him much suffering in prison, did not permit him to carry out his intention. Saint-Cyran died of a stroke on October 11, 1643. His funeral was attended by five bishops and by a future queen of Poland, Marie de Gonzague, and he was buried in an austere little church not far from Port-Royal-de-Paris, Saint Jacques d'Hautes-Pas.[74]

The first phase of the Jansenist movement ended with Saint-Cyran's death. This phase—begun in 1609 when Angélique Arnauld closed the doors of Port Royal to worldly influences, including her own father—came to an end six years before the faculty of theology of the Sorbonne began to consider the heretical implications contained in Jansenius's *Augustinus*. The most prominent features of what came to be known as Jansenism manifested themselves in the reforming zeal and the intense piety of Angélique Arnauld and Abbé de Saint-Cyran, which—although characteristic of the Counter Reformation—nevertheless antagonized authorities of Church and state during the Richelieu era.

Angélique encountered substantial opposition to her efforts to reform Port Royal—not only from unresponsive nuns but from her father, who resented losing control over his daughter. Because she insisted on placing the convent under the jurisdiction of authorities firmly committed to the ideals of the Counter Reformation, and because she set high standards for confessional direction, the abbess earned the enmity of influential abbots and bishops. A charge of heresy was first brought against Port Royal in 1633, seven years before the publication of the *Augustinus*, and although the charge was successfully refuted by the nuns with the help of Saint-Cyran, Angélique's uncompromising standards of reform made Port Royal and those associated with it vulnerable to future accusations by authorities suspicious of an attitude of independence that might, from their point of view, become subversive.

Saint-Cyran's piety and his strict ethical standards eventually led to his imprisonment at the fortress of Vincennes, two years before the publication of Jansenius's *Augustinus*. To many, his opinions about the nature of penitence appeared to be too demanding and discouraging for the ordinary sinner. Angélique, who adhered to the same high standards, was criticized by no less a figure than Saint François de Sales because her convictions were elitist and therefore detrimental to the Church's efforts to sustain weaker souls. Furthermore, the belief that salvation was attainable for only a few intrepid souls hampered the missionary activities of the Church.

Excessive piety was also politically dangerous, as Richelieu made clear in his *Political Testament*, intended for the benefit of Louis XIII. "I will content myself," he wrote, "with observing that, although devotion is necessary for kings, it ought to be devoid of overscrupulousness. I say this, Sire, because the sensitiveness of Your Majesty's conscience has often made you fear to offend God in reaching even those decisions which you cannot abstain from making without sin." The cardinal-minister may have had Saint-Cyran and the nuns of Port Royal in mind when he said in the Testament: "Since princes are expected to establish God's true church, they should be very thorough in banishing all false imitations of it, which are so dangerous to the state that one may say with complete truth that this kind of hypocrisy has always been used to clothe the enormity of the most pernicious undertakings. Many people who are as weak as they are malicious, sometimes use this as a kind of ruse. Particularly is this the case in approaching women, since their sex is more given to transports of devotion which is, however, of so little depth that they are vulnerable to such stratagems, as they depend less on real subsistence than upon cunning."[75]

Equally disconcerting to religious and political authorities was the total rejection of worldly values and worldly influence that was an integral part of the belief of both Angélique and her confessor. It was this attitude that enraged Angélique's father when he was prevented from entering Port Royal in 1609 and that infuriated Chancellor Séguier when he realized that he had lost one of his best lawyers, Antoine Le Maistre.

The same attitude of independence that characterized many of Angélique's actions was reflected in Saint-Cyran's refusal of numerous benefices that might have compromised his spiritual integrity by involving him to a greater extent in worldly affairs. It was reflected as well in the refusal of the *solitaires* to join religious orders and in their desire to regulate their own activities in consultation with confessors who were of their group. This independence and sense of self-sufficiency, caused by a profound personal commitment to God and by a detachment from all worldly influences, was bound to displease religious authorities, who preferred attitudes of conformity and submissiveness among the faithful. Such independence was also intolerable to a government seeking to establish greater control and uniformity throughout the kingdom. Furthermore, Saint-Cyran's political opinions antagonized Cardinal Richelieu and the other royal officials. At a time when France was hard pressed in its war against Spain and when many of the king's subjects suffered from acute economic hardship, the crown regarded as extremely dangerous, *dévot* ideals that criticized the war effort on the grounds that it was against another Catholic country and not in the best interests of French society.

These essential characteristics of French Jansenism—profound personal commitment to God, psychological detachment from the world and its ways, reforming zeal, and *dévot* ideals—aggravated the tensions that existed between the followers of Angélique Arnauld and Saint-Cyran and the authorities of Church and state throughout the long reign of Louis XIV, which began five months before the death of Saint-Cyran.

III. *Jansenism and the Fronde*

As a result of the death of Louis XIII, which occurred only a few months after that of the formidable Cardinal Richelieu, a political crisis began to develop in the spring of 1643. Louis XIV, only five years old at the time, was too young to assume the powers of the crown, and for the third time in less than a century, these powers were transferred to a regency council. The Queen Mother, Anne of Austria, was called upon to organize such a council capable of maintaining royal authority and of protecting it from those at home and abroad who sought to weaken the kingdom. As in the case of Catherine de Médicis after the death of Henry II in 1559, and as in the case of Marie de Médicis in 1610, after the death of Henry IV, the formation of such a council proved difficult because of the competing interests of the great nobles who sought to dominate the government. To make matters worse, the reorganization of the king's government took place at a time when the kingdom was involved in a costly and dangerous war with Spain. To the annoyance and chagrin of the princes of the blood and other grandees of the realm, the queen chose Richelieu's protégé, Cardinal Mazarin, a foreigner, to be her closest advisor on the council. Once again, a cardinal-minister was chosen to govern France during a difficult period. And just as Richelieu had been the object of numerous conspiracies designed to overthrow him and to alter royal policy, so too was Mazarin subjected to conspiracies that contributed to the Fronde, the major uprising that plagued the kingdom throughout the regency period (1643-61). The acrimonious religious quarrels relating to Jansenism emerged during the era of the Fronde and were directly related to it.

These religious quarrels centered around two works: Jansenius's *Augustinus* and Antoine Arnauld's *De la fréquente communion.* Cornelius Jansenius was born in the Dutch Netherlands in 1585, began his theological studies at Louvain, and continued them at

the Sorbonne in Paris. After his years of collaborative study with
Saint-Cyran, Jansenius returned to the Spanish Netherlands to be
ordained a priest. In 1619 he received his doctorate at Louvain,
where he was retained as a professor. The influence of Baius was
still strong at Louvain, and the young theologian became interested
in the problem of grace and free will. This interest was heightened
by the Arminian controversy that divided the Dutch Calvinist
church at the time, and he followed closely the proceedings of the
Synod of Dort (1618-19). Early in his career, Jansenius decided
to write a treatise that would explain, in definitive terms, Augustinian theology pertaining to grace and free will. The ensuing work,
the *Augustinus*, was begun in 1628, but frequent interruptions
prevented the work from being completed until 1636, the year its
author became bishop of Ypres. Jansenius died of the plague in
1638, and his magnum opus appeared two years later.

The *Augustinus* consisted of three parts. The first undertook to
explain Pelagian and semi-Pelagian doctrines and to expose their
errors in exhaustive fashion. Saint Augustine's concept of grace
was incapable of being understood, according to Jansenius, without reference to these heresies. Pelagianism, in effect, denied
original sin and asserted that natural man was capable of acquiring
eternal life on his own merits and by his own faculties, whether
or not he was in the Christian fold. Why, demanded the Pelagians,
should a man, untainted by corruption at birth, be condemned
because he was never given tne opportunity to know the Christian
God? This was a question, of course, that intrigued seventeenth-
century freethinkers including La Mothe Le Vayer, the author of
De la vertu des payens. In the second part of the work, Jansenius
argued that, in matters pertaining to grace, Saint Augustine was
the ultimate authority, and in the third part, he considered the
fundamental relationship between man's free will and divine grace.
The Augustinian argument reasserted by the bishop of Ypres
emphasized the crippling effect of Adam's fall on human nature.
Man's will, capable before the Fall of choosing on its own between
good and evil, was now capable only of evil unless aided by God.
Left to its own devices, the human will was filled with love of self,
and consequently all natural acts were based on *amour-propre* and
were therefore damnable in the sight of God. Only when divine

grace infused it with love of God was the will released from the necessity of evil and inspired to do good. In forceful and un-compromising language, Jansenius stated that man was totally dependent upon God's grace in order to choose good and act meritoriously.

The bishop's ponderous opus reflected the influence of Baius and other theologians affected by the "Augustinian strain of piety," and the ideas contained in it were somewhat similar to those expressed by the abbé de Saint-Cyran in his penitential writings. The two men had maintained their relationship ever since their student days, corresponding frequently between 1614 and 1635—when France became involved in the Thirty Years' War and sending letters abroad became more difficult. Saint-Cyran visited his friend at Louvain in 1621 and at the frontier town of Péronne in 1623. Another encounter took place in France in 1625. Jansenius and Saint-Cyran worked together to promote Augustinian penitential theology within the Church, and they hoped that the Oratory, the secular order founded in France by Bérulle, would be the means by which this theology would triumph over the less demanding penitential theology espoused by the Jesuits, among others. Some contemporaries of the two men maintained that Saint-Cyran had almost as much to do with the *Augustinus* as Jansenius, but the work reflects the theoretical and abstract theo-logical interests of the bishop more than the pragmatic penitential concerns of the abbé. Saint-Cyran obtained a copy of the *Augustinus* while in prison, but his health was so bad and his other devotional obligations so compelling, that he may have been unable to do more than peruse it. Yet he is said to have admired the work. His close friend, the *solitaire* Lancelot, wrote in his *Mémoires*: "He [Saint-Cyran] often spoke of the book as a most important devotional work, it being impossible to be truely pious . . . without understanding the miserable condition to which we have been reduced as the result of original sin and the need that we have of being sustained each minute by God's grace in order not to fall."[1]

Neither the Society of Jesus nor Molina's *De concordia liberii arbitrii* was mentioned specifically by Jansenius, but by clear im-plication he identified both with the Pelagian heresy. The Jesuits at Louvain, aware of Jansenius's project long before its publication, tried to have it suppressed on the grounds that it violated the papal ban on theological discussions pertaining to grace. Once again the university was in an uproar, as it had been in the days of the Baian controversy, and Jansenius's defense of Augustinian theology caused considerable commotion in France. Richelieu and a number of bishops wanted the work condemned by both the Sorbonne and the papacy. The cardinal disliked harsh theology that discouraged Christian initiative, and he was not likely to be favorably disposed to another work by the author of *Mars Gallicus*. After some delay, Pope Urban VIII issued an encyclical, *In eminenti*, in 1643, proscribing Jansenius's work on the grounds that it violated the ban on such discussions. The Jesuits in France aggravated Gallican prejudices by publishing *In eminenti* before it had been registered by the parlements. Had Richelieu been alive, he might have been able to put enough pressure on those bastions of Gallicanism, the Parlement of Paris and the Sorbonne, to obtain a condemnation of the *Augustinus*, but his death and that of Urban VIII in 1644 left a power vacuum that made further controversy inevitable. *In eminenti* had little effect in France, where editions of Jansenius's work multiplied.[2]

The counterattack against the *Augustinus* in France was launched by a member of the cathedral chapter of Notre-Dame-de-Paris, Isaac Habert, in a number of sermons preached during the winter of 1643 and in a polemic entitled *Deffense de la foy de l'église*, published in 1644. Habert stressed the fact that the late bishop of Ypres had relied too heavily on Saint Augustine in interpreting Church doctrine pertaining to grace, and he developed the theme that the orthodox position of the Church on the matter was based on the opinions of a number of early and medieval theologians. Habert also denounced what he described as the cabal that was being formed at Port Royal under Saint-Cyran's auspices (the abbé having only recently been released from prison), for the purpose of propagating heretical beliefs. Thus for the second time in a decade, both Port Royal and its spiritual director came under suspicion of heresy.

Habert's denunciations inspired the youthful Antoine Arnauld to retaliate in the form of a polemic entitled *Apologie de Monsieur Jansenius* (1644), in which the late bishop's arguments were recapitulated and the supreme authority of Saint Augustine as the "docteur de la grace" were strongly reasserted. So infuriated was Habert by this work that he appealed to Rome to condemn eight propositions drawn from the *Augustinus*. Arnauld responded with a *Seconde apologie*, published in 1645. The bitter debate between Habert and Arnauld caused quite a stir within the French Church. Those who supported Habert sought to identify Jansenist arguments with Protestant belief by maintaining that the positions of both with respect to grace were the same; those who were sympathetic to Jansenius and Arnauld argued that the Augustinian doctrine of grace as interpreted by the bishop of Ypres was orthodox Catholic doctrine and that any deviation from it was dangerous innovation that smacked of Pelagianism.

The quarrel over the *Augustinus* was exacerbated by another dispute generated by an important work of Antoine Arnauld's, entitled *De la fréquente communion*, published in 1643. Arnauld had promised Saint-Cyran that he would vigorously defend the abbé's ethical principles against all who sought to undermine them, and *De la fréquente communion* (published in the year of Saint-Cyran's death) was, in effect, a restatement of those principles, constructed around the question of the role of the sacraments in the process of absolution. The number of times the Christian ought to partake of the sacraments was an issue hotly debated among theologians. Some, including the Jesuit confessor Sesmaison, author of a brief work entitled *Question s'il est meilleur de communier souvent que rarement*, asserted that weekly communion was beneficial to the sinner and did not require extraordinary efforts other than his intention, at the moment of receiving it, of mending his ways. Other theologians, including Saint-Cyran, contended that depriving oneself of the sacraments might be an effective way for a sinner to develop his commitment to God's purpose. To a lady who had written him at Vincennes that she had been unable to attend Mass because of ill health, Saint-Cyran replied that her sickness ought to have been beneficial to her, because the isolation of the sickroom had provided her with the solitude necessary to rededicate her life to God. "There are times," he said, "when God prefers deprivation of the sacraments to frequent usage."[3]

In *De la fréquente communion*, Arnauld undertook to present the Jansenist position on penitential discipline as the only Catholic position, and, as was the case with all respectable theological arguments of the period, he buttressed his arguments with references to the works of the early Church fathers as well as to those of the recently canonized saints, Carlo Borromeo and François de Sales. Furthermore, he claimed that the doctrinal definitions of the Council of Trent on penitential matters implied support of his position. Echoing Saint-Cyran, the young scholar asserted that the spread of heresy during the sixteenth and seventeenth centuries had been caused by the gradual weakening of devotional practices. In order to turn back the tide of Protestantism and to undertake a successful reformation of the Church, a return to the penitential practices of the primitive Church was essential. By "primitive Church" Arnauld meant the Church in the time of Saint Augustine. Rejecting what he took to be the prevailing view within the seventeenth-century Church, that ecclesiastical discipline varied according to time and circumstance, Arnauld insisted that the principles of the early Church must be adhered to at all times if the institution were to survive. The primitive Church functioned according to the ideals of the patristic thinkers, "and it was in that time that the Church was completely constructed . . . in the perfection of its virtue and in the order of its discipline."[4] This discipline included public penance by which the sinner humiliated himself before God and his fellow parishioners, as well as periodic absention from the sacraments. For Arnauld, the essential feature of this discipline was separation from Communion for the unrepentant sinner. What he found objectionable about the devotional practices of his own time was the inclination of the sinner, encouraged by his confessor, to take Communion as often as he liked. At issue was not so much frequent Communion but the attitude of the sinner. If he were unrepentant despite frequent Communion, the pain of deprivation might cause him to change his ways. "For as participation in the body of the Son of God is the greatest good that can happen in the world, deprivation of his body is, without doubt, the greatest ill."[5]

Despite the accusations of his critics, Arnauld had no intention of downgrading the sacraments; he wished to make the sinner worthy of the sacraments. Nor did he intend to deny the priest the mystical power of absolution. The priest played a vital role in the redemptive process because as confessor he had the obligation to determine the disposition of the penitent. Because his power of absolution was so great, the priest was also obliged to prepare the penitent carefully for the moment when he was to be absolved of his sins. "He who believes himself to be guilty of mortal sins, if he is not disposed to remain away from the Eucharist despite the orders of his confessor, and if he is unable to defer participation in these holy mysteries, because they are yet too disporportionate to his weaknesses, in order to procure for himself a more perfect cure by means of penitential actions, he reverses the principal part of the sacerdotal blood of Jesus Christ."[6] Abstention from the sacraments was a form of public penance.

For what penance would be more agreeable to God, and in a sense more public, than for a sinner to break entirely with his enemy, the world, and in plain view of everyone to renounce forever the pleasures, or rather the follies, of our time; to renounce all sorts of pretensions in order to embrace a holy and religious life; to withdraw in solitude following the example of so many saints, or to choose the depths of a monastery in order to satisfy the justice of God with continual tears; to sacrifice without end the blood of a heart wounded with sorrow and love? . . .[7]

Solitude and introspection, dominant themes in the prison writings of the abbé de Saint-Cyran, were reiterated in *De la fréquente communion.*

If we feel in the depths of our heart a detachment from worldly things and an attachment to God, a distrust of the pomp and vanity of this century and a joy in the expectation of eternal goods, a mortal fear of falling into God's disfavor and an earnest desire to please him in all things, a firm intention to flee all occasions in which we might commit a sin, and finally, a veritable disposition within ourselves to abandon father, mother, brothers, sisters, relatives, goods, fortunes, honors, worldly esteem, rather

than to forsake the service of God. . . . If we find all these dispo-
sitions in our hearts at least to some degree . . . then we will have
some reason to believe that we love God.[8]

Without intending to minimize the importance of the sacraments,
Arnauld nonetheless limited their powers by making their effects
conditional upon the disposition of the sinner. The Eucharist had
little power to purify the Christian whose resolve to reform himself was ephemeral and who relied on the mysteries inherent in
Communion to cover up his infirmities.

Whereas the doctrinal intricacies emanating from the discussions
centered around the *Augustinus* were intelligible only to learned
churchmen, the issues dealt with by Arnauld in *De la fréquente
communion* were of concern to every sincere Catholic. What was
disconcerting to many about the latter work was that it placed
greater responsibility upon the individual and made it harder for
him to receive absolution. Many Catholics—including the Jesuits,
Saint Vincent de Paul, and the pious regent, Anne of Austria—felt
that the Jansenists were putting redemption out of the reach of
the ordinary person. The Jesuits believed that their moral precepts were within the capabilities of the ordinary sinner and that,
although these precepts accommodated human weakness, they in
no way compromised the faith. But if the Jesuits were able to put
the Jansenists on the defensive by identifying the *Augustinus* with
Protestantism, they were themselves on the defensive against
charges that they compromised Christian ethics. Arnauld did not
hesitate to exploit this issue, as Saint-Cyran had done in his Petrus
Aurelius writings. He castigated the Jesuits in a number of pamphlets, much to the satisfaction of his supporters.

Some of these supporters in the clergy were willing to go to
even greater lengths than Arnauld himself in restoring the public
penance recommended in *De la fréquente communion*. When Jean
Callaghan, a friend of Saint-Cyran's, was appointed vicar of the
parish at Cours-Cheverny near the town of Blois in 1651, he
immediately introduced rigorous penitential practices, including
fasting, abstention from wine, prolonged silences, and delayed
absolution. For striking a priest, a practice not uncommon in an
era when the distinction between priest and layman was often
obscured by the bad habits of the clergy, Callaghan forced a

woman to kneel for three consecutive Sundays at the entrance of the church, imploring the forgiveness of God and of the parishioners attending Mass. The curé also abolished unnecessary religious processions and other religious practices tainted with superstition. The Jesuits, who maintained a college in nearby Blois, were alerted to these "innovations" and immediately launched a campaign against Callaghan. In pulpits throughout the diocese, the leading Jesuit preacher at the college thundered against the dangerous heretical practices, and the diocese became so deeply divided over the quarrel that Callaghan was forced to abandon his parish in disgust two years later. Thus were the issues that separated Jansenists and Jesuits joined at the parish level.[9]

Among the more controversial issues contained in *De la fréquente communion* was its introduction written by Martin de Barcos, a nephew of Saint-Cyran and his successor as abbot of the Benedictine monastery of Saint-Cyran. Barcos referred to Saints Peter and Paul as "the two heads of the Church that make but one," thereby seeming to question the primacy of Peter, the first disciple of Christ. Pope Innocent X, whose authority rested upon the fundamental Catholic belief that Saint Peter alone was head of the Church, was alarmed by this apparent affront to his dignity, and the proposition was condemned in 1645. The pope was reluctant, however, to involve himself in the internecine quarrels that plagued Catholic France. He did not wish to offend the Jesuits, nor did he wish to offend those bishops who regarded *De la fréquente communion* as a manifestation of genuine piety. Premature intervention in French religious affairs was likely to arouse Gallican sensibilities to the point where papal authority might be in jeopardy.

The regent was not in a position to take the sort of drastic action that Richelieu had carried out against Saint-Cyran in 1638. The government was in the process of consolidating its power, but as the Fronde was soon to reveal, its position was far from secure. In March 1644, Mazarin suggested to Arnauld and Barcos that they go to Rome to explain their beliefs to the pope. Although not particularly religious, and indifferent to innocuous doctrinal questions, the cardinal-minister was as aware as his predecessor had been that bitter religious quarrels might provoke political upheavals. But his suggestion violated the basic Gallican principle that, wherever possible, religious matters should be settled in France and not in Rome. Reaction from the Parlement of Paris and the Sorbonne was so strong that Mazarin did not press the point.

In 1649, the syndic of the theological faculty of the Sorbonne, Nicholas Cornet, selected seven propositions—extracted, he claimed, from bachelors' theses—which he invited the faculty to examine for possible heretical implications. Some theologians thought that the syndic was subtly attacking the *Augustinus* because of its influence within the university, but Cornet adamently insisted that he did not have the work in mind. Efforts to get the faculty of that august body to rule clearly against the propositions proved fruitless, and so, despite Gallican prejudices, an appeal was made to Rome for a ruling. The appeal took the form of a letter to Innocent X written in January 1651 by Isaac Habert, who had recently been named bishop of Vabres. Six years earlier, it will be remembered, Habert had selected eight questionable propositions from Jansenius's work that were similar to those propositions selected by Cornet. Before being sent to Rome, the letter was circulated among the French bishops, seventy-eight of whom endorsed its contents by adding their names to it. Eleven bishops wrote independently to the pope, objecting to Habert's letter. Innocent X listened to the arguments of Jansenists and their enemies who, unlike Cornet, did not refrain from ascribing the propositions to the *Augustinus*. Two years passed before the pontiff issued an encyclical dealing with the propositions.[10]

The quarrel over the propositions occurred at a time when the kingdom was profoundly troubled by political and social unrest that reached a high-water mark between 1648 and 1652, when widespread rebellion posed a serious threat to the absolute powers of the crown. This rebellion, known as the Fronde, was caused by a number of factors. The war with Spain, begun in 1635, continued after the Treaty of Westphalia had brought the Thirty Years' War to a conclusion in 1648, and it involved military operations on three fronts: the Spanish Netherlands, the Pyrenees, and northern Italy. The war was unpopular with those political and religious leaders who disliked fighting against a Catholic power, and it became increasingly unpopular within all segments of society as the government increased old taxes and established new ones to continue it. Royal tax commissioners antagonized nobles, provincial and municipal officials, and judicial authorities, whose rights and privileges were placed in jeopardy by the unending quest for new funds to support the military effort. In many parts of France, peasants resorted to violence in order to protect their meager resources from the clutches of royal tax collectors. The government's efforts to increase its sources of income aggravated an economic crisis brought on by a dwindling supply of precious metals and a series of poor harvests increased prices and diminished the food supply. To make matters worse, Mazarin, the dominant figure in the government, was heartily disliked, particularly by those princes of the blood and great nobles who believed that their rightful places in the royal councils were being denied them by this foreign protégé of Richelieu's—whom they had also detested because of his infringements on their prerogatives. The intensity of the Fronde reached a point where Mazarin was forced to withdraw from the kingdom twice—in 1651 and again at the end of 1652. Even after he returned to Paris in February 1653 to take up the reins of government (which he did not again relinquish until his death in 1661), Mazarin believed that his position was insecure. The struggle with Spain dragged on until 1659, creating a dangerous situation particularly on the northern frontier, and two principal Frondeurs were still at large: the prince de Condé, a distinguished military commander, who was with the Spanish armies, and the cardinal de Retz, archbishop of Paris, who was in Rome—where he was in a position to stir up more trouble for the French government.

A crucial question concerning the Jansenists was their role in the Fronde and in the subsequent unrest that plagued Mazarin until his death. The Jansenists themselves insisted that they were obedient subjects of the crown. Antoine Arnauld emphasized his loyalty to the king, and his brother Henri was appointed bishop of Angers because of his services to Mazarin. Pascal's sister and biographer, Madame Périer, maintained that her brother, who became associated with Port Royal during the period of the Fronde, resisted every attempt to enlist him in the rebellion.[11] Racine, a pupil at the Little Schools at the time, wrote in his history of Port Royal many years later:

> . . . it was the doctrine of Port Royal that under no conditions could a subject in good conscience rebel against his legitimate prince and that even if [he] were unjustly oppressed, he was obliged to suffer oppression and to demand justice only from God, who alone may call upon rulers to account for their actions. These [principles] have always been taught at Port Royal. . . . A great many people know that during the civil war, confessors in Paris gave absolution indiscriminately to those who were involved in rebellion as well as to those who supported the crown. The priests of Port Royal were firm in their refusal to absolve those who were opposed to the king.[12]

While emphasizing the Port-royalists' loyalty to the crown, Racine admitted that they may have been indiscreet in their associations with *Frondeurs.*

> Besides, whatever the principles cherished at Port Royal concerning fidelity and obedience to legitimate authority . . . the king was convinced that the [Port-royalists] were not favorably disposed toward his person or toward his state; and without thinking, they strengthened this conviction by their association, however innocent, with Cardinal de Retz and by their inclination, more Christian than judicious, to receive many people either disgusted with the court or in disgrace, who sought consolation from them.[13]

While Saint-Cyran and his associates had always asserted loyalty and obedience to the king's person, they were not always favorably disposed toward his ministers. Such an attitude was, of course, characteristic of those who for one reason or another opposed particular policies of the government. The abbé himself had been affiliated with Michel de Marillac, leader of the conspiracy to overthrow Richelieu that culminated in the Day of Dupes. One of those who attended Saint-Cyran's funeral was Marie de Gonzague, deeply implicated in the Cinq-Mars conspiracy in 1642, the final attempt to destroy Richelieu. The granddaughter of the duc de Mayenne (the last leader of the rebellious Catholic League), Marie de Gonzague was also a friend of Angélique Arnauld, who maintained a correspondence with her after Marie had married the king of Poland. Other *Frondeurs* with close ties to Port Royal included the princesse de Guémenée, and the duchesse de Chevreuse. The duc de Luynes, son of the duchesse de Chevreuse and brother of Cardinal de Retz's mistress, built a residence in 1652 close by Port-Royal-des-Champs, where he was in contact with the *solitaires*. Writing to the duke in the last year of the Fronde, Antoine Arnauld commiserated with him at having to take up arms. "I share your feelings about the difficulty one experiences when one is obliged to take up arms to defend oneself and to risk not only one's own life but the lives of others."[14] The tone of the letter reveals a measure of sympathy for the duke's cause and no indignation whatsoever at his taking up arms against his sovereign. One of the most prominent *Frondeurs*—the king's cousin, the duchesse de Longueville—also built a villa next to Port Royal after the Fronde and became the protectress of the convent. While some of these associations may have been innocent from the Port-royalists' point of view, there is considerable evidence to suggest that at least one of them, Arnauld d'Andilly, engaged in pamphleteering against Mazarin.

Robert Arnauld d'Andilly, eldest son of Antoine and Catherine Arnauld, was born in 1588. An ambitious young man, he entered the service of the *surintendant des finances*, the duc de Schomberg, in 1617 as his chief assistant. After Schomberg's downfall in 1617, d'Andilly attached himself to the king's brother, Gaston d'Orléans, receiving the appointment of general intendant of the duke's household. Despite a brief fall from Gaston's favor in 1626, Arnauld d'Andilly maintained good relations with the duc d'Orléans, whose rebellious activities disturbed the reign of Louis XIII and the early reign of Louis XIV. He received a pension from the duke in 1636 and again in 1637, and when Gaston died in 1660, Arnauld d'Andilly wrote to a friend: "In truth, I have need of consolation at the loss that I have experienced as a result of the death of this prince. No one knew him better than I did. I loved him very much, and he always treated me with the greatest kindness and affection."[15] In 1634 Richelieu appointed Arnauld d'Andilly intendant of the Army of the Rhine, and in the following year Arnauld d'Andilly sent a letter to the stadtholder of the Dutch republic, praising the Franco-Dutch alliance so much deplored by *dévots* and by Jansenius, whose *Mars Gallicus* appeared at about the same time. Arnauld d'Andilly's opportunities for further advancement in the king's service were curtailed after the arrest and imprisonment of his close friend, the abbé de Saint-Cyran.

Shortly after Richelieu's death, Arnauld d'Andilly, still aspiring to high political office, addressed two *mémoires* to the Queen Mother (both written in 1643). The first, entitled "Avis à la reine pour attirer les bénédictions de Dieu sur la France," endorsed Richelieu's prohibition against dueling, but it criticized the luxurious habits of the court. Luxury was antithetical to the Christian spirit, and it constituted a drain on French resources not only because of the need to maintain splendid establishments but also because of the pensions by which the king supported impoverished and often undeserving nobles. The *mémoire* stressed the importance of offering positions in the government on the basis of merit rather than on the basis of right or privilege. Awards of offices and honors based on merit would, in Arnauld d'Andilly's opinion, encourage competition among responsible candidates as to who would best serve the true interests of the king, whereas awards based on right and privilege would encourage selfishness and jealousy among candidates more anxious to gratify their own ambitions than to serve the public interest. New offices, wrote Arnauld d'Andilly, ought to be created to advance the interests of the state instead of the needs of the individual. Appointments based on merit benefited the army as well as the magistracy and the Church.[16] The second *mémoire*, much longer than the first, bore the title "Mémoire pour un souverain." It reiterated some of the points made in the "Avis à la reine," and it offered further suggestions in favor of a more Christian government. The king had certain moral responsibilities, asserted Arnauld d'Andilly. He was obliged to award ecclesiastical benefices to persons noted for their piety, and not on the basis of social status. The sovereign ought to punish blasphemy severely, as in the days of Saint Louis, and to discourage luxury "that on the one hand is the ruin of the nobility, which, finding itself impoverished, becomes a burden to the state, and on the other hand spreads like poison among the inferior orders [of society]." He ought to provide as much as possible for the welfare of the poor, "there being nothing more contrary to the Christian spirit than to permit those who are members in Jesus Christ to die of starvation." In the *mémoire*, Arnauld d'Andilly attacked venality as harmful to the state because the functions of offices that were bought instead of earned by those who held them were employed in the interests of private gain rather than of the public welfare. Arnauld d'Andilly advised the regent, when levying taxes, not to place too heavy a financial burden on those elements of society least able to bear it, and he insisted that the rich bear a fair share of the tax load. The king ought to tour his realm from time to time, listening to grievances and becoming more familiar with conditions throughout the land. Furthermore, the king ought to know who among his subjects had reputations of being wise and virtuous and were capable of giving him honest counsel. The royal counselor who is not selfish is a true friend "who forgets himself and thinks only of acquiring servants for his prince, the love of his subjects, the esteem of his neighbors, and the admiration of all the world."[17] These two *mémoires*, which reflect the concerns of one who had considerable experience in financial administration, reveal a desire on the part of the writer to influence a change of policy. Although Arnauld d'Andilly did not call for an end of the war with Spain, his suggestions were reminiscent of those made by Michel de Marillac in 1629, when Louis XIII was being called upon to decide between a policy of peace and retrenchment and an aggressive anti-Habsburg foreign policy. Finally, the *mémoires* reflect Arnauld d'Andilly's desire to assume office in the royal councils. Although Anne of Austria may well have read the *mémoires*, she did not offer Arnauld d'Andilly a position in government, whereupon he decided to renounce his worldly ambitions once and for all and to retire to Port-Royal-des-Champs. Mazarin pursued Richelieu's policy vigorously enough to cause the rebellion known as the Fronde to break out in 1648.

During the Fronde, opposition to government policy and to Cardinal Mazarin in particular was often expressed in the form of pamphlets—known as *Mazarinades*—many of which were anonymous. One such pamphlet, bearing the title *Avis d'état à la reine*, appeared in 1649 and was signed by "Le Solitaire" writing from "the desert," two terms usually associated at the time with Port-Royal-des-Champs. The regent, according to the *Avis*, ought to respect the traditional social orders of the kingdom as well as its fundamental laws, because the king's authority depended, to a large extent, on both. Many of the difficulties presently experienced in France were caused by financial mismanagement, by bad appointments to political and ecclesiastical offices, and by continuing the exhausting war with Spain. Le Solitaire insisted that the way to overcome these problems was to dismiss Mazarin, who had usurped the powers of the crown, and whose policies were tyrannical. The Queen Mother should then resolve not to appoint another first minister and to heed instead the advice and counsel of persons noted for their virtue and merit. The author of the *Avis d'état* praised the good intentions of the Parlement of Paris, at that time deeply involved in the Fronde. Another *Mazarinade*, couched in similar language and containing many of the opinions expressed in the *Avis d'état*, appeared in 1652 under the title *La vérité toute nue, ou advis sincere et désintéressé sur les véritables causes des maux de l'estat et les moyens d'y apporter le remède*. The anonymous author of this polemic stated emphatically that France was being punished for her sins by means of civil war and that the hour of sincere repentance was at hand. The kingdom was being destroyed by a disastrous financial policy and by a tyrannical first minister who, like his predecessor Richelieu, had produced nothing but disorder and anarchy. Mazarin encouraged luxury among the courtiers and even went so far as to squander a fortune, while the rest of the country suffered under the weight of an ever-increasing tax burden. While the author of the pamphlet insisted that he did not approve of rebellion against royal authority, he argued that it was inevitable given the ruinous policies of the government. Addressing himself to the boy king, the pamphleteer urged the dismissal of Mazarin.

Choose for ministers the great and virtuous personages of your kingdom. Hold the name of favorite in horror, remembering the evil caused by those who have held such positions that had fatal consequences for your kingdom. Reestablish order in your finances, banish luxury, enrich your provinces by reviving commerce on land and sea. Ask the assistance of God so that, by a miraculous change worthy of the eldest son of the Church, piety succeeds impiety, justice succeeds injustice, discipline succeeds license, order succeeds disorder, modesty succeeds luxury, and a golden century succeeds the most unfortunate century that has ever been.[18]

Only by restoring peace at home and abroad could the king hope to accomplish this transformation.

There are some differences between the two pamphlets. In contrast to the earlier polemic, *La vérité toute nue* deplored the irresponsibility of the Parlement, and whereas the *Avis* had very little to say about Cardinal de Retz, *La vérité toute nue* spoke disparagingly of Retz's boundless ambition. But on the whole, both *Mazarinades* contained similar views. Both emphasized the need for wise and virtuous counselors, sound financial administration, the curtailment of luxurious habits, and a greater concern for the poor. Both expressed opinions very similar to those that had appeared in the *mémoires* written by Arnauld d'Andilly to the Queen Mother in 1643. Were all four pieces—the two *mémoires*, the *Avis d'état*, and *La vérité toute nue*—written by the same person? A copy of the latter pamphlet—with notations in his handwriting in the margins—appears among Arnauld d'Andilly's papers at the Bibliothèque de l'Arsenal—the only such pamphlet in the collection. Another copy of the same piece, contained in a collection of *Mazarinades* in Leningrad, bears marginal comments ascribing it to Arnauld d'Andilly. Finally, an anonymous document located in the Cabinet des Manuscrits at the Bibliothèque Nationale entitled "Avis charitable au Sieur Arnaut Dandilly sur une de ses pièces intitulée la verité toute nue" also attributes the *Mazarinade* to him. The weight of evidence strongly suggests therefore that Arnauld d'Andilly was indeed the author of *La vérité toute nue*. There is also considerable evidence to indicate that he wrote the *Avis d'état* three years earlier.[19]

If Arnauld d'Andilly was highly critical of government policies before and during the Fronde, he nevertheless attempted to improve his relations with the court after Mazarin's return to power in 1653. He wrote a number of letters to the cardinal-minister from Port Royal, assuring him of the loyalty and obedience of the *solitaires*.[20] In 1658 he petitioned the king for a position for his son, Arnauld de Pomponne, who eventually attained high office in the government of Louis XIV. In another letter, written the following year, he congratulated Mazarin on the successful conclu-

sion of the long war with Spain. But when the cardinal died in
1661, d'Andilly wrote Louis XIV a letter in which he reverted to
some of the themes that appeared in the *Mazarinades* and in
Arnauld d'Andilly's *mémoires* of 1643. The young king was advised to seek the counsel of wise and virtuous men. Every effort
ought to be made by the king to improve the economy by
abolishing luxurious waste, by establishing trading companies and
a large merchant marine to facilitate commerce, and by looking
after the needs of all his subjects, the poor as well as the rich.
Finally, the king would prove himself to be a great ruler if he
listened carefully to the grievances of his people.[21]

The *dévot* principles asserted by Arnauld d'Andilly during the
era of the Fronde were echoed more discreetly in the letters
written by Angélique Arnauld during the same period, in which
there are innumerable references to the devastating impact of the
war on the countryside as well as to the frightful condition of the
poor Opposition to government policies that appeared to place
the aggrandizement of the state above the welfare of the king's
subjects constitutes an important link between the Jansenists and
those *Frondeurs* who sought a change in policy and ministers. At
the same time, it should be emphasized that there is no evidence
that any of the Jansenist spokesmen took up arms against the
crown. Jansenists were, however, closely associated with those
who did—including the notorious rebel Cardinal de Retz, an association that Racine, in his history of Port Royal, very much regretted.

Jean François Paul de Gondi, Cardinal de Retz, belonged to a
family that had close ties to the *dévot* faction during the reign of
Louis XIII. Because he had been directly involved in conspiratorial
activities to overthrow Richelieu, de Retz was looked upon with
disfavor at court; nevertheless he managed to obtain the appointment of coadjutor-bishop of Paris in 1643 through his family
connections. The position virtually assured the young cleric of
eventually becoming archbishop of Paris when the present archbishop, Jean-François de Gondi, his uncle, died. De Retz became
involved in rebellious activity at the outset of the Fronde and
soon emerged as one of its leaders. In 1652, even though he had
not been excluded from a general amnesty by the government,
de Retz, only recently made a cardinal, was arrested and jailed in

Nantes. His uncle died in March 1654, and de Retz, still imprisoned, became the archbishop of Paris. Four months later, he
managed to escape and to make his way to Rome, where he
created further problems for the French government.

Dr. Retz's association with Port Royal and Jansenism began
even before he became coadjutor-bishop. His father, who had
been a friend of Saint-Cyran's, was outraged when the abbé was
arrested by Richelieu, and his uncle the archbishop had extended
his protection over Port Royal when Angélique Arnauld withdrew
the convent from the jurisdiction of the Cistercians. De Retz
adopted a benevolent attitude toward Jansenism early in his career
because he wished to cultivate a *dévot* image. He performed his
administrative duties in a responsible manner, according to the
ideals of the Counter Reformation, while at the same time
enjoying the pleasures of the flesh. In May 1648 he appeared at
Port-Royal-de-Paris to bless Angélique, who was about to return
to Port-Royal-des-Champs with a group of nuns, and a year later,
when his uncle had suspended the *solitaire* Singlin for having
preached a sermon on grace, de Retz managed to have the suspension revoked. Though certainly not a Jansenist himself, many of
his staunch supporters among the Parisian clergy were.[22] It has
been estimated that of the sixty-eight curés who held office in
Paris between 1653 and 1662, thirty-eight were either Jansenist
or sympathetic to Jansenism.[23] They were attracted to the movement because its penitential ethics provided them with a means of
combating the Jesuits, whom they detested. The quarrel between
the curés and the Society of Jesus was part of the larger jurisdictional dispute between the regular and the secular clergy that
hampered the good works of the Counter Reformation. The curés
resented the growing influence of the Jesuits in the parish, and
very often they were jealous of the prestige of the order. Furthermore, the curés were impressed by the exalted concept of the
parish priest inherent in Jansenist writings, although the Richerist
views of some of the curés were far more radical than those of
Saint-Cyran or Antoine Arnauld. Some curés, including the outspoken Jansenist Duhamel, of the parish of Saint-Merri, had been
friends of Saint-Cyran. Finally, Jansenism provided the curés with
arguments by which they were able throughout the 1650s to

defend what they believed to be their rights and privileges in opposition to higher authorities of Church and state.[24]

Jansenist support for the *Frondeur* cardinal was in part the result of the protection and benevolence that he had bestowed upon them, although some, like Arnauld d'Andilly, disapproved of his irresponsible political actions. When the government arrested de Retz and threatened to have him tried and removed from office, Jansenists and other Catholics in the diocese protested against such an infringement of his ecclesiastical rights and privileges. Staunch episcopal Gallicans, the Jansenists opposed any unwarranted interference by the state in the affairs of the Church. Although the government never succeeded in bringing de Retz to trial, it did exercise what were known as its regalian rights in the archdiocese of Paris,[25] rights that enabled the crown to collect Church revenues when the episcopal seat was vacant. Those who believed that the seat was not vacant deeply resented such a policy. Jansenists also supported the imprisoned bishop, because they were well aware that were he removed from office he would be replaced by the archbishop of Toulouse, Pierre de Marca, one of the architects of the government's anti-Jansenist policies during the 1650s.

The arrest of Cardinal de Retz triggered what some historians have called the religious Fronde, the focal point of which was Paris.[26] Clergy and laity loyal to de Retz once more turned their wrath on Mazarin, who had never been popular in the city. Because of unsettled conditions within the diocese resulting from the cardinal's arrest and his subsequent accession to the office of archbishop in 1654, the curés began to reorganize the diocese in terms of their own interests. They formed assemblies to discuss matters of common concern and advanced the radical proposition that the curé had sole jurisdictional power within the parish. This proposition, a derivation of Richerism, was based on the assumption that priestly functions were delegated to the curé directly from God and not through ordination at the hands of the bishop. The Richerist pretensions of the lower order of the clergy inevitably antagonized bishops and political authorities.

On their own, the curés were no match for the powers of the state, but allied to de Retz, they presented formidable problems for Mazarin. De Retz and the clergy of his diocese acting in his name had the power of interdiction and of excommunication, which, if utilized, would have seriously weakened Mazarin's political authority. Safely ensconced in Rome, de Retz could stir up *dévot* sentiment in France to the point that the regency government might be forced to come to terms with Spain and, quite possibly, to dismiss Mazarin. Furthermore, the exiled cardinal had easy access to Pope Innocent X and, after 1655, to his successor, Pope Alexander VII—both of whom disliked Mazarin and disapproved of French foreign policy. Thus, in the spring of 1656, Alexander VII and de Retz appealed to the French clergy, asking them to put pressure on the government to end the war. The papal letter was intended to dislodge Mazarin, but the clergy remained loyal to the cardinal-minister, and Alexander VII, realizing that the tactic had failed, eventually broke with de Retz, thereby easing the pressure on Mazarin.[27] However, as long as de Retz was at large, with the support of the papacy and of a significant element of public opinion in France, and as long as the war with Spain continued, Mazarin had much to fear. During the Wars of Religion in the sixteenth century, the alliance between zealous Catholics at home and Spanish power abroad had nearly destroyed the French monarchy. Paris in particular was a focal point of *dévot* opposition, which Henry IV overcame only with great difficulty. Fear of this alliance caused Richelieu to imprison Saint-Cyran at the outset of the war with Spain; in the 1650s the same alliance caused his successor to adopt a strong anti-Jansenist policy. Mazarin was well aware of the Jansenist sentiments within the archdiocese of Paris, and he and Chancellor Séguier suspected a connection between Port Royal and the religious Fronde. By suppressing Jansenism, Mazarin hoped to curb rebellious sentiments within the kingdom and also to weaken de Retz's influence in Rome. Because both Innocent X and Alexander VII disliked Jansenism, Mazarin's agents in Rome were instructed to convince the pontiffs that de Retz was a Jansenist and that Mazarin, acting in the name of "the eldest son of the Church" and as a prince of the Church, was serving the interests of Catholicism by suppressing a heretical movement. Mazarin hoped that the papacy would then adopt a more neutral stance in the conflict between the two Catholic kingdoms, thus enabling France to bring the war to a successful conclusion.[28]

When the cardinal-minister returned to Paris in the winter of 1653, the propositions selected by Cornet, the syndic of the Sorbonne, and Habert, bishop of Vabres, were still under consideration at the Vatican. By making it clear to Innocent X that the French government wanted the propositions condemned, Mazarin's representatives in Rome helped to reinforce the arguments of the Jesuits and of other theologians seeking condemnation. Although the pope was suspicious of Jansenist doctrine, which he regarded as innovative and potentially dangerous, he did not want to act precipitately against Jansenius's supporters, because of their influential connections in French episcopal circles. On May 31, 1653, after lengthy deliberations, Innocent issued an encyclical, *Cum occasione*, declaring four of the propositions to be heretical and a fifth to be false. The condemned propositions are as follows.

1.   Some commandments [of God] are impossible to the just, who may wish [to obey them] and may exert all their efforts in that direction; they lack the grace necessary to carry them out.

2.   In the state of corrupt nature, one can never resist interior grace.

3.   In order to act meritoriously or to be blameworthy, it is not necessary that there be in man a liberty that is exempt from necessity. It suffices that liberty be exempt from constraint.

4.   The semi-Pelagians admit to the necessity of an inner prevenient grace for each action, even the act of faith. They are heretics insofar as they believe that man's will may resist or accept that grace.

5.   It is a semi-Pelagian sentiment to say that Jesus Christ died or that he shed his blood for all men without exception.[29]

These five propositions constituted the crux of the acrimonious debate over free will and efficacious grace, but they were couched in such general language that they were capable of several interpretations.

Certainly the condemned propositions related to some aspects of Jansenism. The first proposition reflected a belief that the will is helpless to accomplish good without the aid of divine grace, even though it desires the good. In his "Petit catéchisme," Saint-Cyran had stated that it is not enough for a man to know the commandments of God: " . . . it is necessary for that knowledge to be accompanied by God's grace, without which a knowledge of the commandments is detrimental rather than profitable to those who have it."[30] Innocent X regarded the propositions as heretical because they seemed to deny the traditional doctrine of Christian liberty, by which a sinner accepted or resisted God's grace. This is apparent in the condemnations of propositions two, three, and four. Because Christian liberty had been under attack since the Reformation, the pope was determined to protect the principle that a Christian must participate freely in a meritorious act.

Jansenist theologians, while maintaining the helplessness of the human condition and the efficacy of grace, would not admit that their belief in any way contravened the doctrine of Christian liberty. Saint-Cyran wrote that grace freed the will from the constraints of original sin.[31] "Thus we see that there are two ways of interpreting the proposition that grace cooperates with the will," wrote Antoine Arnauld, "one Catholic and the other Pelagian. The Catholic interpretation is that grace cooperates with the will by causing it to determine to do good, forming within it the desire [to do good]. . . . The Pelagian interpretation is that grace cooperates with the will by helping it after the will has determined on its own to do good."[32] Resorting to the Cartesian argument that the understanding would not reject a clear and distinct idea that was presented to it, Arnauld maintained that the will was incapable of rejecting that which would achieve happiness. Acting according to its own promptings without the aid of grace, the will would inevitably determine happiness on the basis of self-interest, but acting according to the prompting of grace, it would inevitably determine happiness on the basis of God's intent. Just as a clear and distinct idea determined the understanding, grace determined the will in the same way. In neither case was human liberty impaired, because constraint was not involved.[33]

The pope had claimed that the fifth proposition was false because it denied that Christ has died for all men. The Jansenist position on the extent of Christ's redemptive powers was asserted by Antoine Arnauld as early as 1644. He argued that God obviously did not want all men saved, because otherwise he would not have made membership in his Church a necessary precondition for salvation. The existence of millions of non-Christians was proof of God's intentions.[34] Christ died for all men in terms of the amount of redemptive power that he had at his disposal, but not in terms of the number of souls actually redeemed.[35] Some three decades later, the Jansenist theologian Pasquier Quesnel underlined the ambiguity of the fifth proposition. "Jesus Christ died for all [men] because he offered a ransom sufficient for all, but in effect, he did not die for all men because all men have not received the fruit of his death . . . but only those to whom the merit of his passion has been communicated."[36] As was invariably the case with the Jansenists, the fifth proposition was interpreted in such a way as to emphasize the wretched plight of mankind and the infinite capacity of God.

Consisting of such ambiguities, the five propositions allowed a great deal of room for future disputes, and, what is more, the encyclical condemning them never referred to Jansenius's work, leaving open the question of whether or not the propositions were in fact to be found in the *Augustinus*. Innocent X was trying to steer a middle course between absolute acceptance or rejection of Jansenius's interpretation of the Augustinian doctrine of grace. He also wanted to make certain that the Church was in no way condemning Augustinian doctrine itself. He told one of Jansenius's supporters shortly after promulgating the encyclical that "he had not condemned Saint Augustine's and Saint Thomas's [Aquinas] teachings with respect to efficacious grace."[37]

Cardinal Mazarin knew well enough that *Cum occasione* was not an absolute condemnation of the *Augustinus* and that further religious quarrels were likely to ensue. He also knew that he faced the problem in France of overcoming Gallican resistance to publication of the encyclical, of the sort that had rendered the first anti-Jansenist encyclical of Urban VIII ineffective. From his point of view, it was imperative that the five propositions be attributed to Jansenius, and to this end he convened a number of bishops residing at court in the spring of 1654 to obtain their support. At the same time *Cum occasione* was distributed to all the bishops of France to be published in their dioceses. The archbishop of

Sens issued a pastoral letter critical of the encyclical, in which he stated his disappointment that the bishops in assembly had not been permitted to rule on the orthodoxy of the propositions before the matter had been deferred to Rome. After several deliberative sessions, the prelates brought together at the Louvre by Mazarin concluded that the propositions in question were indeed to be found in the *Augustinus*, and the entire French episcopate and the pope were notified of this decision. When informed of these proceedings, Innocent at first remarked that the bishops had gone beyond his intention of not specifically referring to Jansenius or his work, but after Mazarin's emissaries persuaded him that Jansenism was a highly subversive movement, he agreed to write a letter to the French bishops attributing the propositions to Jansenius.

The Jansenists had been disappointed by *Cum occasione*, but they appeared willing to respect the encyclical as long as it did not specifically refer to the *Augustinus* and as long as there was no question of official condemnation of the Augustinian doctrine of grace as they interpreted it. Arnauld d'Andilly tried to use what influence he had at court to assure Mazarin that the Port Royal circle was loyal to the king and to the Church. The Jansenists seemed inclined to refrain from further doctrinal disputes in order to avert outright condemnation,[38] but Mazarin's hostility coupled with their own polemical inclinations made such silence impossible.

A number of anti-Jansenist pamphlets were published in 1654 and 1655, some of them inspired by Mazarin. One such pamphlet entitled *Inconveniens d'estat procedans du Jansénisme* (1654) undertook to prove the dangerous nature of Jansenism. Jansenists— asserted its author, the Sieur de Marandé—regarded the fundamental laws of the kingdom as being based on a contract between the king and his subjects, "according to which, when the king wishes to levy new taxes and promulgate new legislation, he has to have the contract in hand in order to show his people that his demands are in conformance with the clauses and conditions of the treaty he had made with them."[39] The king was bound by the contract, the basis of all law. If his subjects were persuaded that the king was attempting to impose legislation on them in violation of the contract, they were justified in revolting against his authority. The political opinions of the Jansenists, to Marandé's way of thinking, were subversive not only because they were based on an inviolable political contract but because they denied the subject free will, by which he was able to choose between a legal and an illegal act. Compelled by a natural inclination to do evil, the subject was not responsible for his actions and was therefore not liable to punishment by the state. If beliefs of this sort were permitted to circulate about the kingdom, argued Marandé, then justice would be based upon force and violence rather than upon divine sanction.[40] Finally, the pamphlet contended that, by their attacks on pomp and luxury, the Jansenists were undermining the established order "because it is true that the opulence and splendor of the great families assures the prince against popular turmoil and disorder. People who have nothing to lose and nothing to fear are inclined toward disorder and confusion."[41] This defense of pomp and luxury, so distasteful to Jansenists, was reminiscent of Richelieu's opinion, expressed in his *Political Testament*, that luxurious and magnificent surroundings were the mark of a great king. Marandé's accusations were intended to frighten public opinion already sensitive to contemporary radical political ideas emanating from the English civil war.[42]

In February 1655 there occurred an event that heightened the tensions already existing between the Jansenists and their enemies. The duc de Liancourt was refused the sacraments by a Parisian priest because of his Jansenist connections. Three weeks later, Antoine Arnauld issued a polemic entitled *Lettre à une personne de condition*, vehemently protesting the event, while his brother Arnauld d'Andilly wrote Mazarin justifying the Jansenists' need to defend themselves against unwarranted persecution. Several months later, Antoine Arnauld wrote a *Seconde lettre à un duc et pair* addressed to the duc de Luynes, *Frondeur* and patron of Port Royal, in which he again objected to the insult to Liancourt and insisted that the five condemned propositions were not to be found in the *Augustinus*. Arnauld's two letters caused the Sorbonne, under the careful supervision of the government (Chancellor Séguier attended the meetings of the faculty with archers at his side), to censure him for his refusal to submit to the authority of the Church. On February 16, 1656, Arnauld was excluded from the faculty of the Sorbonne. Ironically, sixty-one years earlier, the faculty had publicly thanked Arnauld's father, who "defended with much zeal and effort the rights of the University [against the Jesuits]. . . . The university feels obliged under oath to render services to Monsieur Arnauld and to his children with the same zeal that good clients owe to a defense counsel who has defended their honor, rights, and reputation."[43]

In the autumn of 1655, as the Sorbonne was preparing to act against Antoine Arnauld, the assembly of the clergy, meeting as usual every fifth year to consider its "free gift" to the crown, was asked by Mazarin to endorse both the encyclical *Cum occasione* and Innocent X's letter to the French bishops attributing the five propositions to the *Augustinus.* This was an unusual procedure because for the first time such an assembly was asked to consider doctrinal questions in addition to its usual gift. After some debate over whether it was competent to deal with such matters, the assembly agreed to endorse both documents, and shortly thereafter it endorsed Arnauld's expulsion from the Sorbonne. Still in session in 1656, the assembly drew up a formulary to be signed by all members of the French clergy—regular and secular—promising obedience to the papal decrees. Like the Sorbonne, the assembly of the clergy found it impossible to resist the pressures of the crown. Its members were persuaded that obedience to the government whenever possible was the surest means of preserving the fiscal privileges of the Church. This policy enabled the government to use the assemblies to increase its authority over the French Church. In 1656 Mazarin succeeded in getting the assembly of the clergy to proclaim that it was entitled to speak in the name of the French Church as a whole, an assertion that met with some opposition from bishops jealous of their episcopal rights. These measures constituted an important achievement in Mazarin's campaign against the Jansenists.[44]

Alexander VII, who succeeded Innocent X in 1655, contemplated issuing his own pronouncement against Jansenism. In fact, the new pope disliked the movement so much that he even suggested to the French ambassador in Rome that the nuns and *solitaires* of Port Royal be dispersed. Nevertheless, his hostility toward Mazarin and his anti-Spanish policy was also great, and this caused him to delay issuing his encyclical against Jansenism. He preferred instead to move against Mazarin by writing a letter to the French clergy in March 1656 calling for peace between the warring kingdoms. Only after his attempt to weaken Mazarin had failed did Alexander realize that it was in the Vatican's interests to reach some sort of accommodation with him. Cardinal de Retz withdrew from Rome, and the papal curia began work on a third anti-Jansenist encyclical, *Ad sacram*, which was received at the French court in March 1657. This document stated in no uncertain terms that the five propositions were to be found in the *Augustinus* and that they were condemned in the sense of Jansenius's meaning. When Mazarin immediately set out to register the encyclical with the Parlement of Paris, a step that was necessary in order for it to have the full force of law in the kingdom, the parlement offered some resistance to the encyclical on the usual grounds that it violated Gallican liberties.[45] A *lit de justice* was required before the appropriate legislation was enacted in December 1657, although not without a statement at the proceedings issued by the *avocat général* that "encyclicals against Jansen should be administered through the authority of the king, who is the arbiter in these matters."[46] Mazarin's final act against the Jansenists was taken in 1659, when he closed the Little Schools.

In that same year France concluded a successful treaty with Spain, the Treaty of the Pyrenees. With de Retz's influence on the wane as a result of both his abandonment by Alexander VII and his own ineptitude, and with the long war over, Jansenism and the religious turmoil in Paris caused by the religious Fronde became less of a threat to the regency government. When Mazarin died in 1661, he turned over to Louis XIV not only a kingdom at peace but instruments in the form of three anti-Jansenist encyclicals and the formulary drawn up by the Assembly of the clergy in 1656, endorsed by the highest authorities in Church and state, with which to end the religious Fronde and to suppress the subversive heresy forever.

IV. Port-Royal-des-Champs
The Development of a Frondeur Mentality

In the autumn of 1655, a few months before his expulsion from the Sorbonne, Antoine Arnauld withdrew from Paris to Port-Royal-des-Champs, which had been abandoned by the nuns in 1625 because of the unhealthy conditions that prevailed in that part of the valley of the Chevreuse. During the Fronde, however, Mère Angélique had returned to the ancient convent with a group of nuns, anxious to escape from the troubled capital. The *solitaires*, who had lived in the Faubourg Saint-Jacques near Port-Royal-de-Paris during the 1640s, took up residence at the Grange, a short distance from Port-Royal-des-Champs. They made the dilapidated buildings inhabitable once again and reestablished the gardens under the supervision of Arnauld d'Andilly, who was chiefly responsible for making the wilderness around the convent bloom with flowers and fruit trees as never before. Thus it came about that at the very time when Mazarin was making every effort to suppress Jansenism after his return to power in 1653, Port-Royal-des-Champs, in rustic elegance, became in effect the spiritual and intellectual center of the movement. The activities that took place there inspired the Jansenist movement throughout France and established the basis of Jansenist opposition to ecclesiastical and political authority during the era of the Fronde.

Among the *solitaires* residing at the Grange during the 1650s was Pierre Nicole, who was born in Chartres in 1625. His father, Jean Nicole, was a fairly prominent lawyer, with ties to literary circles in Paris. Pierre enrolled as a student of theology at the Sorbonne, where he was particularly influenced by teachers inclined toward Jansenism, and his bachelor's thesis on grace was among those suspected by Cornet and others of containing heretical implications. The subsequent move to reduce Jansenist influence at the Sorbonne caused Nicole to terminate his theological studies and to withdraw to Port-Royal-des-Champs. Although two of his cousins were nuns at that institution, Nicole's decision to become a *solitaire* resulted from his close association with two spiritual directors of Port Royal, Guillebert and Singlin. At Port Royal, Nicole became a teacher at the Little Schools, one of the *solitaires'* major projects, and in 1654 he became the secretary of Antoine Arnauld, who needed someone to help him translate Latin texts. Nicole eventually became one of the most prominent Jansenist writers of the seventeenth century.[1]

An even more prominent writer affiliated with Port Royal during the 1650s was Blaise Pascal. Pascal was born at Clermont-Ferrand in 1623, the son of Etiènne Pascal, a prominent magistrate in that city and a member of its social and intellectual elite. Perhaps because the provincial atmosphere of the Auvergne was too stifling, Etiènne decided in 1631 to move to Paris, where he had no difficulty establishing relations with the important intellectual circles of the time. Interested in the latest literary and philosophical developments and disgusted with the Scholastic tradition that weighed heavy on the educational structure of France, Etiènne educated his son and two daughters himself. By insisting on a thoroughly modern educational approach, Etiènne contributed much to Blaise's interest in mathematics and physics and to his daughter Jacqueline's literary interests. Having sold his magisterial office, Etiènne Pascal invested some of his income in government bonds. The value of these bonds suffered a sharp decline in 1638, due to the government's fiscal policy, and Etiènne and other bondholders protested vehemently to Chancellor Séguier. Sensitive to any criticism in this period of national crisis, Richelieu ordered Etiènne Pascal's arrest, but before the order could be carried out Etiènne escaped to the Auvergne, leaving his children in the care of relatives. A year later, Richelieu encountered Jacqueline Pascal, who was taking part in a children's theatrical performance arranged for the cardinal-minister's entertainment. Charmed by the little girl, Richelieu took her on his knees and asked her if there was anything that he could do for her. When Jacqueline replied that she wanted her father back, Richelieu forgave Etiènne, who returned to Paris immediately. Shortly thereafter, Etiènne Pascal was sent to Rouen by the government to help reestablish order in that Norman city, then in the midst of a violent revolt against the government. Etiènne Pascal moved his family to Rouen in 1640. The Rouen experience was important for the family, and particularly for Blaise, who remained there until 1647. The Pascals saw firsthand the results of revolt and repression, and in later writings Blaise emphasized the need for political obedience. Blaise helped his father in his work and invented a calculating machine to record tax revenues more accurately, an invention that contributed to his growing reputation as a mathematical genius. At Rouen the Pascal family was profoundly affected by the religious currents that pervaded the city in the years immediately after the revolt. Among the priests with whom they came in contact was Jean Guillebert, curé of Rouville and friend of the abbé de Saint-Cyran. Guillebert, who was to play an important role in directing Nicole toward Port Royal, was not the first link between the Pascals and Jansenist circles. When the family had originally moved to Paris, it had taken up residence in the parish of Saint-Merri, whose curé, Duhamel, was also a friend of Saint-Cyran's. Duhamel subsequently became one of the leading spokesmen of the Parisian curés during the religious Fronde. Under Guillebert's supervision, Blaise read the spiritual letters of Saint-Cyran, Antoine Arnauld's *De la fréquente communion*, and an opuscule of Jansenius's translated by Arnauld d'Andilly in 1644, entitled *Discours sur la réformation de l'homme intérieur*. Though much impressed by the penitential ethics of the Jansenists, the young man refused to renounce the world and its ways or to repudiate his worldly ambitions. In 1647 Pascal, whose health was never very good, was ordered by a physician to return to Paris and to distract himself with any amusements that might help to take his mind off his physical condition.

When Pascal returned to Paris, his reputation as a mathematician and inventor was known throughout Europe. Leading scientists sought him out—including Descartes, who met him at least twice. Between 1647 and 1651 he was preoccupied with the problem of the existence of a vacuum, a problem that was then causing some scientists to challenge the traditional assumption that nature abhors a vacuum. Pascal's famous experiments with mercury led him to disagree on the matter with both Descartes and the rector of the Jesuit College of Clermont, Father Noel, who prided himself on his own knowledge of the subject. Pascal's *Experiences nou-*

velles touchant le vide was written in 1648. In addition to being an important statement in favor of experimental science, its publication provided the occasion for his first polemical encounter with the Jesuits.

While Blaise Pascal continued to make his way in the world as a prominent Parisian intellectual, his sister Jacqueline, who had shown considerable promise as a poet, decided to take the veil and retire to Port Royal, a decision that was bitterly opposed by her father. After Etiènne's death in 1651, however, Jacqueline entered the convent and became Sister Euphémie. Although the question of their inheritance from their father and a suitable dowry for the convent caused Blaise to resent his sister's decision and to quarrel with her for a time, the complicated negotiations leading up to her admission to the convent increased Pascal's contact with Port Royal and reinvigorated his religious sentiment. On the night of November 23, 1654, Pascal had an ecstatic religious experience, later recorded on a piece of paper that he carried on his person for the rest of his life.

> "God of Abraham, God of Isaac, God of Jacob,"
> not of philosophers and scholars.
>
> Certainty, certainty, heartfelt, joy, peace.
> God of Jesus Christ.[2]

This "night of fire" resulted in Pascal's placing himself under the spiritual direction of Singlin. Although he never became a *solitaire*, he visited Port-Royal-des-Champs from time to time during the 1650s, and his subsequent religious writings were permeated with Jansenist spirituality. While Pascal regarded himself as a friend of Port Royal, he continued to maintain his worldly connections and to pursue his scientific interests.[3]

Among the *solitaires* then in residence in the wilderness around Port-Royal-des-Champs was the venerable Arnauld d'Andilly, who in 1654 had entered into a secret correspondence with Mazarin. D'Andilly hoped to use what prestige he had at court for the protection of the Port Royal circle, while Mazarin was eager to maintain contact with the Jansenists, in order to keep an eye on their activities.[4] As has already been pointed out in the preceding chapter, d'Andilly assured the cardinal-minister that his associates at Port Royal would not engage in polemics after the publication of *Cum occasione* as long as the Augustinian doctrine of efficacious grace was not in jeopardy. When the duc de Liancourt was denied the sacraments in 1655 because of his Jansenist connections—thereby causing Antoine Arnauld to write his *Lettre à une Personne de Condition*—Arnauld d'Andilly justified his brother's letter in a communication sent to Mazarin on March 9, 1655, on the grounds that any Christian had the right to defend himself publicly against accusations of heresy.[5] Antoine Arnauld's *Seconde Lettre à un Duc et Pair* was written in response both to Mazarin's invitation, through Arnauld d'Andilly, to explain more fully his position on the five propositions and to continuing public attacks against the Jansenists.[6] Again in defense of his brother, Arnauld d'Andilly wrote that " . . . any Catholic who is unjustly accused of heresy being obliged in good conscience to defend himself, a theologian devoted to the Church would do wrong if by maintaining a criminal silence he betrayed himself by not letting all the world know of the purity of his sentiments." When it became clear that Antoine Arnauld was to be censured by the Sorbonne, Arnauld d'Andilly wrote Mazarin that his brother "would rather die a thousand times than in any way to maintain a belief not based on the abiding and pure sources of the tradition of the Church."[7] This defiant statement was a clear indication that the Port-royalists would not submit to any doctrine imposed upon them by any authority if it did not conform to their own interpretation of ecclesiastical tradition.

On January 23, 1656, shortly before the theological faculty of the Sorbonne reached its decision to censure Antoine Arnauld for his defense of the duc de Liancourt and to expel him from its ranks, there appeared an anonymous letter, widely circulated, defending Arnauld. This was the first of eighteen such epistles written between January 1656 and March 1657, which became known as *The Provincial Letters*. Their author was Pascal, who wrote them in consultation with Antoine Arnauld and Nicole. The third letter, written on February 9, 1656, just after the theological faculty reached its decision, deplored the unjust condemnation of Arnauld's religious belief.

It is not the sentiments of M. Arnauld that are heretical; it is only his person. This is a personal heresy. He is not a heretic for anything he has said or written, but simply because he is M. Arnauld. This is all they have to say against him. Do what he may, unless he cease to be, he will never be a good Catholic. The grace of Saint Augustine will never be the true grace, so long as he continues to defend it. It would become so at once, were he to take it into his head to impugn it. That would be a sure stroke, and almost the only plan for establishing the truth and demolishing Molinism; such is the fatality attending all the opinions which he embraces.[8]

After defending the doctrine of efficacious grace as set forth by Arnauld and other Jansenist theologians, Pascal proceeded to attack the penitential ethics of the Jesuits. Addressing an imaginary Jesuit confessor in the fourth letter, Pascal exclaimed: "Blessings on you, my good father, for this way of justifying people! Others prescribe painful austerities for healing the soul; but you show that souls which may be thought desperately distempered are in quite good health. What an excellent device for being happy both in this world and in the next! I had always supposed that the less a man thought of God, the more he sinned; but, from what I see now, if one could only succeed in bringing himself not to think upon God at all, everything would be pure with him in all time coming."[9] According to Pascal, the ethical precepts of the Society were designed to compromise Christian principles with worldly aspirations. This accommodating and obliging posture made it possible for Jesuit confessors to permit noblemen to defend their honor without violating divine law (the reference here was to dueling), to permit merchants and bankers to demand higher interest rates without disobeying the Church's injunction against usury, and to approve of simony. Jesuit moralists, in short, were willing to accommodate self-interest wherever necessary. Understandably then, wrote Pascal, the Jesuits defended the doctrine of attrition against that of contrition, the doctrine so essential to the penitential beliefs of the Jansenists. Another fictitious Jesuit theologian is made to assert in the tenth letter that

the fathers of our College of Clermont have maintained . . . "that attrition may be holy and sufficient for the sacrament, although it may not be supernatural"; and . . . "that attrition, though merely natural, is sufficient for the sacrament, provided it is honest." I do not see what more could be said on the subject, unless we choose to subjoin an inference, . . . that contrition, so far from being necessary to the sacrament, is rather prejudicial to it, inasmuch as, by washing away sins of itself, it would leave nothing for the sacrament to do at all. That is, indeed, exactly what the celebrated Jesuit Father Valencia remarks. . . . "Contrition," says he, "is by no means necessary in order to obtain the principal benefit of the sacrament; on the contrary, it is rather an obstacle in the way of it . . . ." Nobody could well desire more to be said in commendation of attrition.[10]

Put on the defensive by this devastating critique of their ethics, Jesuit theologians argued in reply to the *Provincial Letters*, that their precepts did, in fact, reconcile divine imperatives with human frailties and worldly necessities. In his *Résponses aux Lettres Pro vinciales* (1658) the Jesuit confessor to the young Louis XIV, François Annat, who later resigned this position to protest the king's illicit relations with Louise de La Vallière, maintained that there were certain precepts set forth in scripture that were unequivocal and therefore applicable to all circumstances. There were, however, many complex ethical problems for which theologians provided conflicting precepts. The confessor was obliged, in these situations, to provide the penitent with a suitable course of action. Several factors had to be taken into account in selecting precepts. They ought not to contradict the universal teachings of the Church; they must emanate from a respectable theologian, they ought not to relate to conditions that no longer existed; and they ought to be based to some extent upon reason and common sense. The Church, wrote Annat, did not expect the sinner to follow rigid principles that prevented him from having any peace of mind or that were beyond his capabilities.[11]

There were, to be sure, some similarities between the ethical teachings of Jesuits and Jansenists. Spiritual directors in both camps recognized the need to tailor their advice to the spiritual needs of the individual. Saint-Cyran had been as insistent as the Jesuits on this point. The significant difference between the two positions, however, occurred in their respective conceptions of the responsibility of the individual. The Jesuits emphasized obedience to the Church, but they were prepared to admit that the Church might alter its requirements to suit changing circumstances. Ecclesiastical discipline in the seventeenth century could not be the same as in the thirteenth or, for that matter, in the era of the primitive Church. The Church in its wisdom was capable of making the necessary adjustments to changing circumstances of time and place. By its mystical powers of absolution, derived from the infinite mercy of God, the Church was able to buttress human frailty. The responsibility of the individual, therefore, was to submit to the authority of the Church, and to take advantage of its healing power by frequently partaking of the sacraments. The Jansenists, on the other hand, placed much greater emphasis on the responsibility of the individual Christian. They too stressed the importance of obedience to the Church, but their ethical principles raised the possibility, at least by implication, of a conflict between an individual entirely committed to God's purpose and ecclesiastical authority tainted by earthly considerations. By emphasizing the rigorous penitential obligations of the individual, the Jansenists appeared to limit the redemptive powers of the Church.

The significance of the *Provincial Letters* to the history of Jansenism is that they reasserted arguments pertaining to efficacious grace and contrition that had aroused the authorities of Church and state since the days of Saint-Cyran at the very moment when Mazarin and the papacy were trying to suppress those ideas. They set forth Jansenist positions with respect to social issues in language and in form designed to have a maximum effect on public opinion. Issues that had until recently been discussed only in Latin or pedantic French by scholarly theologians were now brought to the attention of the public in a manner calculated to attract its interest. Finally, *The Provincial Letters* provided reinforcement for the Parisian curés in their efforts to defend their rights and privileges against the Jesuits and against the government.

The curés of Paris were delighted with *The Provincial Letters*, and when a rather feeble defense of Jesuit ethics, *Apologie pour les casuistes contre les calomnies des jansénistes* written by Georges Pirot, appeared in 1658 after the publication of the final Provincial Letter, they sought to have the work condemned by the Sorbonne and by the French bishops. In order to sustain their assault on Jesuit laxity, the Parisian curés, through their assemblies, authorized the publication of ten *écrits*, which appeared between January 1658 and June 1659. These *écrits* were written by Pascal, Antoine Arnauld, and Nicole and were then ratified by the corps of curés. Pirot was accused in the *écrits* of propagating lax maxims that would inevitably trouble the consciences of decent Christians, and his *Apologie* was referred to as "a seditious and schismatic enterprise" that, if not suppressed by the Church, would cause parishioners to look with suspicion on their legitimate pastors who opposed such corrupt ethical precepts.[12] This concern that legitimate pastors would be separated from their flock was based on the awareness of Parisian curés that their authority within the parish was diminishing. The tone of the *écrits* was militant.

Scripture teaches us that Jesus Christ brought not only peace but also the sword and divisiveness to the world because all means are necessary in their proper time in order to defend the truth, the benefits of which are the ultimate goal of all Christians, war and peace being only the means to that end. Each is effective only insofar as it aids the truth. Christians know that it is for this reason that Scripture proclaims that there is a time for war and a time for peace (Eccles.iii:8). It does not state that there is a time for truth and a time for lies. It is better that a scandal occurs than that the truth is abandoned.[13]

These words, written by Pascal, reveal the close connection that existed between the writers of Port Royal and the Parisian curés whose activities on behalf of their jurisdictional rights and their exiled archbishop constituted the religious Fronde. Mazarin was well aware of this connection. It strengthened his conviction that Jansenism was a seditious movement, and he attempted to have at least one of the *écrits* suppressed.[14]

When Alexander VII's encyclical *Ad sacram* had been received in France and was being considered by the Parlement of Paris, an anonymous pamphlet entitled *Lettre d'un avocat au parlement à un de ses amis* (1657) appeared. Its author was none other than Antoine Le Maistre, who twenty years earlier had announced his intention of having "no further commerce either orally or in writing with the world, which will think me lost." Realizing that the encyclical might provoke the Gallican prejudices of the parlement, the former lawyer asserted that the document was a means by which the pope was attempting to establish the Inquisition in France. Since the great majority of the French clergy, according to Le Maistre, supported this attempt because they were afraid of losing their lucrative benefices, the parlement was obliged to intervene. "This is not a matter of religion but of politics."[15] Le Maistre invoked the *appel comme d'abus*, a procedure by which the parlement received appeals from ecclesiastical jurisdictions. While the French sovereign courts regarded this procedure as an essential prerogative, the clergy for the most part regarded it as an encroachment on the prerogatives of the Church. The *appel comme d'abus*, insisted Le Maistre, prevented the establishment of an Inquisition and preserved Gallican liberties. "If papal encyclicals impose a spiritual control over the mind of the people, then it will be in vain that the parlements will be able to resist Roman encroachments on the temporal powers of our Kings."[16] The Parlement of Paris was reluctant to register *Ad sacram*, not because of sympathy for Jansenism,[17] but because it objected to papal interference in what it regarded as French affairs. Parlementary efforts to oppose the inclinations of the crown, however, were substantially weakened after 1653—for which reason the sovereign court eventually registered the encyclical, after assurances from Mazarin that its judicial prerogatives were intact.

The Port-royalists were desperately trying to defend their fundamental beliefs, threatened as they were by Mazarin and by the papacy. In order to enlist support for their cause, they actively supported the Parisian curés, whose resentments against the Jesuits and higher authorities had contributed to the religious Fronde. So too did they appeal, though somewhat less successfully, to the Parlement of Paris, whose resistence to the crown had also contributed to the Fronde.

Polemical activities did not entirely absorb the energies of the Jansenists associated with Port Royal. They worked in the fields and gardens around the convent, and some of them continued to translate devotional works. Arnauld d'Andilly, for example, translated a life of Saint Theresa at the same time that he was negotiating with Mazarin to prevent further persecution. Of utmost importance to Port Royal were the Little Schools, founded in 1638 under the auspices of Saint-Cyran. These schools endured a precarious existence. They were first set up at Port-Royal-des-Champs, but students and teachers were forced into hiding after the arrest of the abbé. After another brief sojourn at the *Champs* between 1644 and 1646, the schools moved to the Faubourg Saint-Jacques in Paris. The increasing number of students caused the institution to separate into three groups in 1653, one returning to Port-Royal-des-Champs, another establishing itself at a chateau in the valley of the Chevreuse, and a third group moving to a house near Versailles. Forced into hiding once again in 1656 because of Mazarin's efforts to suppress Jansenism, the Little Schools were dispersed forever in 1660. The schools never contained more than fifty students at a time, but their influence was far greater than their size because of the reputations of distinguished teachers and students and because of the important pedagogical treatises that emanated from them. Among the more prominent teachers were Claude Lancelot, biographer of Saint-Cyran and author of some of the most important grammars of the age; Pierre Nicole; Wallon de Beaupuis; and Pierre Coustel, author of one of the better known treatises (published after the closing of the schools), *Les Règles de l'education des enfants.* Among the more prominent students were Jean Racine and the historian so much admired by Gibbon, Sébastien Le Nain de Tillemont.

The purpose of the Little Schools, as conceived by Saint-Cyran, was to sustain the baptismal innocence of children until they were mature enough to take care of their own spiritual needs. Saint-Cyran and those who effected his ideas believed very strongly that the child ought to be treated as a child and not as an adult. The child was weak and needed support, for which reason the teacher had to know the individual characteristics of each child. Pupils at the Little Schools were allowed time to play games and to relax in the fresh air because their teachers felt that too much time in the classroom was injurious to their learning capabilities. Religious instruction was, of course, essential to the curriculum. The students learned the catechism written especially for them by the abbé de Saint-Cyran, they listened to readings from scripture, and they spent time in prayer. The curriculum also laid heavy stress upon the classics. A thorough knowledge of Latin and Greek was necessary for a better understanding of the ecclesiastical tradition.

Training in classical languages, according to the pedagogues of Port Royal, strengthened one's knowledge of scripture and tradition (as was evident in the writings of Jansenist theologians), but knowledge of the classical authors was also important. Saint-Cyran, encountering some children reading Vergil, said to them: "Do you see that author there? He is damned, yes damned, by writing such beautiful verse, because he did it out of vanity, and in order to please the world. But you must sanctify yourselves by learning these verses, because you must learn them in order to please God and serve the Church. You must offer your study to God and be faithful to him."[18] Although the ethical principles of the authors of antiquity were inspired by concupiscence, nevertheless Christians might still benefit from reading them in order to learn more about true virtue as well as to develop their judgment. Le Nain de Tillemont later wrote that pagan moralists, while not virtuous from a Christian point of view, were virtuous from a pragmatic point of view. Seneca and Marcus Aurelius, by means of their reason, advocated rules of conduct that improved the quality of life on earth. For this reason, their works might be read profitably by the Christian pupil. Of Seneca, Tillemont wrote, "What we have to do is to benefit from his writings, which God has preserved for us and through which God speaks to us, because everything that is true comes from the Truth, no matter what the source."[19] Nicole maintained that children ought to study pagan writings because "they contain a number of useful things in them,"[20] but the teacher had to know how to convert these writings to a Christian purpose.

History was taught in the schools because it contained useful facts. By studying the past, the pupil learned to evaluate human conduct. Geography was of value in that it stimulated the child's curiosity. "One ought to strive," wrote Nicole, "to inspire a healthy curiosity in children to see strange and interesting things and to have them learn the reasons for these things. Such curiosity is not a vice at their age, because it opens their minds and turns them away from profligacy."[21] Mathematics and physics were also recommended by Jansenist pedagogues. In the opinion of Nicole and of Coustel, all subjects were of value as long as they helped to develop the child's judgment—an essential purpose of Jansenist pedagogy.[22] A sound curriculum should be flexible enough to suit the capabilities and the needs of the individual child. Poetry might be of value to children with vivid imaginations but of less value to those of a more pragmatic turn of mind. History and geography were useful to children endowed with good memories. Effective teaching, taking the child's interests to heart, made studies "appear as more of a game or a diversion than a dull and constraining pastime." Employing a term made famous by John Locke, Coustel, in his *Règles de l'education*, referred to the child's mind as a *tabula rasa*[23] capable of good and bad impressions and receptive to religious instruction. The teacher tried to make as many good impressions as possible on his student's mind while it was still young and malleable. Jansenist educational theory stressed clarity of thought and expression, for which reason Port-royalist teachers developed new methods of teaching grammar and logic. Proper religious instruction together with sound rhetorical and philosophical training provided the student with the means of developing his judgment so that he might better understand his Christian obligations.

In their teaching and in their discussions among themselves, Arnauld, Nicole, Pascal, and the *solitaires* devoted a great deal of thought to the utility of reason and philosophy. In his attack on the Jesuit Garasse in 1626 and in his prison writings, the abbé de Saint-Cyran maintained that reason was harmful to piety because it fostered pride, and that contemporary intellectual currents in particular constituted an obstacle to the acquisition of virtue. Modern learning, he wrote, "is for the most part philosophical and dependent on reason, which the Apostle [Paul] called the wisdom of the flesh and therefore the enemy of God. It is the enemy of the faith that does not reason, as Saint Thomas says at the beginning of the *Summa*. Many new conclusions have been reached [by today's philosophers] that have nothing to do with ancient religious traditions in which Christian virtue and the Catholic Church are rooted."[24] Expressing his contempt for efforts by scholars to reconcile religion and philosophy, the abbé argued that the Church would be better off if it depended less on reason and philosophy. This distrust of intellectuality constituted a strong current in Jansenist thought and belief. Jansenius himself in a brief essay, *De la réformation de l'homme intérieur,* published posthumously in 1642, wrote that the human mind was inclined to inquire into everything, the secrets of nature, the affairs of state, and even the sacred mysteries of religion. The desire to acquire knowledge merely for the sake of knowledge was sinful because it was motivated by pride and distracted the penitent from his religious duties. "Should we find it strange if, when we have looked within ourselves and have elevated ourselves to contemplate the incomparable beauty of eternal truth where certain and salutary knowledge of all things resides, this multitude of images and phantoms with which vanity has filled our hearts and minds attacks us and drags us down and seems to inquire of us, 'Where are you going, all covered with spots and so unworthy of approaching God? Where are you going? ' And thus in solitude are we justly punished for the sins that we have committed while trafficking in the world."[25]

The belittlement of reason and the human capacity for self-delusion were themes very much in evidence in the *Pensées,* written during the period of Pascal's association with Port Royal. He had read Jansenius's essay, an important influence on his spiritual development.[26] In the *Pensées* Pascal wrote: ". . . Man is nothing but a subject full of natural error that cannot be eradicated except through grace. Nothing shows him the truth, everything deceives him. The two principles of truth, reason and senses, are not only both not genuine, but are engaged in mutual deception. The senses deceive reason through false appearances and just as they trick the soul, they are tricked by it in their turn: it takes its revenge. The senses are disturbed by passions, which produce false impressions. They both compete in lies and deception."[27] The mind, said Pascal, is dominated by imagination, which manages to thwart reason at every turn. Worldly reputations are established by the imagniation. A preacher is considered great not because of what he has to say but because of his appearance and the pleasing quality of his voice. The fine robes of magistrates render their judgments excellent in the minds of their listeners; the caps of doctors, rather than their healing powers, inspire respect in their patients. Imagination is the major influence on the formation of opinion in which are rooted human values.[28] Man's powers of self-deception are extraordinary. He spends so much time thinking about the future that he is unable to live in the present, and he is full of contradictions—proud one moment, bored and wretched the next. "How absurd is reason, the sport of every wind!" [29] Many of Pascal's psychological insights stressing man's wretchedness were derived from his readings of Montaigne's essays as well as the works of Saint-Cyran and Jansenius.

Yet the Port-royalists believed that reason had its uses. The abbé de Saint-Cyran sponsored the Little Schools because he believed that intellectual pursuits, under proper guidance, were beneficial to the Christian. In *De la réformation de l'homme intérieur*, Jansenius stated that "it is the rule of Christian life not to transform into an evil and superfluous curiosity the intention to learn and to understand that of which [one] is ignorant. There are certain things that one must understand in order to sanction or approve conditions. We must be instructed in those things that one must seek out or avoid in order to live in a Christian manner and to fulfill our obligations." [30] In acquiring an understanding of the true nature of religious belief, reason played an important role by providing clear explanations and descriptions of the Catholic tradition. The *solitaire* Le Maistre de Sacy and Pascal both appealed to reason in their efforts to prove that Moses was the author of the Pentateuch, that the history of the Hebrew people was historic proof of the truth contained in the prophecies that preceded the coming of Christ. [31] In the *Pensées*, Pascal wrote: "Submission and use of reason; that is what makes true Christianity." [32] By this he meant that Christian principles had to be instilled into hearts through grace, but into "minds with reasoned arguments." If the truths of the Christian religion depended entirely upon reason, it would be stripped of its mysterious and supernatural content. On the other hand, if the principles of reason were offended, then religion became "absurd and ridiculous." [33] Reason ought to submit to divine authority when it judges that "it ought to submit." [34] Throughout the *Pensées*, Pascal stressed the need to recognize and to submit to the true order of things, pointing out at the same time the different means by which man recognizes this order. The mind had its order, and the heart another. The *ésprit géométrique* (reason) provided a different kind of knowledge from that provided by the *ésprit de finesse* (intuition). Reason drew "absurd" conclusions when it refused to accept the true order of the universe. "One must know when it is right to doubt, to affirm, to submit. Anyone who does otherwise does not understand the force of reason. Some men run counter to these three principles, either affirming that everything can be proved, because they know nothing about proof, or doubting everything, because they do not know when to submit, or always submitting because they do not know when judgement is called for."[35]

One section of the *Pensées* is devoted to persuading a freethinker of the efficacy of the Christian religion. The freethinker ought to wager in favor of God's existence, because he has everything to gain in the way of everlasting happiness if God does exist and nothing to lose if He doesn't. Fascinated by mathematical probabilities, Pascal had written a treatise on roulette in 1658, the same year in which he very likely began to outline his prospective magnum opus, a defense of the Christian religion, in the form of notes that were later published as the *Pensées*. Pascal suggested the wager in order to convince the freethinker by appealing to his rational self-interest. The freethinker would necessarily choose the option that provided him with the greatest happiness for the longest period of time, that option favored as well by the law of probability. Having opted in favor of God, the freethinker was advised by Pascal to undertake certain spiritual exercises by which he might become converted and acquire faith. Reason was once again shown to be a tool to be used in the service of religion, in that it was a possible means by which the unbeliever was persuaded of the necessity of belief.

Although philosophy, with its roots in pagan thought and its humanistic inclinations, was looked upon by Jansenists with some misgivings, many Jansenists still read not only the philosophers of antiquity but contemporary philosophy as well. This interest cannot be ascribed merely to Pascal's mathematical genius or to Antoine Arnauld's intellectuality. The discussions that took place at Port-Royal-des-Champs[36] indicate that interest in philosophy was widespread, although by no means universal, among the disciples of Saint-Cyran. In his memoirs, the *solitaire* Fontaine describes a conversation that took place between Pascal and Le Maistre de Sacy at Port Royal sometime during 1655.[37] The account of the conversation begins with a brief description of Pascal, "a man admired not only in France but throughout all of Europe"[38] because of his brilliant mind and his mathematical accomplishments. Sacy had been asked by Singlin to talk to the mathematician, in order to instruct him in religious matters and to disabuse him of the value of natural science. What impressed Sacy in his dialogue with Pascal was that, although the latter was ignorant of the truths embodied in sacred literature, he seemed nonetheless to be intuitively aware of them. Astonished at Pascal's perceptiveness, Sacy began by asking him who his favorite philosophers were. Pascal replied that he was most impressed by the philosophies of Epictetus and Montaigne. Epictetus, the Greek stoic of the first century after Christ, emphasized man's obligations, including the most important obligation to serve God, but he also stressed the fact that God provided man with the means to perform these obligations and the freedom to choose whether or not to serve God. "Man might by means of his own capabilities know God, love and obey him, cure himself of his vices, acquire all the virtues, and render himself holy enough to become God's companion." Montaigne, on the other hand, threw everything in doubt and rejected certainty of every kind. "In the mind of this independent genius, it is a matter of complete indifference whether one takes one side in a dispute or another, because he is able to show the weakness of either side. Having taken his position in universal doubt, he has fortified himself by his triumph and by his defeat." The two philosophies, Stoic and Pyrrhonic, complemented each other perfectly, in the mind of Pascal, because each in its own way achieved some understanding of the truth. "The reason for this is that these two sages of the world treat the same subject from opposite points of view. One attributes [man's] greatness to nature, and the other his weakness to nature, a contradiction inexplicable to reason. But faith resolves the contradiction. All that is weak pertains to nature, and all that is strong pertains to grace. This is the astonishing new union that God alone teaches, and that he alone can achieve, and it is nothing but the image and effect of the ineffable union of the two natures that exist in the unique person of a God-Man."[39] In short, according to Pascal, neither philosophy contained the whole truth, but each contributed to a paradoxical view of human nature that was satisfactorily explained only by Christian belief. Sacy's response to Pascal's exposition was to warn that only those readers with the intellectual capacity to utilize pagan philosophy in behalf of Christian truth ought to read worldly philosophers. Others, who might be misled by such philosophers, ought to limit their reading to Christian texts.

The dialogue between Pascal and Sacy is significant for a number of reasons. It provides a key to the *Pensées*, in that, taken together, Epictetus and Montaigne revealed the paradoxes in human nature that Pascal emphasized throughout his last work. Epictetus argued that man was capable of everything, Montaigne argued that he was capable of nothing, and Pascal argued: "Let us conceive that man infinitely transcends man, and that without the aid of faith he would remain inconceivable to himself, for who cannot see that unless we realize the duality of human nature, we remain invincibly ignorant of the truth about ourselves."[40] The dialogue also reflects the two major concerns of the Jansenists. Epictetus represented the Pelagian strain within Christian thought that asserted itself strongly in the Christian humanism of the sixteenth and seventeenth centuries and that the Port-royalists considered heretical. Montaigne, on the other hand, represented the Pyrrhonist current that threatened religion as well as philosophy and led to libertinage. Finally, the dialogue reflects an attitude toward philosophy that was typical of Jansenist thought. Worldly philosophy was dangerous because it was misleading to the Christian who was not on guard against the pitfalls of human vanity and delusion. Yet worldly philosophy might be of some use to the reader insofar as it contained certain truths about human nature that facilitated religious belief. As Fontaine pointed out in his memoirs, both Pascal and Sacy came to an understanding of Christian truth in different ways—Pascal through worldly philosophy and Sacy through reading Saint Augustine. Fontaine did not point out, however, that Augustine's understanding of human nature was derived from his reading of pagan philosophers; however, this fact may well have been in the minds of other Jansenists.

The Jansenists' interest in the philosophical developments of their own century is manifested by the influence of Cartesian thought within the movement. Descartes's philosophy was a subject much discussed at the residence of the duc de Liancourt in Paris, at the little villa of the duc de Luynes at Port-Royal-des-Champs, and elsewhere. There are records of conversations dealing with such questions as the nature of the universe and the nature of beasts, questions that fascinated philosophers of the seventeenth century.[41] Antoine Arnauld's interest in Descartes's philosophy dated from the 1640s, when he and the author of the *Meditations on First Philosophy* entered into a correspondence relating to some of the theological implications of the *Meditations*. In his letters to Descartes, Arnauld was primarily concerned that the former's speculations be restricted to the realm of nature, in which reason was able to operate, and that they not be allowed to penetrate the realm of grace. "M. Descartes may now judge how necessary it is to distinguish between those things because of the danger that many of those who today are inclined toward impiety might be able to use these words in order to combat the faith and the truth of our belief."[42] Once reassured that Cartesian philosophy did not prejudice Christian truths, Arnauld became a Cartesian. What appealed to the author of *De la fréquente communion* about Descartes's metaphysics was the sharp distinction made between the spiritual and the material. Unlike Pascal, who believed that Descartes was too bold with reason, Arnauld was certain that Descartes had not confused the natural and the supernatural. To prove the point he cited the seventy-sixth principle of Descartes's *Principles of Philosophy*:

Above all we should impress on our memory as an infallible rule that what God has revealed to us is incomparably more certain than anything else; and that we ought to submit to divine authority rather than to our own judgment even though the light of reason may seem to us to suggest, with the utmost clearness and evidence, something opposite. But in things in regard to which divine authority reveals nothing to us, it would be unworthy of a philosopher to accept anything as true which he has not ascertained as such, and to trust more to the senses, that is to judgments formed without consideration in childhood, than to the reasoning of maturity.[43]

To the objection that Cartesian philosophy undermined the doctrine of transubstantiation by attempting to provide a natural explanation for changes in material substances, Arnauld responded that natural explanations did not necessarily preclude theological explanations. The essence of the wine and water used in the sacraments was indeed motion and extension in natural terms, but their essential sacramental qualities consisted of Christ's body and blood. God achieved the transformation in a mysterious way inexplicable in philosophical terms. From Arnauld's point of view, Cartesian principles made clear the fact that wine and water must be described in entirely separate terms, that is to say, philosophically and theologically.[44] The integrity of the realm of nature and of the realm of grace was thereby maintained. In defending Descartes, Arnauld argued that the philosopher had rectified a mistake made by Schoolmen, which was to confuse the natural and the supernatural. Such confusion led to absurd definitions of the Eucharist that prepared the way for the Protestants' heretical interpretations.[45] Arnauld further argued that, by establishing clear principles upon which rational certainty might be based, Descartes had provided an effective weapon to be used against Pyrrhonists, who, in their efforts to discredit reason, were endangering faith as well.[46]

Not all Jansenists were Cartesians, by any means. Le Maistre de Sacy, who in his conversations with Pascal had expressed a distrust of philosophy, was not interested in the discussions that took place in the valley of the Chevreuse concerning Descartes's new world system. Conversing with Fontaine, Sacy remarked:

God made the world for two reasons . . . one, in order to manifest his greatness, and the other, to depict invisible things in the visible. . . . M. Descartes destroys both. "The sun is a beautiful thing," one says to him. "Not at all," he replies, "It is a mass of metal clippings." Instead of recognizing invisible things in the visible, as in the sun, the God of nature, and to see in its effect on plants the image of grace, he, on the other hand, tries to provide a [natural] reason for everything. I compare [Cartesians] to uninformed people who look at a beautiful painting, and instead of admiring the work, examine each color in particular, and ask, "What is this red here? Of what does it consist?" . . . They do not contemplate the design as a whole, whose beauty has charmed intelligent people who have looked at it. M. Descartes admits, in effect, that he does not intend to explain things as they are. "The world is so big that one can get lost in it," he says, "but I regard it as a set of numbers."[47]

Sacy took a more traditional view of nature, as a reflection of the supernatural to be explained in religious terms. The dualistic aspect of Cartesian philosophy with its mechanistic conception of material substance was repugnant to him. Sacy's distaste for philosophy was again made plain in the same conversation with Fontaine in which he compared Aristotle and Descartes to thieves who had pillaged the Church by subverting its doctrine. Aristotle had perverted the minds of theologians in the late Middle Ages, but in the seventeenth century, the Scholastic synthesis was perverted in turn by Descartes, "like a thief who has killed another thief and taken his booty from him."[48] Sacy, however, was by no means opposed to all intellectual activity, having himself translated the Bible and taught at the Little Schools. For him, scripture, works of piety, and the book of nature provided adequate means for the Christian to contemplate truth. Philosophy, to his mind, was at best an unnecessary diversion and at worst a dangerous influence that threatened to undermine religion. Other Jansenists were equally hostile to Cartesian philosophy in particular. Louis-Paul du Vaucel, a Jansenist agent at Rome at the end of the century, was unable to interpret Descartes in the same way as Arnauld. Whereas Arnauld accepted both natural and mystical explanations of the wine and water used in the sacraments, Vaucel insisted that any attempt to provide a natural explanation threatened the doctrine of transubstantiation. As though anticipating the materialist philosophy of the Enlightenment, Vaucel was distressed by the mechanistic view of nature provided by Descartes because it threatened to engulf man himself, who would no longer be described in spiritual terms at all.[49]

Pascal's objections to Cartesian philosophy are well known. In the *Pensées* he described that philosophy as "useless and uncertain," and he claimed that it contained strong deistic implications insofar as God exists only to set the world in motion, after which he withdraws into himself.[50] For Arnauld, Cartesian philosophy preserved Christian truth by distinguishing between the divine and the natural orders; for Pascal, Cartesian philosophy sought to eliminate the divine order altogether. Nevertheless, Descartes's influence on Pascal's thought is indisputable. Pascal accepted the Cartesian explanation of material substance, and he agreed with Descartes that reason was a useful means of understanding nature. When the author of the *Pensées* called Descartes's philosophy useless and uncertain, he meant that the famous method was ineffective as a means of directly comprehending the Judeo-Christian God.[51]

The influence of Descartes is very much in evidence in the most important educational treatise produced by the Jansenists, *La logigue, ou l'art de penser*, better known as the *Port Royal Logic*.[52] Written at Port-Royal-des-Champs by Antoine Arnauld in collaboration with Nicole and very likely Pascal for the edification of the son of the duc de Luynes, the first edition appeared in 1662. By 1685 six editions had appeared in French and two in English. The *Logic* contains the basic pedagogical principles of the Jansenists that were reflected in the curriculum of the Little Schools, as well as their concern for establishing the proper way to think.[53] In the introduction to the work, the authors stated that "precision of thought is essential to distinguish truth from error in all walks of life by means of sound judgment, rendering it as exact as we can."[54] Faulty judgment is the cause of philosophical and theological errors and civic offenses, and the *Logic* was intended to clear up the intellectual confusions caused by the long-lingering Scholastic tradition that was so offensive to Saint-Cyran and his followers. Aristotelian philosophy was useless because it taught nothing new, and it prevented the mind from acquiring any new knowledge of nature.[55] The preface to the second edition (1664) contained an attack on the tyranny of Aristotelianism as strong as any set forth by Bacon or Descartes.

. . . it is a great inconvenience to feel obliged to approve everything said by him [Aristotle] and to take as the rule of truth his philosophical doctrines. . . . The world can no longer suffer such a contraint and restores itself imperceptibly to the possession of a natural and reasonable liberty, allowing approval of what is judged to be true and rejection of what is thought to be false. In those disciplines which treat of things beyond reason, reason submits itself to authority. There reason must follow another light, which can be no other than the light of divine authority. But in human sciences, which claim to depend only on reason, reason is well justified in not abandoning its own light to accept the light of authority.[56]

Reasserting arguments that appeared in the *Pensées* written at the same time as the *Logic*, the *Logic* insisted that freedom of reason pertained only to nature, that in the realm of grace, reason was helpless. Divine authority, to which both faith and reason submitted, governed meritorious actions. Reason was incapable of judging whether an action was redemptive in the sight of God, and therefore incompetent "within the province of morals."[57] Rejecting the authority of Aristotle in the natural world and the authority of reason in the realm of grace, the authors maintained in the face of Pyrrhonism that the mind was capable of being certain about many things. "Untroubled by the vain arguments of the Pyrrhonists, true reason ranks each thing appropriately, doubting what is doubtful, rejecting what is false, acknowledging in good faith what is evident." Pascal had written virtually the same thing in the *Pensées*.[58]

Logic, according to the *Art de penser*, must have a utilitarian function. It has no value in and of itself, but it provides a method by which men in all walks of life may avoid errors. "Logic is the art of directing reason to a knowledge of things for the instruction of ourselves and others. This art consists in man's reflecting on the mind's four principal operations—conceiving, judging, reasoning, and ordering."[59]

Conception related to the origin of ideas. Rejecting Pierre Gassendi's claim that all ideas come from the senses and are, therefore, merely images of the world, the authors stated that "in fact, but few ideas originate in the senses, whose sole function is the excitation of the brain."[60] Certain concepts occurred to the mind because they were clear and distinct, others because they were obscure and confused. The clear and distinct idea struck the mind sharply, such as the concept of the self, of motion and extension in bodies, and of God. ("Our idea of God is clear since it is sufficient to enable us to know a great many characteristics assuredly found in God alone; our idea is obscure when compared with the idea that the blessed in heaven have of God."[61]) This analysis of concepts was very similar to that set forth in Descartes's *Discourse on Method.*

Having conceived a clear and distinct idea, the mind subsequently set about expressing that idea as articulately as possible. The process of fitting the proper words to the proper idea involved judgment, the development of which was so important to the teachers at the Little Schools. "Judgments are propositions expressed by sentences,"[62] and they depend on rules both of logic and of grammar. Grammar was of great concern to the masters of the Little Schools. Saint-Cyran's friend Claude Lancelot wrote Latin and Greek grammars, and he and Antoine Arnauld collaborated on a *Grammaire générale et raisonnée* published in 1660. The authors of the *Grammaire* wrote in the preface: "Those who esteem works of reasoning will find in this work, perhaps, something that will satisfy them, and they will not spurn the subject because, if the word is one of the greatest of man's advantages, it should be of great value to possess this advantage with all the perfection of which man is capable. Such perfection involves not only the proper use of language but also the reasons for this usage, in order to be able to achieve by means of knowledge that which others accomplish merely by custom."[63] Sound judgments established definitions that improved the mind's understanding of things, something that Aristotelian definitions failed to do.

The third principal operation of the mind, according to the *Logic*, is reasoning, by which the mind evaluates arguments. "It is the human mind's limitations which force man to reason."[64] Human fallibility often makes it difficult to determine the validity of arguments because, in human affairs, it is often difficult to establish proper authority. In matters pertaining to faith, "the authority of the universal Church cannot err. We fall into error only when we wander from the Church's authority and refuse to submit ourselves to it."[65] But in matters pertaining to reason, authority becomes less clear. Some men believe something to be true according to the number of witnesses or because a majority of people subscribe to a given opinion. Some people bestow authority on the opinions of the devout rather than upon the opinions of the worldly wise. "Qualifications perplex men; they would everything be black or else white. If a man can be trusted in one thing, he is to be trusted in all; if questioned in one, then questioned in all. Men love shortcuts and absolute statements. But this love is unreasonable. No one person is an authority in all matters."[66] Faulty reasoning, caused by a poor assessment of a man's qualifications, is not as bad as undue deference to the opinion of those of high birth, great wealth, or high office.

Errors of deference spring from the corruption in the hearts of men. Man with his ardent passion for honors and pleasures has a great love for wealth or for any other means to honor and pleasure. Whatever the world esteems we love; whoever possesses what the world esteems we judge happy; and in judging them happy, we place them above ourselves and regard them as eminent and exalted. Our respect for the wealthy passes imperceptibly from their fortunes to their minds. Men seldom do things by halves; we submit to the opinions of the wealthy since we credit a man with a mind as exalted as his rank. Hence, too, the confidence inspired in any affairs negotiated by the rich.[67]

Although unwilling "to give the rules and precise limits of the deference due to authority in human affairs," the authors of the *Logic* insisted that external characteristics such as grandeur, nobility, and wealth should carry little weight in evaluating the truth of an opinion, whereas "age, knowledge, study, experience, wit, energy, memory, accuracy, labor—all contribute to revealing the truth of hidden things and so deserve to be respected."[68] In the last analysis, distinguishing between truth and prejudice caused by external appearance, by self-interest, or by imagination required reliance on one's own judgment and native wit.[69]

The fourth principal operation of the mind set forth in the *Logic* (after conceiving, judging, and reasoning) is ordering, the means by which the mind attempts to demonstrate the truth of things through the proper arrangement of ideas. Sound demonstration depends upon a thorough understanding of the orders or categories of knowledge. Some knowledge is derived from the senses, some comes from self-evident principles, some depends on authority, and some on reason. Sound demonstration also depends upon understanding the limitations of the mind.[70] Geometry provides a means of demonstrating certain truths pertaining to the material world, and it is also capable of determining those orders

or categories beyond the mind's reach. By establishing the proper
order of things, the mind is able to distinguish between those
categories where knowledge depends upon the autonomy of reason
and those where knowledge depends upon authority.

Proper ordering also requires the mind to distinguish between
the nature of divine authority and of human authority. The mind,
according to the *Logic*, should submit without reservations to the
authority of God. Human authority, on the other hand, pertains
to men and is, therefore, subject to error. Reason plays an important role in assessing the veracity of human authority. How, for
example, is the historian supposed to determine whether an event
actually took place in the past? Since he did not personally witness the event, he has to rely upon the authority of others. In
evaluating sources, the historian has to rely on his own judgment
in order to determine which sources are reliable. The judgment of
the historian is, to a large extent, based on common sense. Common sense, according to the *Logic*, plays a crucial role in ordering
everyday life.

The *Port Royal Logic* is vital to an understanding of Jansenist
thought because in the work the authors attempted to establish
an effective method by which the mind might operate in the realm
of nature. In so doing, they brought the reason of the individual
into potential conflict with the conventional authority of the
Church. Jansenists recognized the need to work out a useful
method for logic in order to establish principles of certainty by
which to replace the obsolete definitions and principles contained
in the Scholastic synthesis. The *Logic* was influenced by the ideas
of both Descartes and Pascal, and it provides a measure of the
common ground that existed between two great minds of seventeenth-century France whose views are commonly regarded as
antithetical. The common ground existed because both Descartes
and Pascal realized that the archaic Scholastic synthesis was no
longer responsive to the intellectual needs of the century, and they
feared the growing influence of free thought. Arnauld and Nicole
freely acknowledged this dual influence in the introduction to the
first edition of the *Logic*. The emphasis upon clear and distinct
ideas, the conception of thought as the essence of mind and of
motion and extension as the essence of matter, these were Carte-

sian principles. The emphasis on geometry as a tool for obtaining certain knowledge of the material world as well as a means of understanding the mind's limitations reflected Pascal's thinking.

The *Port Royal Logic* was an educational treatise intended to develop the student's judgment not only with respect to human affairs but with respect to theology as well. Sound judgment, contended the authors, would prevent the individual from being deluded by Pyrrhonists and Aristotelians, and it would protect him from being misled by doctrinal errors that led to heresy. The 1683 edition undertook to clear up Protestant misconceptions with regard to the sacraments. Proper conceptualization and judgment enabled the mind to comprehend the dual nature of the elements used in the Eucharist insofar as they appeared as bread and wine to the senses and as the body and blood of Christ to the mind trained to distinguish between the natural and the supernatural.[71] Many ambiguities that existed in Scripture also became clear by means of effective principles of logic. These principles enabled the mind to construe such sayings as Saint Paul's "As in Adam all die, so also in Christ all are made to live," in a correct manner. "It is certain that many heathen, dying in their infidelity, have not been reborn through Christ and will not partake of that glorious life of which Saint Paul speaks. The meaning of the sentence is this: As all who die, die because of Adam, so all who are reborn are reborn through Christ."[72] Logic, in the minds of the Jansenists, enabled the true Christian to defend scriptural truth against the misinterpretations of the Protestants, who denied the doctrine of transubstantiation, and it also enabled him to interpret correctly the fifth proposition condemned by the papal encyclical *Cum occasione*. Armed with a method for establishing doctrinal certainty, Jansenist theologians were not likely to yield easily in religious disputes, even when asked to yield by the highest authorities of Church and state.

The real significance of the *Logic* lies in its attempt to distinguish between those areas where the mind must submit to authority and those areas where the mind was free to draw its own conclusions. Arnauld and Nicole agreed that the mind must submit unquestioningly to God's authority. They also agreed that all Christians must submit to the authority of the Church. The Church was a

divine institution in that it provided the exclusive means to salvation and it was the guardian of God's truth on earth. On the
other hand, the Church was a human institution insofar as it
consisted of human beings capable of error. Popes and bishops,
children of Adam like everybody else, were capable of faulty
judgments. Implicit in the work is the possibility of a conflict
between theologians construing Scripture and tradition according
to the proper method and ecclesiastical superiors construing Scripture and tradition by means of erroneous principles. The Jansenists
came to regard themselves as "the friends of truth." They acquired
that truth by means of faith and—some Jansenists believed—by
means of logical concepts by which they were able to discern the
truths of the Catholic Church. For this reason they appeared as
formidable opponents to their enemies within the Church who
challenged their commitment to God and their interpretation of
Scripture and tradition.

The Jansenists' conviction that they were on the side of truth
was reinforced by an event that occurred at Port-Royal-de-Paris
in March 1656, shortly after Pascal began to issue the *Provincial
Letters.* His niece, Marguerite Périer, a twelve-year-old pensioner
at the convent, experienced a sudden recovery from an ocular
abscess. Fearful that she might lose her sight, the nuns had applied
to her eye a recently acquired relic, a fragment of Christ's crown
of thorns, and the eye was cured instantly. The conviction of the
nuns and friends of Port Royal that a miracle had happened was
soon verified by religious authorities, and news of the event contributed to the notoriety of the convent. Interpreting it a year
later, Arnauld wrote: "Thus in every quarrel that has taken place
in the Church, and during persecutions that princes have sometimes excited against those who uphold the verities of the faith,
God has only performed miracles in favor of those who are
defenders of his truth. And all the holy writers who have spoken
of these miracles have regarded them as certain proof by which
God has made known to the world the sincerity of the faith [of
those who defend the truth], and the injustice of the persecution
that they have suffered."[73]

Although miracles were proof of sincerity and true belief, the
Jansenists never admitted that a Christian could be certain of sal-

vation. Lack of such assurance strengthened one's faith, according to Arnauld.[74] If God continually revealed his intentions to men, wrote Pascal to his friend Madamoiselle Roannez, there would be little need for faith. God "hides himself ordinarily, and rarely reveals himself to those whom he wishes to engage in his services. This strange secret by which God withdraws himself entirely from the sight of men is a great lesson to bring us to solitude, far from the sight of men."[75] Certainly we must be "concerned about nothing but good works," wrote Saint-Cyran in 1642, but "it is in heaven that we will have the assurance that we have done well."[76] Nicole was emphatic in asserting that the Christian could never be sure whether his good works were a manifestation of divine charity. "Man is never assured of his perseverance or whether his heart is dominated by love of God or love of self, and there is also within him uncertainty with regard to his salvation."[77]

Like Calvinists, however, Jansenists admitted that there were signs (*marques*), or indications of election. Wrote Saint-Cyran to a friend from prison, "In order to engage us, Jesus Christ spoke these great words to his disciples: 'Whoever despises you despises me, and whoever listens to you listens to me.' And whoever is committed to God gladly hears these words of God. And I dare say to you that this is one of the best marks of a predestined soul."[78] On another occasion the prisoner of Vincennes wrote, "The mark of a predestined soul is to be quiet and to listen to the instructions that are given him, according to what David said: 'You have made me hear a word of consolation and of joy, and all the powers of my soul that you have beaten down and humiliated leap up joyfully.'"[79] Angélique Arnauld also found encouraging indications of election: "In order to discover whether we are among the happy number of his elect, we have only to examine our consciences to see whether we have the necessary resolve to commit ourselves to pious practices and to continue them until death."[80] According to her brother Antoine, "Catholics have never denied that there are marks by which true Christians are able to recognize that they enjoy the grace of God; those who above and beyond everything else have made substantial progress in piety and who have a great desire for the things that are God's and greater aversion to sin and to the vanity of the world."[81] In

De la fréquente communion Arnauld again referred to these divine indications: "Just as there are signs that enable intelligent people to recognize a gold mine even though it is hidden in the depths of the earth, or others that indicate that a field is fertile even though it is covered with brush, so there are signs within souls of God's favorable regard that are recognizable to those who know how to look for them even in the midst of disorder. One can say with reason that one of the first and most important signs is that love of Christian truth that is engraved in the depths of the heart."[82] In another letter to Mademoiselle Roannez, Pascal compared God to a prince who has been chased from his kingdom by his subjects. As the prince "has tender sentiments for those who remain faithful to him during a rebellion, so does God consider with particular kindness those who today defend the purity of religion and morals that are under seige."[83] While signs and indications such as the Miracle of the Holy Thorn in 1656 did not provide absolute assurance of redemption, they encouraged the Christian to persevere in his commitment to God. Encouraging indications included genuine piety, an understanding of God's truth, and a willingness to defend the truth against those who sought to destroy it. Since God chose usually to remain hidden from the world, his intentions were made known only to those who in solitude searched their souls for favorable signs, or by the occasional miracle. The Christian, according to Jansenist belief, found the essence of divine truth in the inner recesses of the self. This discovery made him particularly self-reliant and less dependent on the established institutions of the Church.

Armed with certain knowledge of divine truth and with some assurance of divine favor, Jansenists were prepared to combat error. The eighteenth-century Benedictine historian, Charles Clemencet, who was sympathetic to Jansenism, wrote: "One must remark above all that the literary history of Port Royal is quite properly the history of the war of truth against error."[84] The belief that they were "the friends of truth" caused Saint-Cyran and his disciples to be intolerant toward those who were, from their point of view, in error. As the abbé wrote to his protégé Arnauld from prison, "Even if I had committed all the crimes in the world, I would have great confidence in my salvation if God gave me the power to defend his grace not only against heretics but against Catholics as well."[85]

Intolerant toward their enemies, the Jansenists were prepared to become the victims of intolerance because they were willing to suffer for the truth. The willingness, even the desire, to be persecuted on behalf of the truth as they understood it is one of the more common themes in Jansenist literature of the seventeenth century. In another letter to Arnauld, Saint-Cyran wrote: "You have taken an oath as a doctor [of theology] that you cannot violate without perjury or exempt yourself from responsibility by remaining silent when the truth is being slandered, and you are forbidden to renounce principles that are not those of the bishop of Ypres but of Saint Augustine and all the Church. You are ready not only to defend the truth but to die for it in prison or elsewhere, and if this happens to you, you will have received a great gift of grace from God."[86] Shortly after the young lawyer Antoine Le Maistre had abandoned his career, Martin de Barcos wrote him: "Who cannot marvel at God's providence, which makes it possible for a man against whom all the great powers of the earth have combined to be in the best possible position to receive the fruits of solitude and penitence?" "Nothing appears to me more desirable than persecution,"[87] wrote Barcos to Angélique Arnauld who, in turn, wrote a friend that persecution was beneficial "because it purifies us and makes us better able to make use of God's grace, which we have received in so much abundance."[88] At the height of the Jansenist crisis of the 1660s, Arnauld wrote: "The world will see nothing but oppression and destruction while, on the other hand, the angels will see triumph and victory. This is perhaps the way that God will accomplish the dual purpose to be found in his works of blinding and reproaching the wicked and of instructing his elect. For if God permits the ruin of this house [Port Royal], it will be a stumbling block to all those many politicians to whose narrow minds the sight of such destruction will appear a marvelous consequence of their wisdom."[89] The world, contended Pasquier Quesnel, "is more to be feared when it flatters than when it persecutes. The world gives life to that which it destroys."[90] Saint-Cyran's contempt for the persecutorial powers of Church and state of which he was the victim is clearly evident in one of his many letters written from Vincennes: "God often turns kingdoms upside down to redeem one or two of his elect. All that is temporal is nothing, not even monasteries and temples. For God has only need of himself in us, where he has built his true temple. Just as in heaven, where there are many happy souls, there is no temple but God."[91] This acceptance of suffering and persecution as a test of Christian faith and commitment on the part of the father of French Jansenism served as an inspiration to his disciples throughout the century, and it strengthened their resolve not to compromise what they perceived to be the truth. Furthermore, this acceptance of suffering and persecution on behalf of the truth reinforced the *Frondeur* mentality that existed among the Port-royalists during the era of the Fronde. That mentality consisted in part of a *dévot* idealism opposed to the government's war policy and to Cardinal Mazarin's personal power. It contained an affinity for the rights of the rebellious curés in their struggle to maintain their authority in the parishes. Finally, this *Frondeur* mentality contained a philosophical attitude that firmly maintained the intellectual rights of the individual against any authority that might attempt to suppress them. These *Frondeur* sentiments emerged fully developed at the very time when Mazarin, having crushed the Fronde, acquired those instruments—the papal encyclicals and the formulary—by which he hoped to suppress Jansenism.

V. *Droit et Fait, 1661–69*

When Cardinal Mazarin died in March 1661, Louis XIV, then twenty-three years of age, decided to rule the kingdom on his own, without a first minister. In his *Mémoires for the Instruction of the Dauphin*, the king described some of the problems that confronted him when he became sole ruler of France. "Disorder reigned everywhere," he wrote—seemingly unmindful of Mazarin's efforts to establish domestic tranquillity after the Fronde—disorder caused in part by religious disputes:

The Church, aside from its usual troubles, after long disputes over scholastic matters that were admittedly unnecessary for salvation—differences mounting each day with the excitement and obstinacy of tempers and even mingling constantly with human interests—was finally threatened openly with a schism by people all the more dangerous since they could have been very useful, of great merit had they been less convinced of it. It was no longer merely a question of some individual theologians in hiding, but of bishops established in their see, capable of drawing the populace after them, of high reputation, of piety indeed worthy of reverence as long as it was accompanied by submission to the opinions of the Church, by mildness, by moderation, and by charity. Cardinal de Retz, Archbishop of Paris, whom well-known reasons of state then prevented me from tolerating, favored this entire rising sect either from inclination or from interest, and was favored by it.[1]

Further on in the *Mémoires*, the king referred to the "rising sect" by name: "I dedicated myself to destroying Jansenism and to breaking up the communities where this spirit of novelty was developing, well-intentioned perhaps, but which seemed to want to ignore the dangerous consequences that it could have."[2] Like Richelieu, Louis XIV was suspicious of a piety that appeared to be indifferent to worldly authority; and like both Richelieu and Mazarin, he believed that unbridled religious disputes were dangerous to political stability.

In April 1661 a decree from the *conseil d'état* ordered all churchmen in the kingdom to sign the formulary that had been drawn up by the assembly of the clergy in 1657. Bishops were obliged to obtain the signatures even of nuns and lay schoolteachers. The boarders and postulants of Port Royal were expelled from the two convents because of the crown's desire to weaken the prestige and influence of what was generally regarded as the vital center of Jansenism. *Lettres de cachet* were issued to procure the arrests of the spiritual directors of Port Royal, who were forced to go into hiding. Le Maistre de Sacy was eventually arrested in 1666 and was imprisoned in the Bastille along with his fellow *solitaire* Nicolas Fontaine. The text of the formulary is as follows:

I submit sincerely to the constitution of Innocent X of May 31, 1653 [*Cum occasione*], according to its proper meaning as set forth in the constitution of our Holy Father Alexander VII of October 16, 1656 [*Ad sacram*].

I recognize that I am obliged to obey these constitutions, and I condemn with heart and mouth the doctrine contained in the five propositions of Jansenius in his book entitled *Augustinus* that two popes and the bishops have condemned, the doctrine that is not at all that of Saint Augustine, entirely misinterpreted by Jansenius.[3]

Consternation was widespread among the supporters of the late bishop of Ypres. The dictates of conscience had to be weighed against fear of schism. All those known as Jansenists regarded themselves as true Catholics, obedient to the Church. But in their minds the immediate question was whether there were limits to its authority. The issue was particularly sensitive because the authority of the Church was strongly backed by that of a king who did not tolerate opposition. Why were the Jansenists so disturbed by the five propositions if they were subject to different interpretations, and if they were not clearly set forth in the *Augustinus*? Many Jansenists interpreted the propositions as accurately reflecting not only the beliefs of Jansenius, the friend of Saint-Cyran, but of Saint Augustine as well. For this reason they had objected to the Sorbonne's efforts to have them condemned even before they were directly attributed to the *Augustinus*. The Jansenists were even more alarmed when the propositions were ascribed by the Church to the bishop of Ypres. What was of particular concern to Jansenist theologians as well as to the nuns of Port Royal was that the doctrine of efficacious grace, essential to penitential discipline and to spiritual conversion, appeared to them to be at stake.

The Jansenists responded to efforts by Church and state to suppress what they were convinced was fundamental Christian truth by making a distinction between the *question de droit* and the *question de fait*. Antoine Arnauld explained the distinction in a memoir that was not published until after his death. The *question de droit* pertained to doctrine and discipline. Whether a certain doctrine was or was not heretical in the eyes of the Church was a question pertaining to *faith*. On the other hand, the *question de fait* pertained to people and books. Whether the heretical ideas attributed to a certain author were actually expressed in a given book was a question of *fact*.

With respect to the first questions, those pertaining to faith, that is to say doctrine in itself or the general discipline of the Church, when the Church has spoken, and when she has decided on a matter that has hitherto been under dispute, all Catholics must submit to the judgment of the Church and change whatever language or sentiments that they might have used or held contrary to the decision.

But in the last questions, which concern only facts and people, the Church has never attempted to oblige her children to go beyond a submission of humility, or respect and of silence. And often the Church does not expect even that, permitting Catholics to hold opinions contrary to what she has decided with respect to matters of fact.[4]

The Church was infallible in matters of faith, which emanated from divine law, but not in matters of fact, which depended on human judgment, often fallible. In the memoir, Arnauld argued that the crucial distinction between *fait* and *droit* had always been made by the Church, and to prove his point he cited a number of theologians—among whom were Tertullian and Saint Jerome of the patristic era and Cardinal Bellarmine of the post-Tridentine era.[5]

The issues involved in the distinction were complex. The Church was infallible in matters of faith; but what was meant by the

Church, and how did she reach decisions on doctrinal integrity?
Did papal encyclicals constitute final decisions in such matters or
were decisions to be reached only after solemn deliberation by a
general council of the Church? If ultimate determinations were to
be made by councils, then presumably differences of opinion
among theologians and other ecclesiastical officials were permis-
sible until a decision on a particular issue was reached by a council.
There were also problems relating to questions of fact, as became
apparent when the question was raised during the quarrel over the
five propositions. To what extent were those who refused to admit
that the propositions were to be found in the *Augustinus* entitled
to express their opinion? Did the Church have the right to impose
a respectful silence on those among her members who disagreed
on matters of fact? In short, by insisting that a distinction should
be made between what might be called matters of fact and matters
of faith, the Jansenists raised fundamental questions about the
nature of ecclesiastical authority at a time when both Church and
state were particularly sensitive to these questions.

In 1649—when the syndic of the Sorbonne, Cornet, asked the
faculty to examine seven questionable propositions, five of which
were ultimately condemned by Innocent X—Arnauld reacted
quickly with a pamphlet entitled *Considérations sur l'entreprise
faite par Maître Nicolas Cornet*, in which he argued that traditionally the faculty had never formally decided on sensitive
doctrinal questions that caused differences of opinion among
theologians. "When it was seen that there were differing opinions
among the doctors concerning various points of important doctrine," he wrote, "[the faculty] decided that the best way to avoid
serious disagreements of a divisive sort was to leave these questions
alone and to permit each [doctor] his own opinion and to prevent
anyone from condemning the opinions of others."[6] Arnauld tried
to avoid a ruling by the faculty on the difficult issues pertaining
to grace by requesting a certain amount of leeway among theologians on questions of faith. After Innocent X decreed that the
five propositions were erroneous and heretical, and political
pressures on the papacy to identify the propositions with the
Augustinus mounted, Arnauld, in an open letter to the duc de
Luynes, agreed that the articles were heretical but insisted that

they had nothing to do with the opinions either of Saint Augustine or of the deceased bishop of Ypres. He reasserted the conviction he had expressed as early as 1644[7]—that whether or not the five propositions were to be found in the *Augustinus* was a question of fact. "And the more the issue becomes one of determining whether these propositions may be attributed to him [Jansenius] or not, is it not certain that this point of fact like all the others of this sort has nothing to do with the Catholic faith, which is necessarily founded on the written or unwritten word of God, that is to say on Holy Scripture and on tradition." Arnauld declared his willingness to maintain a "respectful silence" on the question of fact and not to engage in any controversy "unless the violence of adversaries and an inevitable necessity to defend the innocence of pious and Catholic persons leads us to break it."[8] Writing shortly after his expulsion from the Sorbonne, Arnauld complained bitterly that people were willing to submit to authority regardless of whether the authority was right or wrong.

The Sorbonne has spoken, and from the point of view of the faculty, that is sufficient, even though the most capable and disinterested persons are opposed to this violence because all the power of the court is employed to oppress a single individual. From their point of view it is an act of great humility to abandon the doctrine of the Holy Fathers. They regard the affairs of the Church from a political point of view. They believe that, in order to be humble, one must be accommodating and prepared to change opinions like everybody else. They believe that one must follow doctrine that is most in vogue and best suited to the world without troubling oneself as to whether it is right or wrong.[9]

Those who compromised the truth, asserted Saint-Cyran's protégé, ought to be treated as heretics—not those who defended it. The mind "finds different reasons for persuading itself that what is most convenient is also the wisest and the most just opinion."[10] Castigating those timid souls who preferred to please men rather than God, Arnauld insisted on the right of a single theologian to defend that doctrine his judgment and his conscience proclaimed to be true against a majority of theologians whose opinions he rejected in the same way that a single bishop had the right to oppose a decree voted upon by an episcopal council that seemed to compromise the truth. To those who believed that violent internecine quarrels among religious authorities might lead to further schisms in the Church, Arnauld maintained that Christians had to defend the truth and "that submission and obedience to legitimate authority does not mean that one has to fail in his duty to God and to his conscience."[11]

Thus in the early stages of the quarrel arising out of the papal condemnation of the five propositions, Arnauld not only emphasized the distinction between matters of fact and matters of faith, but he also appeared to be defending the conscience of the individual in matters of faith. The Church, to be sure, was infallible in matters of faith, but in terms of her earthly structure, she was guided by ecclesiastical officials who, because they were human, were capable of error. For this reason it was quite possible for a pope or even a general council representing the Universal Church to err in questions of fact, and furthermore it was possible for the pope, for theological faculties, and for councils to misconstrue articles of faith. Infallibility in doctrinal matters, according to Arnauld, could only be proclaimed by means of an ecumenical council.[12] Because they were so aware of the large numbers of unqualified officials in the Church who were motivated by interests other than those of God, the Jansenists were prepared for an assault on rigorous and demanding Augustinian theology in the form of a direct attack on the *Augustinus*. "We live in strange times, and the shadows are frightening," wrote Angélique Arnauld in 1656. "Reason and justice seem to have abandoned the earth, which means that we have no other recourse than to heaven."[13]

In the seventeenth *Provincial Letter*, written in 1657, Pascal also discussed the distinction between *droit* and *fait*. Reason and the senses, he argued, must be the only authority in matters pertaining to fact. In the final letter, he contended that reason must be man's guide in the realm of nature just as faith must be his guide in the realm of grace. Pascal made clear that the Jansenists' distinction between *droit* and *fait* was directly related to the distinction that they made between grace and nature, a distinction very much in evidence in the *Pensées* and in the *Port Royal Logic*. Reason must determine whether the five propositions were in the *Augustinus*, just as reason alone must determine whether the earth is round. For Pascal, the Church's insistence that Jansenius was the author of the heretical articles was just as futile as its attempt to condemn Galileo's opinions about terrestrial motion. "All the powers on earth cannot by their authority persuade us of a point of fact any more than they can change it. There is nothing that can make that which is, not be."[14] The Jansenist defense of what they considered to be divine truth was based not only upon the enlightened conscience of the individual but also upon a degree of intellectual freedom.

At the time when the *conseil d'état* ordered signature of the formulary, Cardinal de Retz was still in exile, and the affairs of the archdiocese were being administered in his name by two general vicars, both of whom were sympathetic to Jansenism. In consultation with Arnauld and others, the vicars drew up a pastoral letter stating that the formulary might be signed with the expressly stated reservation appended to each signature that matters of fact ought to be distinguished from matters of faith. Implied in the reservation was the admission that the propositions might be construed in a heretical sense but a refusal to admit that the articles had anything to do with the *Augustinus*. The general vicars' solution to the problem was generally accepted in Jansenist circles. The Parisian curés willingly circulated the letter in their parishes and went so far as to publish a notarized declaration of support for it.[15] The nuns of Port Royal signed the formulary on these terms in June 1661. When he learned of the contents of the letter, Alexander VII ordered the vicars to repeal it. Retz, who had done so much in the past to sustain the rebellious sentiments that were rife among the clergy of Paris, also indicated his disapproval of the vicars' solution. Finally, in a decree issued on July 9, the *conseil d'état* revoked the vicars' instructions. The highest authorities of Church and state demanded signatures from all churchmen, with no reservations whatsoever on the question of fact.

The issue was clearly drawn. Jansenius's supporters had either to repudiate him in obedience to these authorities or to support him in defiance of them. Because of the momentous problems involved in such a decision, there was considerable disagreement among the Jansenists as to the proper course of action. Three points of view with respect to signing the formulary may be discerned among them.[16]

The first point of view was upheld by the venerable Angélique Arnauld, who died in May 1661, before the crisis over signature came to a head; by Antoine Singlin, who died in the middle of the crisis; and by Martin de Barcos, the nephew of Saint-Cyran. Shortly before her death, Angélique wrote:

All sorts of contrivances are sought after to do us harm, and warped justice is being utilized to do us injustice. All this, dear Mother, ought not to trouble us, but we must seek new motives for having recourse to God, in whose mercy we have more to hope than to fear from the designs of our persecutors, who are more to be pitied than we are. I entreat you to believe, dear Mother, that the recent occasion that we have to suffer enables us to attach ourselves more firmly to God by submitting to his holy will and having confidence in his mercy. All our friends pity us a good deal, but not one dares to say a good word in our favor. The friends of our persecutors rejoice and sing out triumphantly that we suffer what we deserve, which is very true, but in a sense very different from theirs. In one sense, our imperfections deserve the harshest treatment, but in another sense, we do not deserve it, because it is the greatest honor to suffer for the truth. Our Lord bestows much grace upon us by letting us be accused and pushed about as if we were the cause of present woes.[17]

Although the abbess believed strongly in the efficacy of persecution, she also believed that the persecuted should suffer in silence. In the last year of her life, she referred again to the benefits of oppression in a letter to a friend: "this visitation [of persecution] is a sign of God's great mercy, and it is absolutely necessary for us to purify ourselves and put ourselves in a proper disposition to receive his graces, which he bestows in so much abundance. For believe me, if God deigns to reveal to us his greatest charitable intention, persecution will precede [this indication]. . . . The best fruit of persecution is humility, and humility is best preserved in silence."[18] To argue or to publicly defend oneself against the charges of temporal or ecclesiastical officials was not regarded by Angélique as a manifestation of humility nor was it so regarded by Singlin, who did not think that the nuns of Port Royal should involve themselves in the dispute over the formulary. Both, indeed, had disapproved of the *Provincial Letters.*

Barcos' initial response to the condemnation of the five

propositions in *Cum occasione* and the attempt in France to force adherence by the entire clergy to that condemnation was to raise the question of the conscience of the individual churchman. In a long letter to the bishop of Comminges in 1654, he asserted that submission to an unjust doctrine ought never to be required by the Church. If one allowed oneself to be guided by the true spirit of the Church, one did not need to be concerned about schism being brought about by the conflict between the conscience of the enlightened churchmen and unjust authority. Those prelates who demanded adherence to the decisions of Rome and of the assembly of the clergy were motivated by political considerations, and therefore submission under such circumstances was not in the best interests of the Church. Barcos accepted the distinction between *droit* and *fait*. The Church, he maintained, ought not to demand absolute submission on questions of fact. On the other hand, those who disagreed with decisions on facts ought to maintain a respectful silence.[19] In the opinion of Saint-Cyran's nephew, ecclesiastical authority should not impose its decisions on matters of fact, because it would disturb the spirit of tranquillity that was essential to the well-being of the Church; in those situations where it attempted to impose these decisions, however, those who disagreed with them ought not to engage in public debates.

Like his uncle, Barcos did not look with favor on those who devoted too much time to writing, speaking, and opinionating (making "too much noise," as he put it[20]) at the expense of introspection and self-purification. "I have always believed, Monsieur, and I still believe," he wrote in 1656, "that in the bad times in which we presently find ourselves, we would do well to defend ourselves by humiliation, by patience, by restraint, and by silence. The rules of true prudence oblige us to do so." Barcos was particularly concerned about the attitude of the nuns of Port Royal with respect to signing the formulary during the critical period between 1661 and 1669. The theological intricacies involved were not the concern of women, he wrote, but of prelates and theologians. Nuns were not supposed to make their own decisions on complex doctrinal questions. They were obliged to obey their superiors. "It is doubtless a sign of strength to bring ruin on your house, but this strength can only be regarded as presumptuous if you raise yourself above your own knowledge by making yourself the judge of matters that you know you are not capable of making, having persuaded yourself that you may prefer your own judgment to that of your superior."[21] Thus Barcos urged the nuns to sign the formulary without making any significant reservation regarding the distinction between *droit* and *fait*. He suggested three possible models for a nun's signature.

1.   I promise to the Church and to my superiors all the respect and obedience that I owe them, not being able to speak of Jansenius because I have read nothing that he has written or because I do not understand him.

2.   I sign in order to render unto the constitutions of the popes all the respect and all the obedience that is owed to them and that the Church has always required under similar circumstances.

3.   I believe all that the Church believes, and I submit to my superiors with a profound obedience, with a profound respect in everything that I owe them, according to the laws and customs of the Church.[22]

Barcos' model statements emphasized obedience and submission, although certain mental reservations may be detected in each one. In none of the models is there a firm condemnation "with heart and mouth" of "the doctrine contained in the five propositions of Jansenius in his book entitled *Augustinus*. ... " Barcos admitted that one might have mental reservations about official decisions of the Church in matters of fact. "All this suffices to say that obedience and submission do not signify interior consent and acquiescence."[23] But he refused to endorse the expressed reservation relating to the five propositions that was to accompany signatures, a tactic advised by other Jansenists. Human judgment was fallible, and although the Church was capable of error in matters involving such judgments, nevertheless, from Barcos' point of view, a question of fact was not worth a quarrel. For Barcos, as for Singlin and Angélique, those who wished to quarrel over such unimportant issues were guilty of prideful conduct, in that they wished to break that silence suitable to humility, and they showed a lack of respect for their superiors. Those who espoused this position signed the formulary because of an indifference to earthly affairs, a desire to obey the Church, and their fear of a schism resulting from further internecine quarrels.

A second attitude toward the formulary involved a refusal to sign at all. This attitude received its most dramatic expression in a letter written by Sister Euphémie of Port Royal (Jacqueline Pascal) shortly before her death in 1661, the same year in which Angélique Arnauld died. After receiving communion, Euphémie concluded that a signature of any kind was contrary to "Christian sincerity."

I cannot hide the grief that I feel at the bottom of my heart to see that those persons to whom God has confided his truth are unfaithful to him, and if I dare say so, do not have the courage to expose themselves to suffering. . . . And what prevents churchmen who know the truth from replying, when the formulary is presented to them to sign: "I know the respect that I owe the bishops, but my conscience does not permit me to agree that something is in a book that I have not read." . . . What do we fear? Banishment for the secular clergy? Dispersion for the nuns as well as seizure of temporal possessions, imprisonment and death, if you will? But is this not our glory, and ought this not to be our joy? Let us renounce the gospel or follow the maxims of the gospel, and let us account ourselves fortunate that we have the occasion to suffer something for justice.

To those who raised the possibility of excommunication, she replied: "But who does not know that nobody may be cut off from the Church in spite of himself, and that Jesus Christ, being the only one who unites his members to him, one may be deprived of the signs but not the effects of that union as long as one preserves his charity, without which no one is a living member of the holy body."[24] Taking exception to the argument that women should yield to their superiors, Euphémie stated that, if bishops had the courage of women, then women ought to have the courage of bishops.

This uncompromising posture, which rejected any idea of a signature accompanied by a reservation with regard to fact, was adopted by Euphémie's brother Blaise, who in the summer of 1661 wrote a short piece that has been preserved under the title *Ecrit sur la Signature.* Those who signed the formulary without any reservations were not only condemning the doctrine of Jansenius but were also condemning the sacred doctrine of efficacious grace. Those who signed in such a way as to indicate respect for the papal ruling on the matter of faith contained in the five propositions were guilty of an abomination before God. Although Pascal admitted the distinction between *droit* and *fait* in the *Provincial Letters*, he had reached the conclusion by 1661 that signature of the formulary, even with the appended distinction, involved a condemnation of the doctrine of efficacious grace.

Having written his *Ecrit sur la Signature*, Pascal withdrew from the controversy. His health suffered further deterioration, but he still managed to perform charitable acts and to work out a system of public transportation for the city of Paris. In August 1662 Pascal died, "in perfect submission to the Church and our Holy Father, the pope,"[25] according to the priest who administered the last rites. These facts—that Pascal disagreed with Arnauld and Nicole on the issue of the formulary, that he no longer engaged in polemical activity on behalf of Jansenism, and finally that he died in obedience to the authority of the Church—have been interpreted by some as an indication that Pascal had abandoned Jansenism. Yet there is no evidence that Pascal retracted any of his religious beliefs expressed in innumerable writings since 1656. If he felt he died in perfect submission to the Church, such an attitude might easily have been expressed also by Arnauld and others, who regarded themselves as good Catholics and obedient to the Church in matters in which they believed that they ought to be obedient. Faced with immanent death, it is more than likely that Pascal decided to devote his efforts to spiritual preparations in the hope that God would never abandon him.[26] The decision to remove himself from the quarrel and to become almost entirely preoccupied with devotional activities of a personal nature was characteristically Jansenist.

Another Jansenist who took an intransigent position similar to that of the Pascals was Guillaume Le Roy, Abbé de Hautefontaine. As early as 1656, Le Roy had been in correspondence with Arnauld on the matter of the formulary, and he had become unalterably opposed to any signature that appeared to condemn Jansenius's views on grace. In a pamphlet entitled *Lettre sur la constance et le courage qu'on doit avoir pour la vérité*, published in 1661, Le Roy asserted the fundamental Jansenist theme that the true Christian must suffer for the truth. The Christian must seek solitude in order to learn the will of God and to renounce self-interest. The effect of this process of purification resulting from isolation and introspection, wrote Le Roy, was that one became possessed by God and independent of men. A Christian wholly devoted to the service of God and entirely detached from human interests was capable of making kings tremble and of invincibility in the face of his enemies. Furthermore, a man entirely dedicated to the service of God was obliged to resist commandments from ecclesiastical superiors that were in violation of God's law.[27] Le Roy went so far as to write the king's minister, Michel Le Tellier, a family friend, in 1663: "As for the formulary, my conscience does not permit me to sign it, because it confuses *fait* and *droit* by converting fact into an article of faith, and because I am convinced that the doctrine of Jansenius is not that which is attributed to him, but is the pure doctrine of the Church."[28]

Abbé Le Roy elaborated on his reasons for not signing the formulary in a declaration that he issued at the end of the year 1663. He refused to sign because he would be acting against his own intelligence and conscience in order to please the world. He disliked troubling "the true and precious" peace in his heart in order to achieve an illusory peace in the Church because the pope and a handful of bishops were not infallible, and because that element within the Church favored by the worldly "powers of the century" was not representative of the interests of the true Church. The true Christian, rather than submitting to worldly authority as Barcos urged, was supposed to resist, according to Le Roy, to the extent of refusing to sign and suffering the consequences. Unwilling to remain silent, the Abbé implored his friends, including the nuns of Port Royal, not to give in, and he took pride in heading all his letters "At Hautefontaine, where we do not sign the formulary."[29]

The third attitude prevalent among the Jansenists with regard to signature was that taken by Arnauld in 1656, in which the five propositions were recognized as heretical though not to be found in the *Augustinus*. Other Jansenists including Nicole, Le Maistre de Sacy, Le Nain de Tillemont, and Lancelot followed Arnauld in making the distinction between *fait* and *droit*. Arnauld, to be sure, had grave reservations about the doctrinal issues embodied in the propositions, believing that they were capable of being construed in both a heretical and an orthodox sense. He also thought that ultimate decisions on doctrinal questions should only be made by a general council of the Church. Nevertheless, when the king decided to reimpose the formulary in 1661, Arnauld and Nicole agreed that the best way to defend Jansenius and the doctrine of efficacious grace was not to challenge the propositions on doctrinal grounds but to insist instead that they were not to be found in the *Augustinus.* By arguing that the papacy was trying to extend its authority beyond acceptable limits, into areas where reason ought to be autonomous, Arnauld hoped to evoke a sympathetic response from French Catholics, both laymen and clergy, who disliked what appeared to be Rome's pretensions of doctrinal infallibility. Arnauld therefore proposed that good Catholics sign the formulary, adding a statement to the effect that, although they submitted on the question of *droit*, they preferred to maintain a respectful silence on the question of fact. In this way, he and his associates believed, no harm would be done to the doctrine of efficacious grace. "Whatever designs some people have in these times to weaken the doctrine of grace, that doctrine that emphasizes the necessity of a truly efficacious grace for every pious action and that moves the will in an invincible manner . . . will remain as long as the Church." Having determined upon a course of action that would, in his opinion, protect Jansenius, Arnauld was prepared to resist the authority of Church and state with the same vigor as the abbé Le Roy, who refused to sign at all.

It is to the truth that one dedicates his belief, and not to authority unless it is identified with the truth. Otherwise, when that authority is in error, as all the world knows it is possible for popes and bishops to be in matters of fact, one would be obliged to believe in falsehood in deference to authority. And therefore, when for a number of reasons we determine by our judgment that a lesser authority [from an earthly point of view] has the truth on its side, and that a much greater authority does not, it is to act against both God's order and against the nature of our mind not to place ourselves on the side that possesses the clearest indication of the truth.[30]

Arnauld's appeal was to the judgment of the individual, which, if properly trained according to the principles laid down in the *Port*

Royal Logic, would be able to determine the truth with some degree of assurance in matters of fact.

Arnauld therefore rejected all efforts to reach a compromise on the formulary that implied submission to illegal authority in matters of fact. In 1663, the bishop of Comminges attempted to work out an arrangement that would satisfy Jansenist consciences as well as the requirements of Church and state. The bishop secured the cooperation of a Jesuit theologian and two or three Jansenists as well as encouragement from the government. Arnauld was invited to participate in the deliberations, but to the distress of some of his friends, he refused. To Singlin, one of those who urged him to adopt a more conciliatory attitude, on the grounds that the tranquillity and stability of the Church were being undermined by violent internecine quarrels, Arnauld replied: "One must do all that one can in good conscience for the peace of the Church, and one is released from this obligation only if an act that appears in itself to be to the advantage of the Church offends his conscience. . . . " Arnauld distinguished between worldly friendships and Christian friendships. "Freedom of sentiment is the most essential part of Christian friendship. It is not like worldly friendships that are held together by dissimulation and flattery because there is no regard for truth. There is no obligation in the other [Christian friendship] that must not yield before what one owes God and his conscience. . . . "[31] Despite the fact that the bishop of Comminges appealed to the pope to lend his support to the negotiations, his efforts failed. A satisfactory solution that did not explicitly condemn Jansenius could not be worked out.

In 1662, Cardinal de Retz, worn out by the intrigue and conspiracy that had governed his actions for almost thirty years, resigned the office of archbishop of Paris. As expected, Louis XIV immediately appointed Pierre de Marca, archbishop of Toulouse, to the vacant seat. De Marca was a deadly enemy of the Jansenists, one of the architects of the government's anti-Jansenist policy during the era of the Fronde. At this point fate intervened in the form of a fatal stroke suffered by the archbishop-designate. The king next appointed his former tutor, Hardouin de Péréfixe to the office, but because relations between France and the Vatican continued to be badly strained, Péréfixe had to wait almost two years before receiving confirmation of his appointment by the pope. Between the summer of 1662 and the spring of 1664, the archdiocese was virtually without a bishop. During this time, the government's campaign to destroy Jansenism abated somewhat, perhaps because it was feared that aggressive action against the movement when the situation in the archdiocese was still unsettled might stimulate those rebellious sentiments that existed within the clergy of the city during the preceding decade. Once the new archbishop assumed his seat after papal confirmation, the oath of loyalty to him taken by the curés would make it difficult for them to disobey him. The curés had justified their actions during the Fronde on the grounds that they were obeying their rightful superior, de Retz.

When Hardouin de Péréfixe finally assumed office in the spring of 1664, he issued an order demanding signature without reservation but, in effect, accepting the distinction between *droit* and *fait*. The clergy in the archdiocese were asked to sign the formulary—submitting to the authority of the Church on the question of *droit* because of a divine obligation, while submitting to the authority on the question of *fait* only because of an obligation to respect the decisions of superiors in the Church. In the mind of Péréfixe, the question of fact did not impose on the Christian the divine obligation to believe—only a human obligation to obey one's superiors in the interests of order and stability in the Church. The archbishop's concession was hardly any concession at all, because all clergy were required to sign with no expressed reservation. Shortly after the order was promulgated, a pamphlet entitled *De la foy humaine* appeared, written by Pierre Nicole, whose position on the signature was the same as Arnauld's. According to Nicole, the archbishop's demand for submission on the question of fact could easily shatter the unity of the Church. If each bishop set himself up as an authority on questions of fact, disagreement among bishops would eventually lead to a proliferation of sects such as was occurring within Protestantism. The beliefs of one diocese would be as different from those of another as the tenets of Anabaptists were different from those of Socinians. Men were so inclined toward error, contended Nicole, that if the authority of the Church rested to a considerable extent on the fallible judgments of bishops, there could be no unity within the Church. Furthermore, Calvinists, who were always seeking to undermine Catholicism, would be able to fortify their contention that Catholicism destroyed Christian liberty. Worst of all, obedience to episcopal authority in matters of fact would enable superior officials to extend their power over grammar, philosophy, and geometry as well as over history. Péréfixe's order was therefore rejected by Nicole on the grounds that it constituted an unwarranted extension of ecclesiastical authority into an area where reason ought to be autonomous.

This law of nature commands men to make legitimate use of their reason, and it is clear that any human commandment that would compel him to make poor use of it would be contrary to the law of nature.

Now it is to make good use of reason to allow oneself to be persuaded by evident things, and in consequence, it would be an unjust commandment that forbids one to submit oneself to evidence.[32]

The crisis over the signature reached a dramatic climax at Port-Royal-de-Paris during the summer of 1664. An extensive record of what took place there between 1661, when Louis XIV first attempted to impose the formulary, and 1669, when the Peace of the Church was concluded, is contained in a three-volume work published in the eighteenth century entitled *Divers actes, lettres, et relations des religieuses de Port-Royal-du-Saint-Sacrement touchant au sujet de la signature du formulaire.*[33] The nuns at both convents had come to regard their late confessor, the abbé de Saint-Cyran, as a saintly man. Pictures of him were to be found in their cells, and relics such as bits of his hair and the water in which he had last washed his hands were believed by some of the nuns to have restorative powers. Furthermore, Angélique and Agnès Arnauld and the spiritual directors, Singlin and Le Maistre de Sacy, insisted on a rigorous penitential attitude among the nuns, who firmly believed in the doctrine of efficacious grace. The nuns also believed that Catholic doctrine was under attack from within the Church, and they were horrified by the persecution not only of Saint-Cyran but of Arnauld, Nicole, and the *solitaires*, all of whom they regarded as holy men. The nuns heartily disliked the Jesuits, whom they looked upon as the chief source of corruption in the Church, and the *Relations* are filled with bitter comments about the hated order. During the crisis over the formulary, one nun dreamed that she saw a chariot with the emblem of the cross on the door being driven by the devil, who turned out to be the king's Jesuit confessor.

The nuns' conviction that they were on the side of truth was reinforced not only by dreams but by miracles such as that of the Holy Thorn, which took place in 1656, and another one that was supposed to have occurred in January 1662. A young nun, Catherine de Champaigne, niece of the renowned painter Philippe de Champaigne, had been unable to walk since 1660. On December 26, 1661, Mère Agnès began a novena, not for the purpose of seeking a cure, but in order to support the young nun's ordeal. (The scene of Mère Agnès kneeling beside Catherine's couch was committed to posterity by Philippe de Champaigne in a painting that today hangs in the Louvre.) On January 6, 1662, while attending mass, Catherine felt a sudden urge to walk, and raising herself up from her couch, she discovered that she was able to do so. Fortified by miraculous interventions such as these, many nuns were prepared to suffer intense psychological hardships in emulation of Saint-Cyran, who had taught them to defend even the smallest truth.

The new archbishop of Paris, Hardouin de Péréfixe, presented himself at Port-Royal-de-Paris on June 9, 1664, and for nine days interrogated the nuns individually in order to extract a signature from each of them. Finding herself alone in the presence of the archbishop, each nun was compelled to decide whether to obey her conscience or ecclesiastical authority in the form of the harassed but determined Péréfixe, who on several occasions lost his temper at the unyielding sisters.[34] Several weeks later, Péréfixe returned to the convent accompanied by two hundred archers in order to remove twelve intransigent nuns and place them in other convents throughout the city. Those nuns who remained at Port Royal were placed under the supervision of nuns from another order. Nuns who refused to sign without express reservation were deprived of the sacraments and were denied access to sympathetic confessors. The psychological hardships experienced by the nuns, vividly described in the *Relations*, were of great magnitude. Chastised by the archbishop, cut off from the others in many instances, denied the rites of the Church, and acutely aware of differences of opinion among sympathetic theologians as to a proper course of action, each nun had to make her own decision. Each was forced to choose between the advice of Angélique Arnauld, who on her deathbed had counseled silence and submission, and that of Jacqueline Pascal, who urged resistance.

There were three groups among the nuns of Port Royal with respect to the question of the signature; those who signed, those who signed and then retracted, and those who, following the advice of Arnauld and Nicole, refused to sign without distinguishing between *droit* and *fait*. The first group included Flavie Passart, who had entered Port Royal in 1648 and was a prominent figure in the convent. Sister Flavie had initially refused to sign, taking Jacqueline Pascal's position that even a signature making the distinction between *droit* and *fait* did not safeguard the doctrine of efficacious grace. But during the critical summer of 1664, influenced by Singlin (who urged submission), Flavie began to fear that an intransigent attitude on the part of the nuns and the Jansenists as a whole would lead to schism. This fear caused her to sign. "God will not ask for an account of the affairs of the Church in His judgment," she told her colleagues, "but He will judge us according to the Rule [of the order], and according to obedience to superiors."[35] For Flavie Passart, obedience to God meant obedience to the Church, and refusal to respect the decisions of her superiors in the Church was not only in violation of her vows as a nun but also of her obligations as a Christian. Like Martin de Barcos and Saint-Cyran, she understood that the Church was not likely to survive another schism.[36] But Flavie's decision to bow to the wishes of the archbishop was in its own way as courageous as the decisions of the other nuns to resist, for by submitting, she subjected herself to the scorn and abuse of her uncompromising sisters.

Among the second group of sisters at Port-Royal-de-Paris, those who signed and then retracted, were Marie-Angélique Arnauld d'Andilly and Madeleine de Saint-Candide le Cerf. Marie-Angélique, the daughter of Arnauld d'Andilly, was one of the twelve nuns removed from Port Royal. She and her aunt, Agnès Arnauld, were placed in a convent in the Faubourg Saint-Jacques. There "I experienced spiritual pains so intense for over a month that only God knows about them. I was subjected to such terrifying doubts and obscurities that I often found myself doubting whether I believed in God." Deprived of sacramental comfort and unable to communicate her feeling to her aunt, who was very ill, Marie-Angélique experienced all sorts of psychological pressures to sign the formulary. What was particularly trying for her was that she was not allowed to confess her sins, and when she wrote to the archbishop requesting permission to confess and to take the sacraments, Péréfixe himself came to the convent to inform her that it was a sacrilege to permit those who were excessively disobedient to participate in the divine rites of the Church. At this point, Marie-Angélique began to waver in her determination not to sign—whereupon the archbishop assigned her a confessor, who informed her that her signature would in no way condemn Jansenius's doctrine but would simply indicate respect for her superiors. At the same time, the confessor informed her that her situation was different from that of her aunt and her sister, Angélique de Saint-Jean. These two nuns, according to the confessor, were justified in not signing because they were convinced that the five propositions were not in the *Augustinus*, but for those like Marie-Angélique, who were not sure about the question of fact, it was better to sign out of fear of disobeying. The despairing nun was unable to decide which course of action would be more offensive to God: obeying the archbishop or refusing to sign. "If someone had given me the choice of going before the Archbishop and signing on the one hand, and going to the executioner to have my head chopped off on the other, I would have gladly gone to the latter in the hope that God would have mercy on me, seeing how afraid I was of disobeying him." Marie-Angélique was brought before Péréfixe once again. She declared that in signing she did not intend to condemn Jansenius, whom she professed to revere "like a saint," but that her signature was simply a gesture of respect for the authority of her superiors in the Church. Péréfixe replied that he would accept the signature in that spirit, although he would not let her express her reservations in the signature. After the nun had signed, Péréfixe said to her: "I forbid you, my daughter, by all the authority I have over you as your archbishop to suffer any pain over what you have just done. I do not want to be bothered by an overscrupulous conscience." Unfortunately, Péréfixe's command notwithstanding, Marie-Angélique suffered spiritual anguish even worse than that she had suffered prior to submission. She concluded that she had been duped and that she had indeed condemned Jansenius by her signature. Receiving no solace from the sacraments, Marie-Angélique refrained from taking them on the anniversary of her vows, much to the horror of the nuns of the convent who did not subscribe to the ideals expressed by Arnauld in *De la fréquente communion*. Upon observing that her guardian nuns were becoming concerned about her lingering doubts about her signature, Marie-Angélique took heart. "I delighted in the discontent that I was causing among those around me, and I began to believe that God had noticed my prayers and my tears." Eventually Arnauld d'Andilly's daughter wrote a letter to the archbishop retracting her signature: "Perhaps I needed the experience that I have undergone in order to learn how little assurance one receives from putting one's trust in men. No matter how hard I tried to follow the advice that people gave me, I was unable to escape the reproaches of my conscience, which had become my accuser and my judge when I had taken the action."[37]

Madeleine de Saint-Candide was also among the nuns removed from Port-Royal-de-Paris in August 1664. At first unyielding on the subject of the formulary, she was even willing to argue with her guardian nuns in a convent in the Faubourg Saint-Antoine. But Madeleine soon began to feel the effects of being deprived of the sacraments and of the counsel of an understanding confessor. Fearing that her unconfessed sins would cut her off from God, she signed the formulary and was permitted to return to Port Royal. There she was appalled at the situation that existed at the convent. The nuns whom the archbishop had installed there to supervise the religious behavior of the remaining resident nuns were, in her opinion, arrogant and domineering, as were the resident nuns who signed. Those who continued to refuse signature were frightened and suspicious. The atmosphere of suspicion and distrust at Port Royal led Madeleine to conclude that such was the effect of submission to an unjust authority, whereupon she wrote a letter of retraction to the archbishop. "From that day on I was deprived of communion, and I returned to combat with my sisters, and all my spiritual anguish was dissolved." God, she said in her letter of retraction, had given her the grace to see that she had committed a sin in signing the formulary "against my own conscience."[38]

The third group of nuns, those who never wavered in their refusal to sign, included Christine Briquet, Mère Agnès Arnauld, and the eldest daughter of Arnauld d'Andilly, Angélique de Saint-Jean. Christine Briquet was a member of a prominent family of the Parisian *noblesse de robe*. Sainte-Beuve described her as "a Gallican doctrinaire," and he was critical of what he considered to be her legalistic rather than spiritual approach to the question of signature.[39] (Christine served as the model for Montherlant's Sister Françoise in his play *Port-Royal*.) She did not hesitate to argue with Péréfixe, who was alarmed by her seemingly disrespectful attitude. When the archbishop accused her of disobedience to the Church because of her refusal to defer to or acquiesce in its decisions, Christine coolly replied that by refusing to sign, she was indicating her unwillingness to lie to the Church as well as her preference for God's law over all other interests. When she was taken from Port Royal and placed in another convent, Christine put herself under the protection of the deceased abbess Angélique Arnauld, and embraced "with all my heart the necessity of living in solitude." Instead of yielding to the pressures to sign from the nun assigned to guard her, Christine experienced the true happiness of suffering for the truth. "God [in] his mercy did not wish me to find any consolation from creatures, and he reduced me to the happy necessity of receiving nothing except from him." Christine was not alarmed by the reports that other sisters of Port Royal had signed, because she trusted what the Gospels taught: "that no one can tear from [Christ's] hands those souls whom his Father gave to him."[40]

Agnès Arnauld, aged and infirm at the time of her removal from Port Royal, was unalterably convinced that persecution at the hands of the archbishop was an indication of God's favor. The nuns must not complain of their lot, she told Marie-Angélique, her niece who shared her exile. According to Agnès, one had to be despised among men in order to humble oneself before God. Describing her aunt in her *Relation*, Marie-Angélique wrote that "as for her [Mère Agnès], she came to realize every day what great mercy God had shown her, and she did not know what she would have done without [the persecution] because never had she seen her faults more clearly."[41]

The experiences of Angélique de Saint-Jean in "captivity," described in her *Relation* and in letters to her uncle, Antoine Arnauld, have been vividly portrayed by Sainte-Beuve and Montherlant. Arnauld d'Andilly's eldest daughter was the dominant figure among the second generation of nuns at Port Royal, and she played an important role in determining Antoine Arnauld's strategy with regard to signature. But unlike Christine Briquet and Agnès Arnauld, Angélique de Saint-Jean experienced severe mental anguish during her exile in an alien convent. Alone in her cell on the first night away from Port Royal, Angélique despaired at being entirely cut off from her sisters, and was during that night "continually involved in the struggle between grace and nature, without any arms to defend myself except the shield of the truth." Nature called upon her to focus on her afflictions, but she was able to sustain herself by recalling Psalm 121: "I will lift up mine eyes unto the hills from whence cometh my strength." Faith triumphed over doubt ("the gates of darkness"), and Angélique endured not only days of solitary confinement but constant pressure from her guardian nuns to obey the archbishop. One nun—a German and the widow of Marshal von Rantzau—who had been converted from Lutheranism, was especially persistent in her efforts to persuade Angélique to yield. Madame von Rantzau castigated Saint-Cyran and Jansenius for their heretical beliefs, and she argued in favor of papal infallibility. Angélique was able to defend herself by maintaining the distinction between *droit* and *fait*. She took pity on those whose religious zeal took the form "of blind obedience, which is their general maxim, and which is an error prevalent among nuns today."[42]

In the solitude of "captivity," Angélique converted her cell into a chapel, where she recited passages from Scripture and chanted portions of the Mass. Deprived of a confessor, Angélique undertook to subject herself to that intensive introspection advocated by Saint-Cyran, by which the Christian becomes aware not only of his inadequacies but of the workings of God's grace within him. One day, while in prayer, God "moved within me in order that I might abandon myself to the conduct of his grace, and in this condition I found that my prayer and admission of misery to God, whose justice I adore, fortified my resolve." Angélique's faith was strengthened by personal religious experience of an intensive kind, and it did not require the spiritual comfort of confession or of the sacraments.[43] As she wrote to her uncle, ". . . whatever good we derive from participation in the Holy Sacraments, the love and desire for which increases every day when we have been deprived of them for a long time, nevertheless if they were restored to us, it might occasion perilous temptations, and if we were permitted to confess without a free choice of confessor, nothing could do us greater harm."[44]

In July 1665, almost a year after he had dispersed the nuns of Port-Royal-de-Paris, Archbishop Péréfixe decided to return all those who refused to sign the formulary or who had retracted their signature to Port-Royal-des-Champs. The convent in the valley of the Chevreuse was subsequently separated from Port-Royal-de-Paris, which from then on housed only submissive nuns. At Port-Royal-des-Champs, the nuns continued to be deprived of the sacraments and of sympathetic confessors. Yet even in 1668, on the eve of the Peace of the Church, they were reluctant to sign the formulary that was the key to that peace, for fear of compromising divine truth. In the minds of these intransigent nuns, a distinction existed between the eternal Church of Christ and his Apostles and the false Church dominated by worldly officials. This distinction was brought out in a prayer offered by the nuns of Port-Royal-de-Paris shortly before the removal of the twelve sisters. The prayer begins with the recitation of a passage from the Gospel according to Saint Luke (18:7) ("And shall not God avenge his own elect, who cry day and night unto him, though he bear long with them?"): ". . . we ask your permission to address ourselves to those excellent princes, your Apostles, and to appeal the treatment that we are receiving to their authority which will always reside in the Church, and which we recognize in those who have succeeded them legitimately, but in whom we do not find a charitable disposition for souls. It is to these pastors [the Apostles] who have not wished to dominate their flock at all that we ask justice against our pastors who rise up against us with a power that you have not given them because it tends to the destruction and not to the edification of souls."[45] For these nuns, the true Church was represented not only in the living spirit of Christ's Apostles but also in the conscience of a single virtuous Christian intent upon defending the truth even in the face of the highest officials on earth.

The nuns' prayer again raised the question of illegitimate authority that Arnauld and other Jansenist writers had been emphasizing ever since the condemnation of the five propositions. It was the key issue in a pamphlet entitled *Apologie pour les religieuses*, which Arnauld published during the critical summer of 1664. Again he asserted the autonomy of reason in matters of fact. The pope's authority in such matters was no greater than that of a historian. "The authority of a historian in and of itself does not require me to believe his account of certain facts. It is the circumstances accompanying his account that makes me believe that they are accurate and that obliges me to believe them. No one may act unreasonably and against the light of common sense."[46] Nuns did not owe the same obedience to their superiors that soldiers owed to their officers; soldiers weren't involved in the decisions that led to a particular war, and even if it were an unjust war, only those in authority were responsible before God. No one would think of making a soldier sign a statement to the effect that he believed a particular war to be unjust. Soldiers rarely engaged in wars because of conviction. Nuns, on the other hand, took up their profession because of conviction with which no superior had the right to tamper. Taking issue with those who contended that the nuns who resisted signature were guilty of pride, Arnauld maintained that true humility consisted of an inflexible determination to serve the interests of God and conscience. He wrote:

There is a perfect uniformity between their conduct in this affair and the rest of their life. This admirable detachment that they have shown with respect to their house, their repose, and all that is dearest to them in the world is directly related to the detachment that they have always professed.

This contempt for everything that is the harshest and most afflicting in this world follows from their life of penitence and mortification, and this antipathy toward all disguise is nothing but the effect of their extreme sincerity. There has never been suffering that has more signs of being of those Christian sufferings that are the recompense and coronation of virtue, and the greatest indication of being of that eternal love that God bears for his elect.[47]

An important point that Arnauld made in the *Apologie* and in other writings was that those ecclesiastical authorities who sought to impose the formulary on people who had qualms about signing it were guilty of what he called the heresy of domination. Ecclesiastical authority was not of the same order as temporal authority, which was based on utility and which from time to time might sacrifice the interests of a few individuals for the sake of the public good. The authority of the Church was not based upon utilitarian principles but on the spiritual needs of its members; therefore, the interests of a few must not be sacrificed to the interests of the Christian community as a whole. "Bishops are so charged with the care of the Church that their primary responsibility is the care of each of their sheep, and they may not show prejudice against one particular individual on the grounds that they are procuring an advantage for the whole body." Bishops and other officials of the Church had no right to act in "an imperious and absolute manner" toward those who might be reluctant about or afraid of a particular course of action, especially those actions that were not proscribed by the laws of God or of nature.[48] If the heresy of domination was allowed to persist within the Church, and if it were permitted to reinforce the papal claim of infallibility, not only would the rights of individual Christian be endangered but also the liberties of the Gallican Church.

The various psychological experiences of the twelve nuns of Port Royal in "captivity" illustrates the importance of solitude and introspection that the Jansenists maintained was so important for strengthening religious commitment. These experiences also illustrate the relative unimportance of external ceremony for those whose faith was secure. The *Relations* describe the need the captive sisters felt for confession and for the sacraments; without the personal commitment to God's truth, however, the sacraments were incapable of providing consolation. Sister Madeleine de Sainte-Candide ultimately decided that obeying the archbishop and partaking of the sacraments was less satisfying spiritually than defending the truth without the aid of the sacraments. This willingness to do without the sacraments was applauded by the former confessor of Port Royal, Le Maistre de Sacy, who was imprisoned for his beliefs. In a letter to one of the nuns, written in November 1664, Sacy wrote: "Please God that there be one [sister] who is willing to expose herself to death without the sacraments in faith and in peace. . . . Happy is the soul that in its last moment gives to Jesus Christ such an effective proof of the sincerity of its faith."[49]

The efforts of Louis XIV to suppress Jansenism met with resistance not only from the consciences of individual Jansenists but also from a handful of bishops who respected the distinction between *droit* and *fait*. Among these prelates were Henri Arnauld, bishop of Angers and an older brother of Antoine, and Nicolas Pavillon, bishop of Alet, both of whom were outstanding representatives of the ideals of the Counter Reformation. Henri Arnauld was appointed bishop of Angers in 1649 because of his diplomatic services to Mazarin. Loyal to the crown, the new bishop entered Angers to find the local governor and elements of the clergy staunch supporters of the Fronde. Although Angers had been pacified, Henri Arnauld was to experience considerable difficulties with recalcitrant clerics in the diocese, difficulties that were aggravated by the bishop's efforts to introduce reforms. In an open letter addressed to the clergy of Angers, the bishop complained of poor discipline, libertinism, and licentiousness within both the secular and the regular clergy of the region. "Some priests," he wrote, "have even renounced the clerical uniform . . . that requires them to maintain a pious interior and a modest exterior that God demands of those who have enlisted in his service. They prefer the insignia of the secular militia, carrying the sword like soldiers or like libertines. They squander the patrimony of the poor on luxuries and debaucheries . . . and they spend the time that ought to be devoted to prayer and study on gambling, at balls, and in other amusements that the Church prohibits."[50] The bishop insisted

upon proper dress for the clergy and a return to the rigorous discipline of the early Church. Because of his reforming efforts, the
bishop encountered from both orders of the clergy violent
opposition that kept the diocese in a state of unrest during much
of his time in office. (He died in 1692.) Like other bishops whom
the Jansenists admired, Henri Arnauld supported the Jansenist
cause, and in an episcopal ordinance published in 1665, he maintained that, although the five propositions were heretical, it was
questionable whether they were to be found in the *Augustinus.*
The bishop of Angers attempted to assert his authority over the
regular clergy within the diocese, and he also insisted upon considerable episcopal autonomy in doctrinal matters. In a letter
written in 1665 to a fellow bishop, Henri Arnauld stated that
obedience to king and pope should in no way compromise divine
truth.

And if, Monseigneur, it happens that, in following these precepts
so indispensable to our duty, we fall into disgrace in the eyes of
men, and if violence and blindness carry things so far that the
sacred dignity of our character is trampled underfoot ... we cannot thank God enough for having given us the grace to expose us
to everything rather than to betray our honor in a cowardly
fashion, or our conscience or the inviolable rights of His Sacred
Spouse, which he acquired with the price of his blood and which
in us he has made the depositaries, and it seems to me that we
need only be concerned about not being cognizant enough of our
duties toward God as so few among the many who abandon him
are. A true bishop ought to prefer God's interests to his own life.[51]

The bishop most admired by the Jansenists was Nicolas Pavillon,
bishop of Alet. As a young man, Pavillon became a protégé of
Vincent de Paul, who persuaded Richelieu to appoint Pavillon
bishop of Alet, in Languedoc. Unwilling to accept office at first
because of a deep sense of unworthiness, Pavillon was eventually
persuaded by Vincent de Paul that it was God's will that he be
consecrated, and he became a bishop in 1639. Alet was a very
poor diocese situated in the Pyrenees. Its clergy were ignorant and
incompetent, and the two monasteries in the area were in serious
decline. Their revenue was so insubstantial that the monks were
forced to beg for food in the villages. The local nobles were

bandits who terrorized the countryside and bullied the Church. The new bishop, entirely unfamiliar with the region, devoted all his energies to the spiritual improvement of his diocese. He donated part of his patrimony to the poor and made frequent visits to the several villages in order to make himself known to both clergy and laymen and to acquire a better understanding of the reforms that needed to be instituted. In order to educate the local clergy to their responsibilities, the bishop inaugurated a series of conferences throughout the area. "Usually I am present [at these conferences]," he wrote, "at which time we spend two or three hours discussing the verities of the faith, God's commandments, the theory and practices pertaining to the sacraments in order that they may be effectively administered to the people. We want to see that other ecclesiastical functions are performed in a competent and pious manner."[52] Uniform penitential discipline was established throughout the diocese, thereby preventing a reluctant penitent from seeking out a less demanding confessor. Public penance was introduced by the bishop, and priests were instructed to read aloud the names of sinners from the pulpit, while parishioners were required to kneel before the entire congregation and to beg forgiveness for such sins as fornication, blasphemy, dueling, and excessive revelry. Pavillon's reputation as a reformer was such that many people journeyed to Alet to see how a model diocese functioned. A longtime friend of the Arnauld family, the bishop of Alet was in close touch with the affairs of Port Royal and was sympathetic to the Jansenist cause. In 1667 the bishop published his *Instructions du rituel du diocese d'Alet*. This work was written in consultation with a number of Jansenist theologians, including Antoine Arnauld, and it enjoyed a considerable success throughout France. It underwent a number of editions despite having been placed on the Index in 1668. The *Rituel d'Alet* stressed the need for genuine contrition on the part of the sinner before he was eligible for the sacraments, and it insisted on the right of the priest to delay absolution in cases where penance had been improperly performed. "Charity does not oblige pastors to condescend to the weaknesses of penitents when such condescension would be prejudicial to their salvation. . . . On the contrary, charity requires pastors to demand of penitents the strength necessary to obey the ordinances of the Church and to oblige them to do sacred violence to themselves."[53] The intransigent moral principles of the bishop stirred up the diocese and even brought resistance from some clerics who regarded them as too demanding; but Pavillon was intolerant of any opposition within the diocese, and he resisted any attempts on the part of king or bishop to encroach upon his episcopal rights. He objected to *Cum occasione* and to the formulary, which he refused to circulate within the bishopric. While most prelates were afraid to oppose the king openly, Alet addressed a letter to his sovereign asserting the right of bishops to deal with matters of faith and discipline without interference from temporal authority.

The opposition to the formulary expressed by the bishops of Angers and Alet, and by those of Beauvais and Pamiers, was based upon episcopal Gallicanism as well as on conscience. Because they believed that they owed their offices to God rather than to king and pope, bishops adhering to this tradition felt that they were directly responsible to God for the spiritual welfare of their respective dioceses. Thus they were bound to oppose any doctrine that did not satisfy their requirements with respect to the religious needs of those placed under their authority. The four bishops were persuaded that a distinction ought to be made between *droit* and *fait*, which the crown refused to accept. Not only were they willing to resist the authority of the *conseil d'état* in this matter but also the authority of the pope. In February 1665, Alexander VII, in response to an appeal from the French king, issued his second anti-Jansenist encyclical, *Regiminis apostolici*. Comparing the Jansenist heresy to a serpent whose head was crushed but whose body continued to thrash about, the encyclical demanded signature of the formulary by all members of the French clergy. It was registered by the Parlement of Paris without opposition, and it was sent out to all the bishops of the kingdom accompanied by a letter in which the king commanded signature "without any distinction, interpretation, or restriction." Despite the fact that signature of the formulary had become the requirement of the highest authority in Church and state, it was resisted by the consciences of Jansenists and by the Gallican sentiments of the four bishops.

Louis XIV's confessor, Father Annat, declared that the pope

had the right to depose disobedient bishops, an opinion that violated the principles of both royal and episcopal Gallicanism. Alexander VII went so far as to have condemned by the Inquisition the pastoral letters of the four bishops permitting signature with reservation as to fact, but in 1667, before he was able to take further action against the Jansenists, he died. The new pope, Clement IX, was a man of moderate temperament. He was aware that a schism might develop in France as the result of aroused Gallican prejudices. Nineteen French bishops who had signed the formulary without reservation had nevertheless publicly expressed their support for the recalcitrant four on the grounds that they had the right to resist demands that infringed on their episcopal rights. To avert further resistance, Clement undertook to achieve an accommodation on the formulary. He obtained the cooperation of two distinguished French prelates, the archbishop of Sens and the bishop of Chalons, as well as the support of the crown. A number of Jansenists were becoming weary of religious disputes, and for this reason, the two prelates, after some maneuvering, were able to establish a generally acceptable compromise. A letter to the pope that was to be signed by the four recalcitrant bishops was drafted. In the letter, the bishops declared their desire to end the troubles that afflicted the Church and expressed their apologies for having contributed to these troubles. They agreed to circulate in their dioceses new pastoral letters requiring signature, accompanied by a vaguely worded statement implying mental reservations as to the question of fact.

After some hesitation on the part of the bishop of Alet and the nuns of Port-Royal-des-Champs, who were still afraid that the doctrine of efficacious grace was being compromised, all parties agreed to what became known as the Peace of the Church (*Paix de l'Eglise*), which went into effect early in 1669, when all the necessary signatures had been collected. The Pope forbade further discussion of the issues arising out of the *Augustinus*, the nuns of Port Royal were permitted to participate in the sacraments once again, Le Maistre de Sacy and Fontaine were released from the Bastille, and Arnauld and other Jansenists came out of hiding. Arnauld was even presented to Louis XIV by his nephew, Arnauld de Pomponne, a minister of state at the time. But the author of

De la fréquente communion was not readmitted to the ranks of
the Sorbonne, an indication that Jansenism was still doctrinally
suspect.

The Peace of the Church was achieved by Clement IX and
Louis XIV because the crisis over the signature threatened the
stability of the French Church and because of the growing opposition (among the higher clergy throughout the kingdom) to any
disciplinary action against the four bishops. The nuns and friends
of Port Royal who insisted on their right to adhere to the dictates
of their consciences were spared further persecution by the Gallican sentiments of many political and spiritual leaders of the
kingdom. But for episcopal intervention, Port Royal might well
have been destroyed in the 1660s and the Jansenist leaders forced
into exile and probably excommunicated. Indeed, the Gallican
tradition may explain the curious fact that the Jansenists were not
excommunicated even though they obviously anticipated such
punishment. Once the bishops intervened on their behalf, any
disciplinary action taken against them by Church or state would
have seemed to many in France to be in violation of episcopal
liberties, and public opinion would have been even more stirred
up than it already was by the publicity that the quarrel received.
The Jansenists were also protected by such powerful figures as the
duchesse de Longueville, the king's cousin, and by other prominent subjects of the crown. Any attempt to ascertain why further
persecution of the disciples of Saint-Cyran was not undertaken in
the 1660s must take into consideration the impact of these disputes on public opinion. Each side issued pamphlets and public
letters justifying its position. Jansenist publicists were keenly
aware of the power of public opinion as a result of the impact of
the *Provincial Letters* in the 1650s, and the nuns of Port Royal
felt compelled to tell their story in print. Angélique de Saint-Jean's
Relation first appeared in 1665 in Arnauld's *Apologie pour les
religieuses.* Given sensitive Gallican feelings and an aroused and
apparently sympathetic public opinion, Louis XIV and the papacy
decided that a compromise would have to be worked out, at least
temporarily.

VI. *After the Peace of the Church*
The Jansenist Critique of Ecclesiastical Absolution

The Peace of the Church proved to be a temporary cessation of hostilities that for almost a decade suited the convenience of all parties involved. The Jansenists, their backs to the wall, wanted to prevent, if possible, the outright condemnation of their beliefs; the papacy wanted to avoid another rent in "the seamless garment of Christ," and Louis XIV, preparing for and then waging war against the Dutch, needed order and tranquillity within the kingdom. Despite the somewhat ambiguous compromise, however, there were Jansenists who continued to feel that the truth must be defended in the interests of personal salvation and ecclesiastical reform, and who were unable to respect the conditions of the truce for very long. There were many opponents of Jansenism who still believed that it was the duty of the Church to extirpate a dangerous heresy and who loathed the challenge to authority inherent in so many aspects of Jansenist thought. Continuing religious quarrels were inevitable. Although the papacy was reluctant to rule again on the doctrinal orthodoxy of Jansenism in the face of Gallican prejudices, the government of Louis XIV could not tolerate for long the continued existence of a movement that seemed to be the source of so much trouble. The *Paix de l'Eglise* depended on the enduring cooperation of all concerned, but cooperation for a long period of time was impossible, given the fears and suspicions in all quarters.

Yet the Peace of the Church provided the embattled convent of Port-Royal-des-Champs with a few years of peace and quiet. During the decade of the 1670s (Sainte-Beuve calls it the "autumn of Port Royal"), it enjoyed the august patronage of the duchesse de Longueville and the marquise de Sablé. The former, well known for her activities during the Fronde, built a house close to the convent. The *solitaires*, including the venerable Arnauld d'Andilly, remained in the valley of the Chevreuse, and the spiritual needs of the Port-royalists were looked after by a number of priests including Le Maistre de Sacy and, from time to time, Antoine Arnauld. Port Royal was again permitted to take in boarders and postulants, who flocked to it in large numbers—evidence enough of its undiminished reputation for piety.

Although they were prohibited from openly discussing matters pertaining to the *Augustinus*, Jansenists continued to write on religious subjects in the years immediately following the Peace of the Church. Arnauld and Nicole wrote polemics against the Huguenots on the eve of the revocation of the Edict of Nantes, which they supported. Works such as *La perpetuité de la foi de l'église catholique touchant l'eucharistie* (1669) were written as much to differentiate the beliefs of the Jansenists from those of Protestants as to ingratiate the authors with the authorities of Church and state. Arnauld, Le Maistre de Sacy, and Lancelot undertook a collaborative translation of the New Testament, which was first published in 1667. Many of the religious writings of the Jansenists in this period were characteristic of their belief. Arnauld, Nicole, and other friends of Pascal gathered up the notes he had made for what was to be his magnum opus in defense of Christianity. These notes were published in 1670 under the title *Pensées de Monsieur Pascal sur la religion et sur quelques autres sujets* and were to undergo successive editions down to our own time. Although this edition of the most enduring of Jansenist works did not include some of Pascal's statements that might have been regarded as violations of the Peace of the Church, it nevertheless contained a strong element of the spirituality that was so characteristic of Saint-Cyran and his followers.[1] Many of the themes contained in the *Pensées* reappeared in Pierre Nicole's most important work, the *Essais de morale*, presented to the public during the 1670s. These essays—admired by Madame de Sévigné, by John Locke, who translated some of them into English, and by Voltaire, among others—were concerned primarily with human nature. In the first, entitled "De la foiblesse de l'homme," Nicole declared that the good opinion that men have of themselves is caused by pride and imagination. These enable them to forget their corporeal and spiritual weaknesses. Men are continually reminded of the frailty of their bodies, he wrote, by such daily needs as hunger and thirst, yet they continue to regard life as something solid. "If the greatest mind in the world were permitted to go without eating for two days, it would become virtually incapable of thought or action." While it is relatively easy to persuade men of their corporeal weaknesses, it is far more difficult to persuade them of their spiritual flaws. Men pride themselves on their virtue, knowledge, and breadth of mind, all of which are based on worldly values and not on Christian ideals. In fact, men are so little aware of their weaknesses that they undertake enterprises that defy common sense.

It is because they forget how fragile life is, and because they have an unreasonable confidence in their ability to escape all dangers, that men resolve to undertake voyages to the end of the world and to fetch themselves to China in order to bring back lacquers and spices. In truth, if they thought enough about it, taking into account what they were risking and what they hoped to gain, they would doubtless conclude that a little gain was not worth the pain of exposing a body as feeble as theirs to so many perils and so many inconveniences. But men blind themselves to their true interests. They love only life, and yet they risk it for everything, and they have agreed among themselves that it is shameful to be afraid of risking life.[2]

To illustrate the diversity of opinions and sentiments among men, Nicole, in an essay entitled *The Prism*, attempted to show how that object might appear to three different kinds of human beings—a child, a philosopher, and a man of the world. For the child, the prism is a plaything, and he is charmed by the beautiful colors. The philosopher finds in the prism an occasion to speculate on the nature of light. For the man of the world, uninterested in philosophy, the prism is a thing of beauty, but because it is of so little value, he pays little attention to it. Men of the world distrust philosophers and children because the former waste their time in idle speculation, and the latter, in idle pursuits. Philosophers distrust men of the world because they are not moved by the beauties of the spirit or of nature, and philosophers are contemptuous of children because they derive too much pleasure from the senses. Children disapprove of no one, for which reason their inclinations are less defective than those of the philosopher or of the man of the world. What is extraordinary about the prism, concluded Nicole, is that it is an object of such beauty and yet of so little value because opinion dictates that the value of an object must be minimal if it is easily procured. It is the same with the beauties of nature, available to everyone, and consequently valueless, whereas an ornate palace is valuable because only a few are able to afford such a luxury. Men's pleasures are inspired by vanity and malice, both of which determine the value of things. The opinions of children are less reprehensible than those of adults, but as they get older, their judgment becomes corrupted by pride and avarice, and their reason is led astray by illusion. The irony of Nicole's use of the prism lies in the fact that he took an object that contemporary philosophers used to achieve a more accurate understanding of color in order to illustrate the mind's ability to create illusions. The prism also served as a means by which Nicole illustrated the effect that faith has on the mind. Just as the prism turns our view of nature upside down, faith "makes us see how little are the great of this world and how great are the little people, how poor the rich and how rich the poor, how miserable the fortunate and how fortunate the wretched. Each rank or degree that we regarded as exalted in terms of honor and felicity now becomes debased in our sight."[3] The abbé de Saint-Cyran had made similar statements to the effect that faith makes men see that those who are regarded as wise in this world are taken for fools in heaven.

For Nicole, coauthor of the *Port Royal Logic*, reason had its uses. Like Pascal, he was concerned about Pyrrhonists who went so far as to doubt even the truths pertaining to Christianity, and like other Jansenists, he was alarmed by the trend toward deism inherent in the bold claims of seventeenth-century rationalism. Nevertheless, although reason was incapable of directly comprehending God, it could lead the sinner to a firmer understanding of himself. "True knowledge of men is the way to peace, and the way to salvation," wrote Nicole in one of his essays,[4] reiterating a point made by Jansenius and Pascal. Self-knowledge enabled a man to understand the workings of self-interest, by which virtue was defined in worldly terms. Courage, for example, was a virtue established by approbation. A man might be considered strong and courageous by others because he had qualities that were generally considered admirable. Self-interest caused men to respond affirmatively to what was pleasurable and negatively to what was painful. The cold light of dispassionate reason, however, revealed that all human beings are weak and entirely dependent upon God's strength and mercy. True courage, contended Nicole, lies in the recognition that worldly virtues are based upon illusions.[5]

Pascal and Nicole were similar in their analyses of the human condition and in their belief that reason played an important role in comprehending divine as well as human truths. Both men appealed to enlightened self-interest, but in different ways. The mathematician resorted to the wager as a means of appealing to the freethinker. Nicole, on the other hand, concluded that objective self-analysis revealed that human actions were motivated either by self-interest or by charity. Although self-interest (the fruit of concupiscence) was the exact opposite of charity (the fruit of grace) their effects were, ironically, the same. In order to illustrate the point, Nicole resorted to Cartesian physics just as Pascal had resorted to mathematics. Descartes had conceived of the material world in terms of motion and extension. Humanity, insofar as it was motivated by concupiscence, might be regarded in the same terms. "Each material particle naturally tends to move, to extend, and to leave its place, but being pressed by other particles, it is reduced to a sort of prison, from which it escapes when it finds itself to be stronger than the bodies around it."[6] The human instinct is to dominate whenever possible, and the individual would try to dominate those around him except that he stands to lose what he already has by opposing a more powerful force in his way. Fear of retribution, therefore, restrains the instinctive inclination to dominate. Almost as strong an instinct is the desire to be loved, and the individual, after careful calculations, realizes that he can make his way in the world more easily by means of the approbation of others than by their hostility. Natural or instinctive self-interest, a socially disruptive force, according to Nicole, yields to enlightened self-interest (that is, self-interest guided by reason), which causes men to regulate their lives by pleasing others. A seemingly humble act might as likely be inspired by enlightened self-interest as by charity, because a particular person might conclude that he had as much to gain in worldly terms by appearing humble.

Enlightened self-interest, according to Nicole, is a means of maintaining social order in the absence of charity. Without order, men would be unable to enjoy their possessions, to travel safely, or to profit from commerce and industry. "Men are devoid of charity as a result of Original Sin," wrote Nicole, "yet they have needs and are dependent on one another in an infinite number of ways. Cupidity has taken the place of charity in order to satisfy human needs in a way that fills one with admiration." Social order rooted in cupidity is a cunningly contrived means by which God enables men to establish terrestrial law and order, without which anarchy would prevail. "No matter how corrupt a society is in the eyes of God, to all human appearances nothing is better ordered, more civil, more just, more pacific, more honest, or more generous. What is so extraordinary is that all these characteristics are animated by self-interest, which is not easily discernible because everything seems to be motivated by charity."[7]

Essential to Nicole's philosophy was the contention that the mind is incapable of ascertaining whether a person is motivated by concupiscence or by grace. God, however, intended such uncertainty in order to encourage humility, because assurance of God's grace might inspire pride.

We always have within us a divine principle or a human principle, the external and sensible aspects of those exercises pertaining to the Christian life. Often we have both together, but we cannot know for certain which of these two principles dominates our hearts and motivates our actions. And although it is our duty to continually purify ourselves of all interest and self-love, we do not know whether this desire to be purified does not come from another interest more spiritual and more subtle. One can desire to be humble for the sake of pride. Thus the actions of the soul involve a vicious circle of reflections on reflections.

Such is the condition in which God has placed us. We are condemned to these shadows by his justice.[8]

Nicole distinguished between the life of the just (the life of faith) and the life of worldly people (the life of reason), but he maintained that the human mind could not differentiate between them.[9] This conception of enlightened self-interest was intended to provide a natural explanation of human activity and at the same time to encourage the penitent to serve God by practicing Christian virtues in the hope that they were genuinely inspired by grace. It was also intended to emphasize the point that reason plays a role in ordering the good life.

Like Saint-Cyran before him, Nicole retained a skeptical view of the value of philosophy even though he contributed to the *Port Royal Logic*, which was impregnated with Cartesian principles. Man must understand, wrote Nicole in one of the essays, that, for the most part, philosophy is nothing but a mass of obscurities and uncertainties. "Men philosophized for three thousand years on various subjects, and then a man [Descartes] appeared in a corner of the earth who changed the entire face of philosophy, who intended to make everyone see that all those who came before him knew nothing about the principles of nature. And these were not vain boasts, because it must be admitted that this newcomer has shed more light on the knowledge of natural things."[10] Yet Descartes, in Nicole's opinion, was unable to provide certain knowledge of nature, his explanations being only probable. Descartes and other philosophers had really only succeeded in revealing man's ignorance and his capacity for self-delusion.[11] Nicole had great respect for Montaigne, whose ideas about philosophy had so much influence on the Jansenists. Montaigne, he wrote, "reveals in a naive way the natural movements of the mind, its different agitations, the half-hearted efforts it makes, and the brutal conclusions that it arrives at after having looked about."[12] Pascal had said much the same thing about Montaigne in his dialogue with Le Maistre de Sacy at Port-Royal-des-Champs. Nicole also admired Sir Francis Bacon, a man "who contributed much to reestablishing common sense."[13] Certainly Bacon's distaste for the learning of the past would have appealed to Nicole, as well as his insistence upon the establishment of useful, rather than misleading, categories. While more inclined toward Pyrrhonism than any of the other French Jansenists except Saint-Cyran, Nicole never repudiated philosophy entirely. He regarded it as helpful in understanding the realities of the human condition and in comprehending at least something about the realm of nature.

The *Essais de morale* constitutes an important expression of Jansenist thought and belief in the seventeenth century. In the essays is to be found that Augustinian spirituality that characterized the religious beliefs of Cardinal Bérulle, the abbé de Saint-Cyran, and Bishop Jansenius, to say nothing of Protestantism. They also reflect the philosophical currents of Pyrrhonism and Cartesianism. The influence of Montaigne, Charron, and Saint-Cyran are apparent in Nicole's analysis of human weakness. Yet there is also apparent a recognition of the utility of Descartes's philosophy in acquiring a better understanding of natural phenomena. Indeed, Nicole went so far as to use the Cartesian principles of extension and motion to explain human motivation. Finally, the dichotomous aspect of Jansenist thought and belief is further developed in the *Essais*. Crucial to the belief of Saint-Cyran and his disciples was the absolute distinction between grace and nature. The Christian comprehends the realm of grace by means of faith, and in matters pertaining to faith he submits to divine authority. He comprehends the realm of nature by means of reason, which must be free to draw its own conclusions. Nicole elaborated on the distinction inherent in Jansenist thought between two kinds of human behavior. In the realm of grace, man is motivated by the spirit of charity, which makes him truly repentant of his sins and helps him to establish a harmonious existence with his fellow creatures. In the realm of nature, man is motivated by self-interest, which causes him to seek absolution for his sins, not because he loves God, but because he fears punishment. But self-interest is also a means of establishing a fairly stable and harmonious social order. By carefully analyzing the ethics of self-interest as well as by emphasizing their beneficial effects, Nicole appears to have anticipated the ethics of utilitarianism that came to full fruition during the eighteenth century.

Another important Jansenist work published shortly after the conclusion of the Peace of the Church was entitled *Abrégé de la morale de l'évangile, ou, considérations chrétiennes sur le texte des quatres évangiles* (1672). Its author was Pasquier Quesnel, born in 1634 the son of a Parisian bookseller and the grandson on

his mother's side of a Scottish nobleman. Quesnel studied at the
Jesuit College of Clermont and at the Sorbonne, after which he
entered the Oratory and was ordained in 1659. At the Oratorian
seminary of Saint-Magloire, the young priest quickly acquired the
reputation of being a devout and conscientious spiritual director.
The *Abrégé* contained Quesnel's devotional ideals, many of which
were characteristically Jansenist. It touched upon the nature of
divine grace, despite the prohibitions of the Peace of the Church.
"The grace of Jesus Christ is an efficacious principle behind everything good, and it is necessary for the start, the continuation and
the accomplishment of every good deed, large or small, simple or
difficult." Quesnel denounced those Christians who relied primarily on human efforts to achieve salvation. "They who defend
human liberty against grace," he wrote in obvious reference to the
Jesuits, " . . . contradict Jesus Christ." The repentant sinner must
undertake demanding spiritual exercises that would detach him
from the world, and he must be prepared to suffer persecution.
"Persecution," wrote Quesnel, "is beneficial because it enables one
to understand the truth."[14] Widely circulated, the *Abrégé* underwent several revised and expanded editions. The edition published
in 1692 bore a new title, *Le nouveau testament en françois avec
des réflexions morales sur chaque verset.* Though approved by the
Sorbonne and by several bishops, one hundred and one propositions from the *Réflexions morales*—which was to replace the
Augustinus as the most controversial Jansenist work at the
beginning of the eighteenth century—were eventually condemned
in the papal encyclical *Unigenitus* (1713). During the crisis over
the formulary, Quesnel was a young priest whose spiritual ideals
were not fully developed. He signed the document in obedience to
his superiors in the Oratory, but in 1673, a year after the publication of the *Abrégé*, he retracted his signature, declaring that he
had given it in ignorance and that he had become firmly committed
to the doctrine of efficacious grace, which he believed the formulary had condemned.

Quesnel's difficulties with the authorities of the Church were
increased by the publication in 1675 of his edition of the works of
Saint Leo, the fifth-century pope who opposed Pelagianism and
who extended the influence of the Roman see. This erudite work

caused the General Assembly of the Oratory publicly to recognize Quesnel, along with Richard Simon and Nicolas de Malebranche, as one of its most illustrious scholars. Quesnel's edition of Saint Leo's works offended the Vatican, however, because it interpreted that pope's thought and action in a Gallican light that appeared to belittle papal authority. Furthermore the Vatican disapproved of Quesnel's assertion of the right of the scholar to investigate freely all sources relating to the history of the Church, without interference from the pope or any other ecclesiastical official. Like Saint-Cyran, Jansenius, and Le Nain de Tillemont, among others, Quesnel endeavored to base Church doctrine on a dispassionate understanding of primary sources, an understanding that could only be achieved, in Quesnel's opinion, through intensive philological analysis. This sort of scholarly activity had in the past thrown certain fundamental Catholic principles open to question and had contributed to the Reformation, but Catholic as well as Protestants theologians continued their investigations throughout the seventeenth century. Indeed, Quesnel's fellow Oratorian Richard Simon—in his *Histoire critique du vieux testament*, published three years after Quesnel's work—was to challenge the authenticity of scripture and tradition in a number of areas. Roman authorities therefore insisted on the right to control scholarly investigations. Despite Quesnel's protestations in favor of the intellectual rights of the individual, his edition of Saint Leo's works was placed on the Index in 1676. Simon's *Histoire critique* was added to it in 1683.[15] Quesnel's fundamental religious beliefs developed independently of the Port Royal circle, although he undoubtedly read the devotional works of Saint-Cyran and others when he was a seminarian. Nevertheless, during the 1670s, a decade before he became associated with Antoine Arnauld, Quesnel exhibited those essentially Jansenist characteristics that had become so apparent at Port Royal in the era of the Fronde—a rigid penitential ethic supported by an uncompromising interpretation of Saint Augustine's doctrine of efficacious grace, as well as a willingness to defend the spiritual and intellectual integrity of the individual against any authority that attempted to compromise that integrity.

The decade following the *Paix de l'Eglise* 'was marked by

incidents that were to contribute to the renewed persecution of the Jansenists. Arnauld and others continued to criticize the activities of the Jesuits, whose hostility toward the followers of Saint-Cyran remained unassuaged. In the very year that the Peace of the Church went into effect, Arnauld began the publication of a multi-volumed work entitled *La morale pratique des jesuites*, in the preface of which he wrote: "Despite what the Jesuits say, the face of the earth has not changed since they came into existence. There is no less simony, usury, impurity, injustice, or violence. Merchants cheat as usual; judges continue to embezzle and extort, and soldiers make it easier to commit these crimes. They make a game of penitential discipline. People do not fear God's punishment, because they are persuaded on the faith of these fathers that it is easy to receive absolution."[16] When Péréfixe, the archbishop of Paris, died in 1671, he was succeeded by Harlay de Champvallon, who was eager to adhere to the terms of the Peace of the Church. To this end, he attempted to suppress the formulary entirely, on the grounds that its continued existence was provocative. Neither king nor pope would consent to the suppression of the formulary, the meaning of which had been rendered indeterminate by the agreements of 1669, and the document continued to stir up trouble. At the University of Angers, for example, Jesuits and Jansenists still quarreled over the *question de fait*. The bishop, Henri Arnauld, declared in a pastoral letter that a clear distinction between *droit* and *fait* ought to be made by those who refused to admit that the five propositions were to be found in the *Augustinus.* Louis XIV, who learned of the quarrels while in the middle of a campaign in Flanders, issued a decree rebuking the bishop and demanding signature without reservation.

In 1679, the Dutch war concluded, Louis XIV was able to devote more attention to domestic affairs again. His cousin, the duchesse de Longueville, patroness and protector of Port Royal, died in that year, facilitating royal action against the convent. Less than a month after her death, the archbishop of Paris ordered the permanent expulsion of the confessors, postulants, and pensioners from Port Royal, in a move intended to cripple the convent by denying it spiritual sustenance and future generations of nuns. The king tried to regain the right to nominate the abbesses of Port Royal, a right that the crown had relinquished in 1629. In a dispatch sent to the French ambassador in Rome requesting him to lay the matter before Innocent XI, the king explained that these actions were being taken in order to maintain the "purity of the faith" as well as public order, jeopardized by the "heretical" activities at Port Royal.[17] Aware of Louis's intentions, Angélique de Saint-Jean, then abbess of the convent, appealed to the pope for protection against the efforts to destroy the establishment. "We must explain to Your Holiness our long suffering and the condition to which we have been reduced because of the unwarranted hatred of those who have desired our destruction for a long time and who do not hesitate to launch the powers of Church and state against us."[18] Displeased with the French king at the time, Innocent XI rejected Louis's request.

Fearful of renewed persecution of the Jansenists, Antoine Arnauld decided in 1679 to go into exile in the Netherlands. Accompanied by his associate of many years, Pierre Nicole, Arnauld sojourned briefly at Mons and at Ghent before settling at Brussels. He never returned to France, but Nicole, after twenty years of harassment and persecution, yearned for Paris, and he soon decided to make his peace with king and Church. Although he had engaged in polemical activities throughout the conflict over the five propositions, Nicole was by nature timid. "I have such a hatred of controversy," he wrote, "that I take no pleasure in being involved in it."[19] His strong convictions enabled him to overcome this timidity during the years leading up to the Peace of the Church, but his preference for tranquillity was very much in evidence in the *Essais de morale*. In an essay entitled "Traité des moyens de conserver la paix entre les hommes," Nicole declared that Christian ethics required peace within communities as well as among them. As in the other essays, Nicole constructed his argument on Christian principle and on enlightened self-interest. One way of maintaining peace was to respect the opinions of others. Men dislike being contradicted, particularly when "wealth, power, and authority imperceptibly influence their opinions." In dealing with persons of this sort, "it is always useful to be on guard not to shock their opinions and sentiments without considerable justification."[20] According to Nicole, the opinions most easily shocked are those formed by generally accepted ideas and values. Matters pertaining to the faith are, of course, above dispute; but in other matters, there is likely to be a wide variety of sentiment that, if unchecked, is likely to cause tensions and unrest. People are usually persuaded by reason or by authority, but most believe what they are told or what they are brought up to believe, which is to say that they are likely to accept the authority of others. Thus, if a man attempts to convince his neighbors that a commonly held opinion is false, and he pits his own reason against the weight of custom, he is likely to stir up trouble. "For just as it is sedition in a state to wish to reform disorders when one is not in a position that gives him the right to do so, it is a sort of sedition when persons who are not in positions of authority challenge prevailing sentiment."[21] Nicole did not entirely repudiate the right to disagree on matters of fact. There are instances, he admitted, when a man has to take a stand on what he knows to be right, but in such instances where generally accepted opinions have been challenged, the challenge ought to be made in a spirit of humility and civility. In any event, the chief responsibility of the Christian, concluded Nicole, is his own salvation and not "that of his brothers." For this reason he ought to resist the temptation to impose his views on others and ought instead to humble himself before God.

In a letter to Harlay de Champvallon, archbishop of Paris, written in 1679, Nicole declared his intention to make peace. He promised the archbishop that he would not "cause you pain."[22] This conciliatory attitude that enabled Nicole to spend the last years of his life in Paris instead of in hiding prompted a sharp rebuke from the intransigent Abbé Le Roy. "The love of liberty and of repose that one can enjoy in this life appears to have caused you to fall into the trap of the enemy. It is altogether astonishing and incomprehensible that a man with such a pure and active mind, and whose reasonings are so penetrating and just has suspended the use of his reason, and does not see that the respect and liberty that one acquires in abandoning the truth and the interest of the Church will produce nothing but frightful trouble and shameful servitude." And, he continued, how much "do these words *libertas summa* teach us in an excellent way that our ultimate repose and liberty lie in our becoming attached to Jesus Christ, crucified and despised by the world, oppressed in his truth and in the truths of the gospel. This liberty in Jesus Christ remains inviolable and entirely perfect in those who possess it even in prison. The closer one approaches the end of one's life, the more one must love the divine liberty of Jesus Christ, which all the powers on earth cannot hurt or destroy."[23] Nicole replied that one did not have to defend the truth by constantly publishing polemics, that in fact the truth might best be defended by maintaining a respectful silence whenever possible.[24] In a second letter to the abbé Le Roy, Nicole added that it was not given to all Christians to defend the truth at all times. Some people were better qualified to defend it publicly because of superior intelligence or a charitable disposition. Some periods were more propitious for public debate than others. Now that the Peace of the Church was in effect, an attitude of conciliation among all parties was necessary.[25]

Nicole had come to the same conclusion reached by Barcos during the crisis over the formulary. Saint-Cyran's nephew had long since retired to his monastery and had cut himself off from the other disciples of his uncle. Both men contended that further quarrels were futile and that their spiritual interests were better served by remaining silent. Silence, to be sure, did not mean total submission. Barcos, when he was advising the nuns on how to sign the formulary, had suggested that one might have mental reservations at the time of signature but that in the interests of public order they ought not to be stated. Nicole said almost the same thing in his exchange of letters with Le Roy and in his essays. One might not agree with one's superiors on a given issue, but the reasons for the disagreement did not have to be proclaimed aloud. Barcos and Nicole refused to challenge further the authority of Church and state because they were indifferent to that authority and were totally absorbed in their own spiritual condition. Nicole continued to write pamphlets criticizing Protestant belief, and he also attacked quietism, but never again, at least in public, did he make the assertions that he set forth in *De la foy humaine*, in which he denied the right of the Church to exercise its authority in areas where reason must remain autonomous.

By voluntarily going into exile in 1679, Arnauld was, in effect, expressing a willingness to proclaim the truth whenever necessary and to suffer for it. One could not remain silent so long as God's enemies sought to undermine the Church. When Arnauld first came into contact with Saint-Cyran, the abbé had urged him to defend penitential discipline against those who would weaken it. The youngest Arnauld's commitment to defend his beliefs may also have been strengthened by his mother's dying wish. Among the papers of the Arnauld family is a document entitled "Paroles de ma soeur Cathérine de Sainte-Félicité écrite de la main de M. Arnauld." After her husband's death, Madame Arnauld retired to Port Royal, where she became Sister Catherine. On her deathbed in 1641, she is supposed to have spoken the following words to her confessor. "I beg you to tell my youngest son that, as he has been engaged by God to defend the truth, I exhort him and beseech him not to slacken in this commitment."[26] Because of his exile, Arnauld was no longer obliged to respect the terms of the Peace of the Church, and he continued to criticize ecclesiastical officials for intruding in areas beyond their competence. In a letter written in 1686, for example, he stated that "an atmosphere of domination over the faith in those things that do not pertain to faith is not likely to make the government of the Catholic Church more charitable and is scarcely suitable to the successor of him who said: *Non dominantes in cleris*."[27] Reiterating the point that he and Nicole had made in the *Port Royal Logic*, Arnauld insisted that the authority of the Church be limited to matters pertaining to faith. The Church was not authorized by God to prohibit the mind from freely investigating the realm of nature. Even Scripture ought not to be accepted as an authority on natural occurrences. Writing in 1691, Arnauld declared that "wisdom requires that in these situations we should not construe the passages wherein it speaks of natural things in such a way as to oppose demonstrable truths and that we believe that the Holy Spirit made the canonic writers speak of these things in terms of commonly held opinions rather than in terms of exact truth, which was not involved and about which God did not intend to instruct men."[28] To accept the authority of Scripture in the interpretation of natural phenomena was dangerous to the faith, Arnauld contended in another letter, written in the following year: " . . . in religious matters, one would do well to follow the judicious advice of Saint Augustine and Saint Thomas, which teaches us to avoid interpreting Holy Scripture in such a way as to cause one to doubt the veracity of God when it deals with natural things. Such interpretations will be contrary to those of intelligent people, whose certainty is derived from reason and manifest experience. Such is the situation now with respect to the question of the earth's movement. Almost all astronomers and philosophers now believe that it moves."[29]

The assertion that God intended reason and experience to be autonomous in the natural sphere touched upon a sensitive issue in the seventeenth century, when philosophers and scientists were challenging traditional concepts of the universe and, indirectly, the authority of the Church. The condemnation of Galileo in 1633 by the Inquisition was an indication of the distrust with which the "new philosophy" was viewed by the Church, which did not hesitate to place Descartes's works on the Index. Arnauld referred to the condemnation of Galileo in a number of writings. He admitted that the Church might have been justified in censoring the Florentine scientist because Aristotle's authority with respect to natural phenomena was more generally accepted at that time and because common sense seemed to support the geocentric theory. Given the progress that had been made in astronomy and physics since that time, however, the same authorities would have great difficulty in not accepting Galileo's conclusions. So impressed was Arnauld with the discoveries in the natural sciences since the sixteenth century that, in the great debate between the Ancients and the Moderns that took place during his lifetime, he sided with the Moderns. In a work entitled *Examen du traité de l'essence du corps,* Arnauld took issue with the opinion that "God does not give to philosophers of today a rational capacity any greater or more illuminating than he gave to those philosophers who lived two thousand years ago. In fact, human nature becomes increasingly corrupt with the passage of time and with it the gradual erosion of natural reason."[30] He argued instead that natural philosophy had progressed substantially since antiquity because of the efforts of Copernicus, Huygens, Galileo, Harvey, and others who refused to be intimidated by the authority of the Ancients, and who relied instead on their own observations and experiments.[31] The Jansenist pedagogue Pierre Coustel, who strongly advocated the teaching of mathematics and physics to children, was also impressed by the progress made in the physical sciences. "As for physics, one must say that it has changed a great deal, and that a number of discoveries have been made and remarkable progress achieved since men have abandoned as fantasies those things that the ancients taught us concerning occult virtues, and the sympathies and antipathies of things; and instead of reasoning according to their false principles, men have endeavored to make a number of experiments and observations. A number of astronomical instruments have been invented, and men have tried to learn about nature in terms of itself and its effects."[32]

Arnauld's defense of free inquiry in the realm of nature was based, in part, on his fear of libertinage. If reason were free to challenge divine authority in the realm of grace, he admitted, Christian truth would suffer at the expense of free thought. But free thought would also triumph if the authority of Church and state was extended to those areas where freedom of thought was permitted by God. The proper order of things must be respected, insisted Arnauld, and in what might be regarded as a postscript to the *Port Royal Logic*, he wrote in 1681: " . . . nothing is more judicious than this rule, to listen to *reason* in the human sciences and authority in matters pertaining to religion. And nothing is more ruinous to either philosophy or theology than to ignore this rule and to do the opposite. People want to *believe* where it is a question of knowing, and they want to *know* when they should content themselves with believing."[33]

The reliance on reason as a means both of defending their beliefs and of discovering more about natural phenomena became particularly apparent among Jansenists of the second generation. Attracted to Christian Pyrrhonism, Saint-Cyran had regarded reason as an instrument of pride. But he would have denied that reason plays no role at all in the life of the Christian. The abbé based his faith upon an intelligent understanding of Scripture and of ecclesiastical tradition. Reason contributed to that understanding, without which faith would become corroded by superstition. Saint-Cyran's major criticism of Father Garasse's *Somme Théo-*

logique was that the Jesuit's attack on Christian Pyrrhonism was marred by error and shoddy scholarship. Unsound scholarship and faulty judgment had contributed to an inadequate understanding of the penitential theology of the Church, for which reason Saint-Cyran encouraged the training of judgment and the proper use of scholarship in the Little Schools. As their beliefs came under attack, even Pascal and Nicole, though attracted to Christian Pyrrhonism to a far greater extent than Arnauld, recognized the need to construct well-reasoned theological arguments to be used against all enemies of Christian truth, Huguenots, Jesuits, and libertines. Condemned for their beliefs, some Jansenists maintained that they were being persecuted by misguided officials who exerted their power and influence unjustly. But the increased reliance on reason caused other Jansenists to return to Saint-Cyran's opinion that too great a reliance on reason was a manifestation of pride. Yet both groups could claim that they were adhering to positions set forth by the abbé de Saint-Cyran. Barcos and Nicole were acting in accordance with the abbé's contention that suffering in silence was particularly beneficial to the soul. Arnauld and Quesnel, on the other hand, were responding to Saint-Cyran's dying wish that the truth should be defended.

Arnauld's conviction that an "atmosphere of domination" pervaded the Church was derived in part from Jansenist ideas about the structure and government of the Church. The Jansenist position on such issues as papal infallibility, conciliarism, the degree of authority pertaining to the bishop in his diocese and to the priest in his parish, and, finally, what might be called the spiritual rights of the laity, were shaped in part by the Gallican tradition—which sharply curtailed the power of the papacy over the French Church—and in part by their own adverse experiences at the hands of what they regarded as incompetent and unjust functionaries. As the century progressed, Jansenists became increasingly sensitive to the abuse of papal power in matters pertaining to doctrine and discipline. They also became more aware of potential conflicts between the responsibilities of the bishops on the one hand and the lower clergy on the other and between the responsibilities of the clergy and the rights of the laity.

The abbé de Saint-Cyran had maintained that the ultimate authority in the Church was the bishops. Christ had bestowed the government of the Church on the spiritual descendants of his apostles. As bishop of Rome, the pope was the first among the bishops.[34] The argument that episcopal authority descended directly from God through Christ and His apostles was very much a part of the Gallican tradition that rejected the papacy's contention that bishops owed their authority to the pope, who alone received his power directly from God. Since the Council of Trent, the papacy, supported by certain Catholic elements, had insisted that the ultimate authority in matters pertaining to doctrine lay with the pope. While Saint-Cyran's writings do not make clear his views on these pretensions of the Vatican, many of his disciples were outspoken in their hostility to them. Wrote Godefroi Hermant, a Jansenist professor of theology at the University of Paris:

The most ardent of these flatterers of the Roman court have had the temerity to maintain in public that the bishops are only vicars and the viceroys of the Holy Father, owing to him alone all their power and jurisdiction. They have even dared preach that there is only one vicar of Jesus Christ, the successor of Saint Peter, the visible head of the entire Church. He alone has the power to decide and enunciate matters pertaining to faith, and everything that he ordains must be received by all the faithful with complete submission as proceeding from an infallible authority. The Church of France, on the other hand, has always professed another doctrine. She has maintained that the bishops' office has no other founder than our Lord Jesus Christ and is not the work of men. Their authority comes from none other than God, who has given them the power to govern their churches and to watch over their flocks as His immediate vicars and apostolic successors. Until recently, it has always been upheld in the Gallican Church that, by virtue of this power, the bishops have the right to judge in all matters concerning the faith and the safety of their flock, and because of this right, they may assemble together when they deem it necessary for the good of their churches, in order to administer to their needs.[35]

Hermant argued that in matters that affected the Church as a whole, the assembled bishops had a greater authority than the pope alone.

Arnauld based his opposition to papal infallibility on episcopal

rights he believed to be guaranteed by the Gallican tradition that
was derived from medieval conciliarism. No papal encyclical or
ordinance had any authority unless it was endorsed by the bishops,
who alone had the authority to publish them in their respective
dioceses. This was, of course, the position taken by the four
bishops during the quarrel over the formulary. When the pope
reached a decision on a doctrinal issue, it required the consent of
the bishops, either individually or as a group. Before consenting
to a papal decree, a bishop was obliged to consult Scripture and
tradition in order to make certain that the opinion contained in
the decree was in conformity with both. If, on the other hand, a
bishop published a book or a pastoral letter for the edification of
his flock, the pope had no right to condemn it on his own. In this
circumstance, it would be the opinion of one man against that of
another. If both men were sincere, it might be difficult to determine whose views more accurately reflected ecclesiastical tradition.
Papal infallibility, from Arnauld's point of view, gave too much
authority to one man who, being human, was capable of error.
"One must not suppose that the pope is the absolute master of
the Church and that he has the absolute power to command as he
pleases, the bishops being nothing more than the executors of his
wishes, without any right to determine what is just or unjust or
what is in conformity with or contrary to Scripture and tradition
in what he says."[36] Christ did not entrust the government of his
Church to one man, but to the entire corps of bishops. The bishop
of Rome, to be sure, was chief among the bishops, but he had no
authority to determine important matters on his own.[37] In earlier
times, general or ecumenical councils were held, over which the
pope presided either in person or through a representative. When
such a council was in session, it was infallible in matters pertaining
to the faith, and its decisions were binding on the Church as a
whole. If a doctrinal dispute occurred during a time when no such
council was in session, the matter then had to be referred to a
future council. The pope had no right to claim even an interim
authority, and to Arnauld's way of thinking, the absolutist pretensions of Rome were all the more reason for reviving the
conciliar tradition, which was obsolescent. To the papacy's
assertion that its dominant position in the Church was derived

from Christ's designation of his disciple Peter as the rock upon which he intended to build his Church, Arnauld replied that the Church was built on Peter's faith in the same way that it was built on the faith of all Christians.[38] Since the Council of Constance in the fifteenth century, according to Arnauld, the Gallican Church had consistently maintained the superiority of a council over the pope, and by insisting on its "liberties," it had succeeded in limiting papal authority in the kingdom. "Although the pope has been regarded as a suzerain in spiritual matters . . . in France, at least, his infinite and absolute power is not recognized, his authority being limited and restricted by the crown and by the rules of the ancient councils of the Church that have been received in this kingdom."[39]

For Arnauld, the Gallican Church was the guardian of religious orthodoxy and the best hope for ecclesiastical reform, but he was alarmed by the threat to its integrity not only from Rome but also from the king. Toward the end of his life, he began to consider the possibility of a national council of bishops, free from both royal and papal control, to protect the interests of the French Church. In order to remove royal and papal influence from episcopal elections entirely, Arnauld advocated a return to the practice of electing bishops by cathedral chapters. Although he never fully developed this idea, he seemed to think that by this procedure bishops would be selected who were pure of heart and sound of doctrine.[40]

Much more complex than their ideas about the relationship between pope and bishops were the Jansenists' ideas about the relationship between bishops and priests. Saint-Cyran and his followers did not question episcopal superiority in the diocese. The abbé proclaimed that bishops were "supreme priests," whose authority over the lower clergy was extensive. The responsibilities of bishops were far greater than those of priests. Although the priest was definitely subordinate to the bishop, the attitude of the bishop toward the priest ought to be that of a father toward his son rather than that of a master toward his servant.[41] Despite Saint-Cyran's respect for the hierarchy in the Church, he was accused by his enemies of harboring presbyterian ideas to the point where Arnauld was obliged to reassert Saint-Cyran's arguments on episcopal powers in 1653. Saint-Cyran's writings, declared Arnauld, made clear "the sacred power that Christ gave to the bishops over priests."[42]

But Saint-Cyran and Arnauld, among others, exalted the office of priest by emphasizing its mystical powers of absolution. It was the highest office God could bestow upon a Christian. This elevated view of the priesthood reappeared in Quesnel's *Réflexions morales*. Essential to the welfare of the Church were enlightened and zealous pastors who would work indefatigably for the sanctification of souls. The priest, according to Quesnel, was the personification of the Church in his parish, obliged to instruct himself and his parishioners and "to defend, to suffer, and to fight for the truth and liberty of the Church without yielding any ground." The priest must be prepared to be "persecuted in order to teach his parishioners that, by suffering, they merit God's grace."[43] Quesnel respected the hierarchical organization of the Church. "Each member of the Church," he wrote, "must be directly united with his bishop and indirectly with the chief of all the bishops, and ultimately with all the bishops of the Christian world, according to the hierarchical order established by canon law. For, in truth, there is only one episcopate."[44] The bishop of Rome was a preeminent figure in the Church because all lower orders were directly subordinate to him, yet he represented the highest authority because he was a part of the episcopacy, which included all bishops to whom God through Saint Peter had bestowed the government of the Church.[45] The pope was the chief spokesman for the bishops and for the Church, and he presided over all councils, but ecclesiastical administration was the responsibility of the bishops as a whole.[46] Throughout the history of the Church, however, there had been general councils convened to consider particularly important problems, and because these councils were ecumenical, they represented the entire Church. Not only bishops but curates and laymen were included, because the universal Church consisted of all Christians. The people might be represented by the emperor, by other royal dignitaries, by lesser magistrates, "or even by the people themselves, as in the time of the early councils, when the people were less numerous and more saintly."[47] An ecumenical council, after study and deliberation, was likely to be guided by the Holy Spirit, in which case it would speak as a single voice without dissension. "Happy is the Church when all the pastors, united in one spirit, endeavor to conserve the treasury of truth. No single person attributes to himself the glory of having made the decision. All act in such a way as to preserve peace within the Church, because all involved love only the Church and its peace and have in mind only the interests of Jesus Christ."[48]

Toward the end of his life, after exile and imprisonment, discouraged by the divisions within the Church caused not only by the papacy but by incompetent bishops and by political interference in the affairs of the Church, Quesnel began to attribute even more authority to the lower clergy. In a letter written in 1709, he asserted that, whereas bishops made the initial decisions in matters pertaining to doctrine, a decision had no binding authority unless accepted by what he termed "the corps of pastors."[49] Reiterating a point made by Saint-Cyran, that priests owed their offices to God in the same way bishops did, Quesnel declared that priests ought not to be blindly obedient to higher authority in the Church. They were obliged by the sanctity of their office to consult their best judgment in making the decision whether or not to consent to an episcopal decision.[50] Not only was it possible for popes to err but councils might err as well, because they consisted of fallible human beings. No decision of a council had any authority unless it conformed to Scripture and to tradition.[51] Quesnel maintained that there were situations in which one honest Christian, no matter what his rank, might alone uphold the interests of God against other Christians who sought to compromise the truth. The virtuous Christian might prefer to remain silent, fearing disciplinary action or convinced that his intervention in behalf of the truth would do no good. Fear of speaking out ought never to prevent the Christian from performing his duties, even if the unity of the visible Church were adversely affected and higher authority contravened. "It is to imitate Saint Paul to suffer unjust excommunication or anathema rather than to betray the truth."[52] Quesnel did not reject the hierarchical order of the Church. In his mind there could be no conflict between its upper and lower echelons when bishops and priests had genuine vocations and were properly instructed in the articles of the faith.

Conflict arose when those less committed to God's purpose inter-
fered with the spiritual obligations of others deeply committed to
God's purpose. Quesnel went much further than Saint-Cyran or
Arnauld in attributing a greater role to the lower clergy in the
government of the Church. But Saint-Cyran had called the priest
"a prince of souls," which in Quesnel's mind entitled him to a
position of responsibility in the conduct of ecclesiastical affairs.
This conclusion seemed all the more necessary given the fact that
the quality of the lower clergy had been considerably improved as
a result of the impact of the Counter Reformation. Furthermore,
Jansenist ideals were particularly attractive to the lower clergy,
which gave the movement strong support in Paris, Rouen, and
other cities. The Richerist principles that had inspired the Parisian
curés during the religious Fronde became more prominent in
Jansenist ideology at the time when the crown and papacy were
making certain that Jansenist sympathizers were not being appointed to high offices within the Church. The close ties that
developed between Jansenists and the lower clergy as the upper
clergy became increasingly hostile toward the movement undoubtedly contributed to the royal edict of 1695, which consolidated
episcopal control over the dioceses.[53]

Jansenists, like other Catholics, continued to maintain the
distinction between clergy and laity, a distinction that Protestants
tended to blur. The layman needed the priest's support in ab-
solving himself from sin, the priest being the earthly embodiment
of the Church empowered to administer the sacraments. But the
Jansenists believed that the clergy should respect the spiritual
rights of the laity, particularly the layman's right to instruct himself in the verities of the faith. One of the sources of corruption
in the Church, in Quesnel's opinion, was ignorance among the
laity as well as among the clergy. One way to rekindle the faith
was through "good books inspired above all by a love of God's
word."[54] With this in mind, Jansenists translated works of the
Church Fathers as well as Scripture. Catholic authorities were wary
of scriptural translations in the vernacular because they were
associated with Protestantism, and because they might violate
interpretations in conformity with Church tradition. A translation
undertaken by Jansenists was particularly suspect, the more so

since the New Testament translated into French by Arnauld, Lancelot, and Sacy appeared during the crisis over the formulary. The so-called *New Testament of Mons* was placed on the Index, and it was the object of numerous attacks, particularly from the Jesuits. In defense of their version of the New Testament, Arnauld claimed that it was necessary to enlighten simple people who were unable to read Latin and Greek and who, prevented from understanding the true meaning of Scripture, might fall prey to heresy. Arnauld applied Cartesian principles to effective translations that illuminated obscure passages and rendered scriptural meaning as clear and distinct as possible.[55] A good translation would promote piety throughout the Church and make Catholic truth more accessible by making the one true Catholic interpretation of the Word evident to any reader properly instructed in the articles of faith.[56] Not all Jansenists favored scriptural translations. Barcos defended scriptural obscurity by saying that it dramatized the mysteries of the faith and served the interests of religion better than clarity did: "But those who are unable to tolerate an obscure word or phrase, but desire everything to be clear and distinct, facile and easy to understand even for the simplest people, will never be edified and will never receive any nourishment. The efforts made to express everything in agreeable terms and in conformity with their humor will have been of little value. These efforts will have only strengthened their weaknesses and their attachment to the pleasurable sensations of the mind which are no less dangerous than those of the body."[57] Arnauld disagreed, however, with the idea that translations in the vernacular were dangerous for the ordinary Christian. "Nothing is more false than the opinion that, in order to profit from sacred writings, one must know Latin and have a profound mind not usually found among ordinary people: women, artisans, villagers, and those sorts of people who for reasons that are totally alien to the Christian spirit are called 'the little people.' For this opinion rests on an equally false premise, that sacred writings are so obscure throughout and so difficult to understand even in matters pertaining to morals that these sorts of people have no right to believe that they will understand them upon reading them."[58]

To deprive the ordinary Christian of the right to read Scripture in the vernacular was to violate Christian liberty, which included the right to obtain a firmer understanding of religious truth. To deny Christians this right was to act tyrannically and in contradiction to the Christian spirit.[59] His dislike of despotic tendencies in the Church caused Arnauld to take a dim view of the Index and other means employed by ecclesiastical authorities to censor books. He believed that more often than not the decision to censor a particular work was based on faulty judgment rather than on sound doctrine. "One thing is very certain," he wrote, "and that is that Jesus Christ expressly forbade the ministers of his Church to act despotically toward those entrusted to their care. Christ's ministers do not have the right to prohibit the reading of useful books out of caprice and without showing cause."[60] Bishops and others were required to explain their reasons for censorship in a way that was persuasive to the honest Christian, by employing sound theological argument. Arnauld was not the only Jansenist to complain of censorship. Pascal maintained that the Inquisition often condemned books *because* they contained the truth. "If my *Provincial Letters* are condemned in Rome," he wrote, "that which I condemn in them is condemned in heaven. *Ad tuum Domine Jesu tribunal appelo.*"[61]

In discussing the nature of Church government, Jansenist writers distinguished between it and temporal government. Because the state was responsible for the maintenance of order, it was entitled to exercise its authority arbitrarily upon occasion, but the primary responsibility of the Church was the spiritual welfare of each of its members. Its function, therefore, was to persuade and instruct rather than to command. "The spirit and rule of ecclesiastical government is humility, instruction, and condescension, and not domination, control, and harshness," wrote Quesnel.[62] Arnauld differentiated between what he called ecclesiastical theology and political theology. Political theology was despotic and founded on human error. Ecclesiastical theology resorted to persuasion as a means of achieving a broader understanding of Catholic truths. It did not have to rely on brutal methods as a means of terrorizing people into submission.[63] The Jansenist conception of a reformed Church involved a pious and enlightened clergy and laity, entirely cognizant of the needs of each individual member as well as of the needs of the institution as a whole. The spirit of charity and benevolence that should prevail in a revitalized Church would prevent it from resorting to the arbitrary methods sometimes employed by the state. The Jansenists believed that the introduction of tyrannical methods in the Church was the inevitable result of the ignorance and vanity on the part of those in positions of authority. The Church was torn apart by conflicts between persons and between orders. The way to combat tyranny and absolutism within the institution was to give greater responsibility to all its members. Quesnel, whose ideas about Church government were more radical than Saint-Cyran's or Arnauld's, expanded these responsibilities to include a greater role in the affairs of the Church for laymen as well as for clergy. The highest authority in the Church, according to the author of the *Réflexions morales*, resided in its entire body, in whose name popes and bishops acted. The consent of the entire body was required in order to validate excommunications, to verify the doctrine of the Church, and to sanction all ecclesiastical appointments.[64] This democratic inclination appeared at the time when authoritarian tendencies in Rome and within the dioceses were increasing, and it made Jansenism all the more distasteful to the authorities at the Vatican and at Versailles.

One problem that intransigent Jansenists were forced to consider as their struggle with religious authorities intensified was the effect of possible excommunication on the resistant Catholic. Addressing himself to this question in a letter to Barcos written from the Bastille, Le Maistre de Sacy said:

If I know that the sentence of excommunication against me is unjust, and if it is impossible for me to make known my innocence, I can celebrate the Holy Mysteries and partake of them, but secretly without troubling or causing a scandal among others. And for the same reason, those who know my innocence although I have been excommunicated may say Mass to me and offer me the sacraments, but secretly. One must act secretly in order to show that even an unjust excommunication is to be feared, because it has been executed in public, and one does not want to cause scandal among men who are only aware of what has been done in public. . . .[65]

Like Barcos, Sacy understood the dangers of schism, for which reason he was opposed to a public outcry against such an unjust action on the part of religious authorities.

One pamphlet, published in 1665, was written by the *solitaire* physician Jean Hamon, who had been one of Racine's teachers at the Little Schools and at whose feet the great tragedian requested to be buried. Hamon asserted that an unjust excommunication could not harm the Catholic who suffered it with humility, because the true bonds linking him to the Church were internal and spiritual. Speaking of the corrupt officials who dominated the earthly Church, Hamon wrote: "They may well deprive us of the sacraments, but they cannot deprive us of the grace of the sacraments. They may cut us off from visible union with the faithful, but they are unable to separate us from the invisible union that the Holy Spirit forms between all the faithful and with Jesus Christ. They can banish us from the physical temple; but they cannot banish us from the spiritual temple, which is nothing else but the body of Jesus Christ. . . . "[66] False excommunications, according to Hamon, were based on judgments that were in violation of the faith and Holy Scripture or were prejudicial to justice and to Christian liberty. Such an excommunication was, to Hamon, in violation of Church tradition as well as of true justice and liberty. Nevertheless, the Catholic threatened with excommunication ought to make certain that his cause was entirely exempt from mortal sin.[67]

Pierre Nicole also considered the question of an unjust excommunication in his fifth *Imaginaire*, written in February 1665.

The life of the faith, which is the life of the just, according to Saint Paul, consists of loving according to the faith, of being afflicted according to the faith, of fearing according to the faith, and finally of regulating all one's movements according to that divine light and not according to the senses of reason. We must fear excommunication in the manner in which the faith teaches us that we must fear it and not according to ideas based on vain fantasies. Now faith teaches us that an unjust excommunication has no effect on the person who suffers it in humility, which does not separate him internally from the Church, and which affects the pastors who unjustly strike their inferiors.[68]

Like Hamon, Nicole made a distinction between the visible and the invisible Church, membership in the invisible Church being essential to redemption. Catholic theologians had always made a distinction between the two churches, but Nicole, Hamon, and the nuns of Port Royal were, in effect, pitting the invisible Church against its visible counterpart. For Nicole, the visible Church was essentially human and subject to error, and therefore an excommunication based on a question of fact could have no effect on the realm of grace, where the invisible Church resided.

Later in the century, Pasquier Quesnel maintained that membership in the invisible Church was determined only by God, whose decision to redeem His elect was infallible and incapable of being altered by human action.[69] "The fear of disgrace or of an unjust excommunication is capable of destroying us. ... We should cling to nothing that men are capable of taking from us if we wish to preserve that which God alone can give us. He can save a soul without sacraments and outside of the external communion of the Church."[70] By distinguishing between the invisible Church established in the realm of grace and the visible Church rooted in nature, Quesnel and others—including the nuns of Port Royal during the crisis over the formulary—were able to resist those superiors and those commandments that appeared to them to be motivated by human considerations. Their attitude toward excommunication strengthened the Jansenists' conviction that they were true Catholics acting in the interests of God's Church against worldly influences that sought to dominate and corrupt it.

VII. *Toward* Unigenitus

The radicalism inherent in Jansenist opinions about the structure of Church government is not to be found in their expressed ideas about the nature of political authority. In this respect, they were royal absolutists. Saint-Cyran, for example, despite his opposition to the policies of the French government, believed that kings were instruments of God's justice, whose power and majesty were sanctioned by God's will. Obedience to temporal authority was required of all subjects. "Of all the commands that God makes to us," wrote the abbé, "the most important is submission and obedience, which obliges us to remain silent and to have great respect for our superiors and not to prejudice them against us in any way, because they are placed over us by God." Obedience even to an unjust ruler was regarded by Saint-Cyran as an exercise of Christian humility.[1] Antoine Arnauld also preached the necessity for obedience to temporal authority. In his polemics against the Protestants, he argued that, whereas Catholics respected temporal authority, Protestants were inclined toward civil disobedience. Citing the rebelliousness of the French Huguenots during the previous century, plainly expressed in such pamphlets as *Vindiciae contra Tyrannos* as well as the rebelliousness of the seventeenth-century English Puritans, Arnauld insisted that Catholics must respect the authority of their prince even if he were excommunicated by the Church—whose powers, some believed, extended to unbinding the ties between the prince and his subjects. "Catholic theologians the most attached to the king are in accord that, being a Christian, a prince may be excommunicated for reasons that are entirely justifiable. . . . Excommunication does not deprive him of his crown, nor does it dispense subjects from obedience."[2] Christian virtue, according to Arnauld, included patience, enabling the subject to suffer persecution at the hands of his sovereign and preventing him from revolting against his lawful sovereign.[3] Jansenist writers attempted to show that the Jesuits, like the Protestants. were disrespectful of civil authority. In the fourteenth Provincial Letter, Pascal accused the disciples of Loyola of justifying regicide and rebellion in contradiction to the Church's teaching that even the unjust prince must be obeyed.

One of Pascal's oldest and closest friends was Jean Domat, who was to become the leading French jurist during the reign of Louis XIV. A Jansenist, Domat opposed signing the formulary condemning the five propositions. Throughout his life he remained closely associated with Port Royal. Named Pascal's literary executor, Domat participated in the editing of the *Pensées* after his friend's death. Domat's ambition was to organize the corpus of French law according to those principles of clarity that inspired the logical and grammatical treatises of Port Royal. The two most important effects of reordering the laws, according to Domat, were "brevity, by which the useless and superfluous are omitted, and clarity, by means of proper arrangement. It is to be hoped that, by this brevity and clarity, it will become easier to acquire a solid knowledge of the laws."[4] In the 1680s, under the sponsorship of the government, Domat began his codification of the laws that was published in 1694 under the title *Les lois civiles dans leur ordre naturel*. The work was prefaced by a short *Traité des lois*, which included a strong endorsement of political absolutism. In Christian societies, according to Domat, "each man is bound to the society of which he is a member, he must undertake nothing that will disturb order, and he must submit to those powers whom God has set over him to maintain that order." "God places kings above other men to serve justice," he wrote[5] for which reason obedience to kings on the part of subjects was a divine necessity.

The political theory of Saint-Cyran, Arnauld, and Domat was derived from the divine order of the universe. Two other Jansenist apologists for absolutism, whose ideas on the subject appeared shortly after the conclusion of the Peace of the Church, derived their political principles from human nature. "The power of kings," wrote Pascal, "is founded on the reason and folly of the people, but especially on their folly. The greatest and most important thing in the world is founded on weakness." To argue that government derived its power from natural law, which in turn emanated from divine law, was unrealistic because, although natural laws might exist, man's corrupt nature made him unable to comprehend them.[6] "Equality of possessions is no doubt right, but as men could not make might obey right, they have made right obey might. As they could not fortify justice, they have justified force so that right and might live together and peace reigns, the sovereign good." Force being the means by which some men establish rule over others, custom sustains that rule.

Custom is the whole of equity for the sole reason that it is accepted. That is the mystic basis of its authority. Anyone who tries to bring it back to its first principle destroys it. Nothing is so defective as those laws which correct defects. Anyone obeying them because they are just is obeying an imaginary justice, not the essence of the law, which is completely self-contained: . . . The art of subversion, of revolution, is to dislodge established customs by probing their origins in order to show how they lack authority and justice. There must, they say, be a return to the basic and primitive laws of the state which unjust custom has abolished. . . . That is why the wisest of legislators [Plato] used to say that men must often be deceived for their own good. . . . The truth about the usurpation must not be made apparent; it came about originally without reason and has become reasonable.[7]

Political argument based on natural law was, in Pascal's mind, not only unrealistic but potentially subversive because it encouraged dangerous speculation about abstract ideals and it repudiated realpolitik, the basis for effective government. The *Frondeurs* were wrong, argued Pascal, because they misunderstood the true basis of politics and were misled by abstract conceptions of right.[8] By grounding political institutions in force and custom, Pascal sought to undermine fundamental arguments justifying rebellion, including arguments from natural law. Yet he recognized the need for good government, and he took an interest in educating princes and noblemen to their political responsibilities. In three little treatises entitled *Sur la condition des grands*, written for the edification of the sons of the Duc de Luynes in 1660 and later published by Nicole, Pascal urged rulers to treat their subjects benevolently—to satisfy their genuine needs, and to redress their grievances. It was in the prince's interests to provide good government, because he would earn the affection of his people, who would be more inclined to serve him. But if the prince based his politics exclusively on the principle of self-interest, he might acquire a good reputation on earth, but at the same time he might displease God. Only if his policies "were inspired by charity and the fruits of charity"[9] was the prince likely to satisfy the needs of his subjects and the commandments of God.

The political philosophy of Nicole, much of which appears in his *Essais de morales*, was somewhat similar to Pascal's. Social structure and political institutions were rooted in man's corrupt nature. Human weakness and selfishness required that the strong establish dominion over the weak in order to prevent anarchy. Man recognized the need for order by means of his reason, and government came into being as a result of this need. Although rulers were initially chosen by the people, once they were in power God made their authority legitimate, and the people renounced their right to reconstitute this authority. Nicole made this point clear not only in his *Essais* but in a conversation that he is reported to have had with a Monsieur Diroire, an account of which is preserved at the Bibliothèque Nationale. "Nicole asserted that the public no longer has any control over the power that it gave to the prince from the time that he was chosen. Monsieur Diroire replied that this was not so, that God gave power to the people, and if there were not such a great fear that widespread disorders might occur during transitional periods, the public would be able to dispose of this power as it saw fit, even to the point of changing governments."[10] Hereditary monarchy was preferable to other forms of government, in Nicole's mind, because political authority was smoothly transferred from one king to another without the need to consider the potential merits of one ruler as compared with another. Sovereignty based on birth was far better than sovereignty based upon merit, because, if it were based upon merit, each individual would think himself better qualified to rule than his nieghbor. An aristocracy based on birth was also preferable to one based on merit because everyone knew his place in a hierarchical social order, and those born to inferior positions might learn the virtue of humility and not disturb the social order by seeking to elevate themselves. Good government was of great concern to Nicole, who also wrote treatises for the edification of young noblemen and who even hoped that he might be appointed a tutor to Louis XIV's son after the Peace of the Church. To this end he wrote a *Traité de l'education d'un prince*, in which he emphasized the need to develop in a prospective ruler a profound concern for the welfare of his subjects. The prince should be taught to recognize those ills that led to civil war through the study of history. Benevolent government, according to Nicole, was justified in terms of both self-interest and charity. Since it was impossible for a human being to determine whether his good acts were motivated by one or by the other, the prince could only hope that his policies were inspired by God's grace.[11]

Not only were Jansenists advocates of absolutism but they also regarded themselves as loyal subjects of the king of France even when they disagreed with him over specific policies. Thus, at the end of his life, after years as a fugitive from royal justice, Antoine Arnauld wrote as follows to his nephew Arnauld de Pomponne, a minister and loyal servant of the crown. "You may imagine, my dear nephew, how hard it has been for me to be regarded as a rebel and a troublemaker, and to know that there are those who have encouraged thoughts in his majesty's mind contrary to the fatherly tenderness that he must bear toward his subjects. . . . This image, I can assure you, does not resemble me at all, and those who know me realize that his majesty has no subject more loyal than I am, more impressed by the glory of his reign, more ardent in support of his true interests."[12] The same sentiments of loyalty were expressed by Pasquier Quesnel in a letter written to Louis XIV in 1703: "Because I defended the sovereignty of kings and their inalienable rights against . . . [the Jesuits], because I exposed in broad daylight the maxims of their schools that are antithetical to the independence of your crown from all earthly powers, and that seek to undermine the inviolable loyalty of your subjects and even the safety of your person, they have sought revenge against me. . . . "[13] Like all who found themselves in disfavor with the king or in opposition to his policies, in the seventeenth century, Arnauld and Quesnel blamed the situation on those of the king's advisers who prevented their sovereign from knowing the truth. This of course, had been the attitude of Saint-Cyran and the *dévots*, who hoped that Louis XIII would dismiss Richelieu and

abandon his policies. This was also the attitude of Arnauld d'Andilly who, during the Fronde, urged the queen mother to rid
herself of Mazarin and his disastrous policies.

Among the most important prerogatives of the crown, in the
minds of the Jansenists, was its obligation to protect the liberties
of the French Church from ultramontanist encroachments, for
which reason they adhered by and large to the principles of royal
Gallicanism. In the preface to the second volume of *La somme des
fautes du père Garasse*, the abbé de Saint-Cyran rejoiced in the
fact that he lived in a kingdom where the Church enjoyed certain
rights and immunities not common in other Catholic states, and
in which the parlements were able to protect these immunities
against foreign attempts to undermine them. Arnauld, the son of
a distinguished and outspoken defender of the rights of the
French Church, was much concerned about the effect of the
doctrine of papal infallibility on those rights. Furthermore, that
doctrine threatened the prerogatives of the king. Once popes
acquired such extraordinary power, what was to prevent them,
asked Arnauld, from claiming that they had the power to dispose
of kingdoms as they saw fit? Here he touched on an issue that was
still sensitive, despite denials from Rome that popes had the power
to depose kings. The independence of temporal power from the
spiritual power of the papacy was a fundamental tenet of royal
Gallicanism, and any Catholic writer who suggested that the king
was subordinate to the pope was liable to be accused of *lèse-
majesté*.[14] Arnauld also upheld the rights of the sovereign courts
to reject offensive encyclicals. "It is the established order in the
kingdom that [the Parlements], invested as they are with the
king's authority, prevent any violation of forms prescribed by
canons and ordinances that might be unjust or might oppress the
king's subjects. And this violation of forms might involve matters
pertaining to the faith or anything else."[15] Quesnel was also a
firm supporter of royal Gallicanism. He too insisted that no papal
decree could have any effect in France without the consent of the
king, the parlements, and the bishops.[16] For the Jansenists, reform
of the Church was possible only within the Gallican framework,
with the king the defender of the immunities of the Church against
ultramontanist influences that might corrupt it. They invoked

certain basic principles of royal absolutism in order to resist the pretensions of papal absolutism.

If the king was the defender of the liberties and immunities of the French Church, he was not himself permitted to encroach upon these rights. On this issue the Jansenists were episcopal Gallicanists. During the Fronde they had defended the rights of Cardinal de Retz against what they regarded as the government's attempts to violate them. A few years after the conclusion of the Peace of the Church, Jansenists again found themselves at odds with Louis XIV, who was again threatening episcopal rights. The crown had traditionally maintained the right of receiving the income from Church property within a given diocese for one year after the death of its bishop. During that time, the king was free to place his own candidates in offices normally dependent on the bishop's choice. These "regalian rights" constituted an important source of income for the crown and a useful means of providing patronage. But not since the thirteenth century had the crown claimed these rights in areas that had been attached to the kingdom, out of respect for the customs and traditions of these areas. Badly in need of financial support for his war against the Dutch, Louis XIV decided to assert his regalian rights over these territories. A decree was issued in 1673 proclaiming the extension of the *régale* throughout the kingdom and applying them retroactively to all the dioceses affected by the decree. Only two bishops, Alet and Pamiers, objected to the king's intentions, on the grounds that extension of these rights constituted an infringement on episcopal rights. These same bishops had objected to the imposition of the formulary in their dioceses during the 1660s. In 1677 the bishop of Pamiers issued a pastoral letter rejecting the application of regalian rights in his diocese, which was affected by the decree, and at the same time he appealed to Pope Innocent XI for support. (The bishop of Alet had died earlier in the year, before he had the opportunity of associating himself with the appeal.) The Pope agreed to take the bishop under his protection, because he regarded the extension of regalian rights as an assault on the privileges of the Church. Louis XIV, on the other hand, regarded papal intervention in the matter as a violation of Gallican liberties, and in 1682 he obtained from an assembly of French bishops four articles restating the Gallican position in extreme terms. The crown was entirely independent from the authority of the Church in temporal affairs, and he was responsible for protecting the customs and traditions of the kingdom. Finally, the assembly declared that the supreme authority in the Church was not the pope but a representative council.[17]

In defense of episcopal rights, Arnauld argued that regalian rights had been granted to the king by the Church and that any extension of these rights required the consent of the Church. Like sovereign pontiffs, Christian kings were obliged to respect canon law, under the authority of which regalian rights were bestowed. The best-known Jansenist tract in defense of episcopal rights was entitled *Traité général de la régale* published in 1681. Its author, Louis-Paul du Vaucel, asserted that the quarrel had been generated by incompetent royal counselors, whose poor advice was a disservice to the legitimate authority of the king as well as to the liberties of the Church. Delving into the history of regalian rights, Vaucel maintained that in the early Middle Ages, the crown's obligation to protect the property of vacant sees had evolved into an untenable right of the crown to enjoy the usufruct of such property as long as a particular see remained vacant. Toward the end of the Middle Ages, it had become the policy of the crown not to extend what had become customary rights further, and not until recently had the government attempted to extend these rights to the newer territories. The bishops whose dioceses were threatened by these illegal and blasphemous pretensions of the crown ought to resist them, said Vaucel, because bishops "are the depositories not only of the faith of the Church but of its discipline, its rights and immunities, as well. Just as there are occasions when they must protect the pure doctrine of the Church by condemning error, so there are occasions when they must defend the liberties of the Church from those who would destroy them." Resorting to a comparison favored by Jansenists, Vaucel insisted that absolute obedience to kings was not required of bishops as it was of soldiers. "Bishops have this in particular, that, being subjects of the king, and belonging to the first order of the kingdom, they are the pastors and fathers of the king by virtue of powers bestowed on them by God. . . . Thus they need not defer to everything that bears the mark of royal authority, especially in ecclesiastical matters. There are times, however, when bishops can give no clearer indication of their fidelity to and respect for the king than to instruct him in the truth and in his obligations." Asserting a basic Jansenist ideal, Vaucel declared at the end of his treatise that bishops must be prepared to suffer for the truth. "It is not enough that bishops speak freely to princes and to the great of this world in defense of the rights and privileges of the Church. They must be disposed to suffer anything rather than to consent to violations and usurpations of these rights."[18]

During the regalian quarrel, the Jansenists found themselves allied with Innocent XI. A man of deep religious feeling, the pope was much interested in sustaining the spirit of the Counter Reformation. He favored the appointment to ecclesiastical offices of men who had experienced a real vocation, and he was opposed to the holding of multiple benefices by one man. Because of his enthusiasm for reform, his election to the papacy in 1676 was well received by the Jansenists. Indeed, the bishops of Alet and Pamiers both wrote letters congratulating him. But Jansenist support for Alet and Pamiers was not based as much on sympathy for the pope as it was upon principles pertaining to episcopal Gallicanism. Just as, in the Petrus Aurelius writings, Saint-Cyran had defended episcopal rights against the encroachments of the Jesuits, and as his disciples defended the same rights of Cardinal de Retz, so too did these disciples maintain the integrity of episcopal authority against royal efforts to infringe on them. So strong a royal Gallicanist was Arnauld, however, that even though he defended episcopal rights against the crown in the regalian controversy, he endorsed the four articles promulgated by the bishops' assembly of 1682. Writing to Vaucel in 1691, Arnauld asserted

. . . that one would do wrong to hide from the king his true interests. There is nothing of importance except the four articles, and on this issue he must remain firm and concede nothing. The extension of the *régale* is of little advantage to the king, and he will lose nothing by conceding the *plene jure* and other similar things. For he will not have fewer benefices at his disposal. . . . But if he yields on the four articles, that will be a manifestation of weakness with respect to an issue on which he should stand fast in order to acquire the glory that will be his if he defends to the end the doctrine of the Gallican Church, which is the same as that of the General Councils of Constance and Basel as well as of those who have in our own time zealously worked for the reestablishment of the discipline of the Church.[19]

The Jansenists not only upheld ecclesiastical rights but also affirmed the right of subjects to advise their prince on particular policies, to respectfully disagree with him on matters of policy and to seek redress of grievances. Indeed their association with the *dévot* opposition had been based on this assumption. "Kings are not well served," wrote Arnauld during the height of the crisis over the formulary, "when they are not told the truth, for the reason that they might at first be shocked. If one perseveres in telling the truth with firmness and with respect, one not only satisfies his conscience, but one may succeed in disabusing his sovereign of wrong impressions that he may have received from others, thereby enabling him to comprehend the truth. For if kings are strengthened in their wrong impressions, they will accustom themselves to governing both Church and state with an absolute authority because they have found no one to resist them."[20] In all fairness to the prince, insisted Arnauld, he must be told the truth by his advisers. Otherwise he might easily violate both divine and human law and might jeopardize the possibility of his redemption in the sight of God. God may require a king to account for his not permitting his counselors to speak freely on matters pertaining to his subjects' welfare and his own.[21] Arnauld believed that subjects should hold their sovereign in high esteem, and therefore he maintained that the ruler ought to be praised publicly as much as possible for worthy accomplishments. On the other hand, if the prince were about to commit an injustice, his counselors ought to warn him discreetly of the danger of such an act, in order not to embarrass him before his subjects.[22] If the prince was under a divine obligation to heed honest advice and counsel, so too was the counselor obliged to tell the truth. God set rulers over men to maintain social order, and because of the devastating effects of civil war, the prince ought to have the power of life and death over his people in order to compel obedience to the law. But a ruler, like anyone else, was capable of error, and while his subjects had no right to take up arms against their prince, they were entitled to attempt to persuade him of the errors of his ways. "Christians ought not to carry obedience to legally established authority so far as to refuse to seek redress of grievances against unjust decrees and against laws condemning innocent people."[23] But obedience to God took precedence over obedience to the prince. "There is always a practical *via media* for virtuous Christians between servile acquiescence that causes them to obey everything that is commanded of them without looking to see whether their consciences are offended, and criminal recklessness that causes them to rise up against legitimate authority under specious pretexts. This *via media* is the firmness of an enlightened soul well aware of its obligations, so that nothing can cause it in any way to act against God's law or to fail in the respect and loyalty owed to the prince." Having failed to persuade the sovereign of the error of his ways by means of reasoned argument, was the virtuous subject then required to submit to the authority of the sovereign? In such circumstances, maintained Arnauld, "the Gospel tells him what he must do, and that is to suffer all things rather than to obey an unjust command, and to allow his own throat to be cut rather than to permit death in his soul by violating God's law." Because the Christian was never authorized to take up arms against his prince, refusal to submit meant exile, imprisonment, or execution.[24] This willingness to suffer in defense of the truth against the oppressive actions of Church and state, based upon the experiences as well as the beliefs of the Jansenists, constituted a form of passive resistance. Another Jansenist statement in support of such resistance appeared in a pamphlet published in 1688, entitled *La régle des moeurs contre les fausses maximes de la morale corrompue.* Its author was Gabriel Gerberon, a Benedictine monk who had long been associated with Jansenism and who had escaped from France in the previous year, when threatened with arrest. No law, asserted Gerberon, whether ecclesiastical or civil, exempted a Christian from his moral responsibility to obey God's law "which is engraved in our hearts and is marked in Holy Scripture."[25] The virtuous Christian must look within himself and must acquire a firm understanding of Church tradition. Once in possession of the truth, "which is nothing but the law of God," he should be able to identify easily those judgments of his superiors that are fallible. One should always be on one's guard against "false prophets in the Church," warned Gerberon, employing a term used by the abbé Le Roy. Such prophets deceived sinners by giving them a false sense of security, by promising them peace, and by assuring them that no harm can come to them.[26] No authority, spiritual or temporal, ought to demand blind obedience from those placed under its jurisdiction. If a prince commanded evil of his subjects, they in turn had the right to remonstrate, on the grounds "that it is more just to obey God than men."[27] If the prince insisted on pursuing a wicked course of action despite the remonstrances, the subjects should be prepared to suffer punishment at the hands of their prince rather than to obey. The only sure guide to virtuous action, contended Gerberon, was the conscience of the individual enlightened by faith. Conscience "is a teacher and director within us that instructs us."[28] Nowhere in the pamphlet did Gerberon claim the right to publicly rebel against higher authority. The righteous were to show their devotion to the truth by suffering at the hands of an unjust authority.

Like other proponents of absolutism, the Jansenists in effect distinguished between absolute and arbitrary rule. The absolute prince recognized that there were limits to his power in the form of such fundamental laws of the realm as the Salic law as well as certain provincial customs and traditions. Indeed, the kings of France swore to protect these laws and customs in their coronation oaths. Arbitrary rule involved a refusal on the part of the sovereign to respect these rights. For the Jansenists, arbitrary rule involved, more than anything else, a refusal to respect the privileges of the Church that the prince was bound to protect or to respect the conscience of the individual obliged to obey God's law. Their obedience to temporal authority was therefore qualified. They would obey the righteous commands of their prince, but they would not obey those commands that violated the dictates of conscience enlightened by grace. While Jansenists rejected active rebellion as a legitimate political action, they chose other means of resistance. If some Jansenists were willing to suffer in silence as an exercise in humility, others chose to speak out in defense of their ideals by publicly justifying their beliefs in the form of polemics, published accounts of their suffering, and other gestures designed to affect public opinion. While some Jansenists looked to the absolute powers of the crown to provide order and stability, they were nevertheless willing to disturb the tranquillity of the kingdom with their vigorous protestations against what they regarded as unjust policy. They justified these protestations on the grounds that they were appeals for redress of grievances and on the grounds that the enlightened conscience must speak out in defense of its rights. If Jansenists like Arnauld, Le Roy, Nicole, Quesnel, Gerberon, or even Pascal were unwilling to resort to the sword, their reliance on the pen in an era of increasing political awareness reflected an apparent recognition on the part of these men that the pen was at least as mighty as the sword as an instrument of resistance. The harsh measures taken against hostile pamphleteers by the government and its own reliance on pamphleteers to generate support for its policies also indicate a profound respect for the power of the written word.

Gerberon's vehement defense of the conscience of the individual appeared during the years immediately following the conclusion of the Dutch War (1672–74), when Louis XIV resorted to more aggressive policies to increase his authority at home and to improve the strategic posture of France on her eastern frontier. His efforts to reduce the influence of Jansenism, his strong assertion of royal Gallicanist principles, and his move to suppress the Huguenots were manifestations of this policy decision, as was the king's determination in 1679 to appoint a new foreign minister. The foreign minister during the Dutch War had been Simon Arnauld de Pomponne, the son of Arnauld d'Andilly. Arnauld de Pomponne entered the royal service shortly after the death of Louis XIII under the sponsorship of Le Tellier. During the Fronde, despite the activities of his relatives and friends at Port Royal, he remained loyal to Mazarin. Indeed, his father's efforts to reconcile the cardinal-minister and the Port-royalists after the former's triumphant return to power in 1653 were due in large measure to his desire to see Arnauld de Pomponne succeed where he had failed. Arnauld de Pomponne married a cousin of the superintendent of finance, Nicolas Foucquet, for which reason he fell from royal favor during the period immediately following Foucquet's arrest and trial. Arnauld de Pomponne resumed his political career as

French ambassador to Sweden and to the Dutch Republic and then as foreign minister. But he favored a more modest foreign policy than the king was willing to accept at the end of the Dutch War, and therefore Louis decided to replace him with the more aggressive Colbert de Croissy.[29] French policies during the 1680s contributed to the disastrous wars that climaxed the Sun King's reign—the War of the League of Augsburg (1689-97) and the War of the Spanish Succession (1701-14). These policies were adopted during a difficult economic period. A declining population increased the tax burden, while famine, plague, and fluctuating prices and income created hardships for the king's subjects at a time when preparations for war required increased tax revenues. The situation in France during the 1680s was somewhat similar to that which prevailed during the decade immediately preceeding France's involvement in the Thirty Years' War. There was widespread social discontent caused by economic hardships, and military preparations aggravated social and political tensions. There were conflicting opinions within the king's council—some advocating a policy of restraint, others urging a more dynamic policy. Religious controversy troubled the atmosphere and, in some instances, contributed to political opposition. Richelieu was confronted with dangerous *dévot* conspiracies as he prepared for war, and while Louis XIV had curbed opposition to his policies to a far greater extent than Richelieu was able to do, voices demanding political reform began to be heard in the land in the 1680s. These voices grew louder after France became involved in war in 1689.

The political opposition that formed in this period around the duc de Bourgogne, grandson of Louis XIV and heir to the throne, was a pale imitation of the much more dangerous opposition that had formed around Marie de Médicis and Gaston d'Orléans at the time of the Day of Dupes. The Burgundy circle included jealous ministerial rivals, discontented nobles, and *dévot* idealists. The dominant figure among the latter group was François de Salignac de La Mothe-Fénelon, appointed tutor of the royal children in 1689. Bishop Fénelon was to become a deadly enemy of the Jansenists, who were not prominently involved in the group. Nevertheless, among those associated with the Burgundy circle was the duc de Chevreuse, grandson of the notorious duchesse de Chevreuse (enemy of Richelieu and *Frondeuse*) and son of the *Frondeur* duc de Luynes, the intimate friend of Port Royal.[30] In fact, the *Port Royal Logic* and Pascal's *Discours sur les grands* had been written for the edification of the young duke, whose political ideals doubtless reflected the influence of the Port-royalists. Among the reforms advocated by the Burgundy circle were the end of oppressive wars, which weighed heavily on the resources of the kingdom; the abolition of luxury and waste; the revival of agriculture; and a sound fiscal policy—reforms that had been urged by the *dévots* during the Richelieu era and particularly by Arnauld d'Andilly during the Fronde.[31]

Dévot ideals began to appear in Jansenist writings after 1679, and Gerberon's broadside in 1683 was in effect, an extreme statement of these ideals. In a letter written to Angélique de Saint-Jean at Port Royal, Arnauld quoted approvingly these lines of Boileau-Despréaux:

> Mais quelques vains lauriers que promettre la guerre,
> On peut être Héros sans ravager la terre.
> Il est plus d'une gloire. En vain aux conquérans
> L'erreur parmi les Rois donne les premiers rangs.
> Entre les grands héros, ce sont les plus vulgaires.
> Chaque siècle est fécond en heureux téméraires,
> Mais un roi vraiment roi, que, sage en ses sujets,
> Qui du bonheur public ait cimenté sa gloire,
> Il faut pour le trouver courir toute l'Histoire.
> La terre compte peu de ces Rois bienfaisans.
> Le Ciel, pour les former, les prépare longtemps.[32]

They expressed political values similar to those expressed in the Mazarinade *La Vérité tout nue* and to those that were to appear throughout the last difficult decades of the reign of Louis XIV. On the other hand, Arnauld supported the French cause during the War of the League of Augsburg—for which, he thought, the pope and the emperor were to blame.[33]

The most important political treatise written by a Jansenist during the seventeenth century was the four-volumed *Institution d'un prince*. Its author was Jacques-Joseph Duguet, born at Montbrison in 1649, the year that the faculty of the Sorbonne began to consider the five propositions. Duguet entered the Oratory, and was ordained in 1677. He was a colleague of Quesnel's on the faculty of the seminary of Sainte-Magloire. He refused the command of his superiors in the Oratory to sign the formulary and eventually left the order. By 1684 Duguet, Gerberon, and Quesnel had become closely associated with Arnauld in Brussels. Explaining his reasons for quitting the Oratory, Duguet wrote in a 1685 letter: " ... I am unable to conduct myself according to the rules that others find beneficial. A person with a peculiar temperament like mine needs a particular kind of situation. ... "[34] Like Antoine Le Maistre and other *solitaires* a generation earlier, Duguet displayed that detachment and independence that characterized the Jansenist mentality. The *Institution* was written in 1699, on the eve of the War of the Spanish Succession, but Duguet refrained from publishing it, perhaps because the work might have embarrassed Arnauld de Pomponne, who was then a member of the royal council. In any event, it was published in 1739, when the issues of war and peace were being hotly debated among the ministers of Louis XV as France prepared to become involved in the War of the Austrian Succession (1740–48).

In the first volume of the work, the author asserted that the prince must place the interests of his subjects above his own. In order to improve the public welfare, he ought to surround himself with honest counselors who were not afraid to speak the truth instead of with flattering courtiers, who only acted and advised in terms of their own selfish interests. "The prince must seek the truth not only with sincerity but even with uneasiness." In the second volume of the *Institution*, Duguet described the characteristics of good government, which he claimed to have learned from reading Tacitus, Cicero, and Marcus Aurelius, as well as from Scripture and the writings of the Church Fathers. Because the dispensation of justice was the fundamental purpose of government, Duguet stressed the need for judges with a true vocation; " ... venality in the magistracy is a disorder contrary to justice."[35] Venality was a corrupting influence because it was rooted in self-interest and because it encouraged the rich rather than the worthy to seek high office. Venality had caused the magistracy to become alienated from the crown, having been transformed from public offices into private property. The prince ought to respect the ancient laws of the kingdom in the interests of justice, because his subjects were more likely to respect laws that had been in existence for a long time. The prince was therefore well advised not to begin his reign by promulgating many new laws without the support of enlightened and virtuous counselors. Obviously referring to the French monarchy, Duguet insisted that the king ought to allow the parlements "a free, sincere, and respectful scrutiny of those laws presented to them for registration." Servile magistrates who agreed with everything that the monarch desired were harmful to the state. The prince who loved the truth ought not to be offended by remonstrances, and those who respectfully disagreed with him ought not to be considered seditious.[36] Duguet maintained that powerful ministers were inclined to stifle dissent, and he urged princes to govern on their own. "There is no better indication that a prince governs on his own than the freedom that he permits superior magistrates to examine legislation presented to them in order that his interests as well as those of justice are well served."[37]

Duguet was not only concerned about the proper administration of justice but about the economic condition of the country as well. Among the first fruits of good government were "prosperous cities, a stable population, and general well-being." The prince ought therefore to be more interested in increasing the wealth of his subjects than in enriching himself. In order to accomplish this, the sovereign should favor agriculture, "the source of true wealth and of riches that have a real value that does not depend on men's opinion. . . . Agriculture makes it possible for a kingdom to be self-sufficient, . . . and it provides the chief source of revenue for the prince."[38] Even if commerce and industry ceased to flourish, agriculture would sustain the populace. Agriculture was not only useful but it was also favored by God—Adam was charged with the cultivation of the Garden of Eden in his innocence before the fall. (Saint-Cyran had maintained that those with the best opportunity for salvation were the lowly peasants who lived in the countryside and cultivated the fields.[39]) Agriculture, by rights the most honored occupation, "is today regarded by prideful opinion as the most vile. Whereas useless arts are protected, and honor is attached to those occupations that serve only to oppress the people, those who work for the prosperity and happiness of others are left in misery."[40] Though less important to the economic well-being of society, commerce and industry should not be neglected. Duguet suggested several reforms intended to improve both, including the reduction of internal tariffs, improved roads, the control of ports by native rather than by foreign interests, and a fleet capable of protecting the sea lanes. Duguet was by no means an unqualified advocate of free trade. "The maxim that commerce should be free is only partially true, and what we have said to this point makes it clear that it is false in a number of ways."[41] He was opposed to the exportation of goods needed at home, and he favored high tariffs on foreign goods in order to encourage domestic industry.

The economic well-being of society depended in large measure on the financial policy of the prince. Ruinous to the ruler as well as to his subjects was the government's habit of acquiring revenue by borrowing money at high rates of interest. Duguet maintained that high interest rates sapped the wealth of both the king and his people. In order to make quick profits, financiers increased the rates during hard times. If the prince was forced to borrow money for lack of a feasible alternative, he should insist on lower rates, and he should set up a sinking fund in order to pay off loans efficiently and with a minimum burden to society as a whole. The prince ought to be careful about excessive taxation that weighed upon the poorer elements of society and about levying new taxes. War was often a pretext for raising taxes, but the prince should make better use of existing sources of revenue by means of the sound administration of the royal domain and by more efficient methods of tax collection. Duguet was critical of the cumbersome fiscal administration of the crown, which reduced revenue without alleviating harassment of the king's subjects. If new taxes were found to be necessary, the prince ought to summon an Estates General or to consult with provincial estates or local notables.[42] War, by its very nature, adversely affected the economic well-being of the kingdom and should be waged only when necessary. "War is sometimes necessary and therefore just." The prince was responsible for the protection of his subjects, but he had no right to extend his territories or to terrify his neighbors. The prince, wrote Duguet, must prefer peace to victory.[43]

The policies discussed in the second volume of the *Institution* pertained to all rulers, Christian and pagan; but in the last two volumes, the author concerned himself with the obligations of the Christian prince, whose interest in the spiritual welfare of his subjects should be uppermost in his mind. To this end, he was required to choose a virtuous confessor to guide his conscience. Such a confessor was more likely to be found from among the secular clergy than among its regular ranks. The regular clergy tended to place loyalty to pope ahead of loyalty to prince, and confessors belonging to orders were often incompetent and deceitful. The secular clergy was more likely to adhere to Gallican liberties.[44] A virtuous confessor would inspire a proper penitential attitude on the part of the ruler as well as an interest in the moral life of his people. Because the Christian prince was under a divine obligation to facilitate the redemption of as many of his subjects as possible, he was required to suppress anything that might give rise to scandal and disorder, to protect the virtuous, to respect the rights and privileges of the Church, and to appoint worthy candidates to benefices. Finally, in defense of the true faith, the prince should be prepared to suffer the death of a martyr.[45]

The *Institution d'un prince* contained a number of political themes that were common to Jansenist writers throughout the century. There are innumerable references to the need for wise and virtuous counselors; these also appeared frequently in the writings of Saint-Cyran, Arnauld d'Andilly, and Antoine Arnauld. Not wishing to criticize the king directly for his anti-Jansenist measures and for what they regarded as other unwise policies, Saint-Cyran and the others chose instead to blame these policies on the advice of incompetent courtiers. All these writers—Saint-Cyran, Arnauld d'Andilly, Antoine Arnauld, and Duguet—shared a common concern for the burdens that war placed on the less fortunate members of society, and both Arnauld d'Andilly and Duguet made specific proposals to alleviate these burdens. Both men attacked venality as injurious to government and society. The *Institution* is a transitional work in that it reflects a concern for issues that were very much a part of seventeenth-century politics as well as an intimation of political problems that were to affect eighteenth-century France. Duguet obviously disapproved of Richelieu and Mazarin, powerful ministers who prohibited dissent and who prevented the crown from pursuing just policies. He was opposed to policies that failed to place the Christian responsibilities of the ruler above all else, and he disapproved of policies that placed the dynastic interests of the crown above the public welfare. In this respect, Duguet's opinions reflected seventeenth-century concerns. His emphasis on the parlements' rights of remonstrance, the rights and privileges of the Church, and the dangers of a financial policy that relied too heavily on government loans related to seventeenth-century issues that were to become very much a part of French political life during the following century. The work was influenced by the mercantilist principles that dominated the economic policies of the French government in the seventeenth century, but its insistence that agriculture was the fundamental source of wealth based on Christian agrarian principles foreshadowed some of the ideas of the physiocrats of the Enlightenment.[46]

Although the measures taken by Louis XIV after the Treaty of Nimeguen to curb Jansenism and to establish religious conformity in the kingdom had deprived Port Royal of future generations of nuns and had forced the Jansenist leadership into exile, religious controversies continued unabated. Jansenist pamphlets received a wide circulation—indicating that the movement in France was flourishing—Huguenot polemics from abroad attacked the despotic regime, and the government was forced to send troops to the Cévennes to quell a Protestant uprising. The quarrel arising out of the mystical movement known as quietism involved such leaders of the French Church as Bossuet and Fénelon and directly affected the Jansenist movement. Finally, the Jesuits aroused indignation throughout France and Europe in their efforts to reconcile Catholic doctrine and Confucianist tradition in order to enhance their missionary activities in China. These quarrels occurred during the last decades of Louis's reign, when famine and war generated increased opposition to royal policies.

The archbishop of Paris, Harlay de Champvallon, died in 1695 and was succeeded by Louis Antoine de Noailles. The new archbishop, though not a Jansenist himself, was favorably disposed toward some of the spiritual ideals of the movement. Furthermore, he was known to be critical of the Jesuits, who were embarrassed by the Chinese issue, which brought into question their ethical principles. The appointment of Noailles as archbishop of Paris seemed to indicate to the disciples of Ignatius Loyola that their influence was on the wane, and they were not likely to overlook an opportunity to humiliate the prelate. A year after Noailles had taken office, there appeared a work entitled *Exposition de la foi touchant la grace et la prédestination.* It had been written by Barcos, long since dead, and was published by the intransigent Gerberon in blatant violation of the terms of the Peace of the Church. Noailles promptly condemned the book, but two years later an anonymous pamphlet, *Problème ecclésiastique,* pointed out that the doctrine set forth in *Exposition de la foi*, condemned by the archbishop, was precisely the same as the doctrine set forth in Pasquier Quesnel's *Réflexions morales*, which he had approved. Very likely written by a Jesuit, the anonymous pamphlet challenged Noailles's competence and aroused public opinion in Paris.[47]

Sensitive Jansenist issues were also involved in a case presented in 1701 to the faculty of the Sorbonne concerning a priest, Louis Périer, a nephew of Pascal's. Périer had never ceased proclaiming the doctrine of efficacious grace and the doctrine of contrition, and on his deathbed he had insisted on observing "a respectful silence" on the subject of whether the five propositions were to be found in Jansenius's *Augustinus.* The question presented to the theologians of the university was whether such an uncompromising Jansenist was entitled to final absolution of his sins. Forty doctors, including seven curés, affirmed the rights of the deceased priest, much to the embarrassment of the archbishop and the consternation of king and pope. The affair occurred just as France became embroiled in the War of the Spanish Succession. Convinced that Jansenist sentiment was powerful enough in Paris to cause the sort of trouble that hampered Mazarin during the religious Fronde, Louis XIV took drastic steps to suppress Jansenism. Because Spain was France's ally, the French king was able to convince his nephew, Philip V, to arrest the Jansenist leaders Quesnel and Gerberon, who had taken refuge in the Spanish Netherlands.

(Arnauld had died in 1694, and Quesnel had succeeded him as the dominant figure in the movement.) Both men were seized and imprisoned in 1703. Gerberon was brought back to France, where he was eventually incarcerated at Vincennes (where Saint-Cyran had spent five years) and was released in 1710 after he agreed under compulsion to sign the formulary. He died a year later. Quesnel managed to escape from prison, but the Spanish authorities had taken possession of his papers and correspondence, which were forwarded to France. Quesnel's papers strengthened Louis XIV's conviction that Jansenism remained a widespread and dangerous movement,[48] and with the help of the Jesuits, he managed to persuade the pope, Clement XI, to promulgate yet another anti-Jansenist encyclical. *Vineam Domini*, which arrived in France in July 1705, specifically condemned the right to maintain a respectful silence on the question of the fact of the five propositions.

In 1703, the year of Gerberon's and Quesnel's arrest, the aging and infirm nuns of Port-Royal-des-Champs were ordered to sign the formulary. Again, as in 1664, they refused to do so without appending specific reservations. The implacable Louis, after some delay, managed to obtain the pope's permission to suppress the convent and to disperse the nuns in 1709. Fearful that Port Royal might become a shrine of sorts, the king had the bodies of the more prominent nuns and *solitaires* moved elsewhere, had the bones of other nuns hurled into a common grave, and had the buildings leveled in 1711. Several years later, Quesnel wrote a fitting epitaph for the ruined abbey: "True consolation comes only from the spirit of God, and on these occasions he only gives it to those who are faithful to the truth and are prepared to sacrifice everything to it. . . . It is indeed a misfortune that a community so beneficial to the Church is disparaged and destroyed. But if it cannot be preserved without harm to the truth, without acting against conscience, . . . then the community ought to perish rather than to prefer those things that are so injurious to God and his truth."[49]

Despite these oppressive measures, the enemies of Jansenism were still convinced that the movement was dangerous. Among these was the bishop of Cambrai, Fénelon. He had been identified with quietism, which the Jansenists, among others, objected to on the grounds that it appeared to undermine penitential discipline. The Jansenists had supported the efforts of the king and Bishop Bossuet to have one of Fénelon's devotional works, *Maximes des saints*, condemned by the Vatican. Seeking to regain favor at court, Fénelon determined to have what he regarded as the most dangerous and influential Jansenist work, Quesnel's *Réflexions morales*, specifically condemned by the pope. He was particularly disturbed by the conciliarist and Richerist implications of the work. Such a condemnation would further embarrass archbishop Noailles, who had approved the work in 1692. With the aid of the Jesuits, Fénelon had little difficulty in stirring up a quarrel over the controversial work to the point where Louis XIV once again requested Pope Clement XI to issue an encyclical. Although reluctant to arouse Gallican prejudices, the pope was persuaded that such an encyclical would be well received in France. *Unigenitus*, the fifth anti-Jansenist encyclical since *In eminenti* was promulgated by Urban VIII in 1643, arrived in France in September 1713; it condemned 101 propositions from the *Réflexions morales*. In language reminiscent of Richelieu's *Testament* and Louis XIV's *Mémoires*, the pope castigated "these seducers full of artifice who insinuate dangerous doctrine under the guise of abject piety and who in seeming saintliness form new sects to lead men to destruction. . . ."[50] Like *Cum occasione*, issued some fifty years earlier, the new encyclical condemned the belief that salvation proceeded from grace alone, without the aid of the human will, and the essentially Jansenist concept that grace liberated the will from the bondage of Original Sin. It also attacked the interpretation of the doctrine of contrition cherished by Saint-Cyran and his followers. But *Unigenitus* went beyond *Cum occasione* and repudiated Jansenist beliefs pertaining to the structure of the Church, the right of informed Christians to interpret Scripture on their own, and the right to translate Scripture into the vernacular in clear and precise language. Condemned as well was the contention that the Church had on occasion persecuted the righteous even to the point of excommunication and that the authority of the Church was limited to matters pertaining to faith and not to fact. *Cum occasione* had defined Jansenism in terms of the doctrine of grace; Clement XI's encyclical extended this definition to include Jansenist beliefs relating to the spiritual renewal of the individual and the institutional reforms of the Church—beliefs that gave greater weight to the spiritual and intellectual integrity of the individual. Still smarting from the impact of the Reformation, which had pitted the consciences of Protestant reformers against its authority, and wary of the challenge to its authority implicit in the natural philosophies of Copernicus, Galileo, and Descartes, the Church could not accept a set of beliefs that seemed to emphasize certain rights of the Christian that might weaken its control over the religious life of its members.

While *Unigenitus* was an expression of ecclesiastical policy, it was also an instrument of royal absolutism in France. Louis XIV, engaged in a long and costly war against a powerful coalition, was unable to tolerate religious dissent among his subjects any more than Richelieu or Mazarin could under similar circumstances earlier in the century. As Clement XI had feared, however, the encyclical provoked Gallican sensibilities in France that made its reception difficult. Bishops residing in Paris were convened in January 1714. Thirty-four agreed to receive the encyclical, nine, including Archbishop Noailles, refused to do so. By insisting that an extraordinary assembly of bishops could impose an encyclical on the entire kingdom, including those dioceses presided over by bishops who disagreed with the majority, Louis XIV once again appeared to be violating episcopal rights. Members of the Parlement of Paris objected to this procedure, making it clear that the king would have difficulty obtaining that institution's endorsement of *Unigenitus*. Undaunted, Louis approached that other bastion of Gallicanism, the Sorbonne, where there was fierce opposition to the encyclical. By forcibly excluding its opponents, the government managed to register the encyclical at a rump session of the faculty. Noailles, on the other hand, refused to submit to the wishes of the king. He declined to receive the encyclical and also prohibited its circulation in the archdiocese. Paris, the source of so much religious unrest since the days of Henry IV, and center of the Jansenist movement, would have to receive the encyclical if it was to have any effect at all. To this end, Louis XIV decided to convoke a national council, representing the French, for the purpose of condemning Noailles. A declaration calling for such a council was to be registered without discussion by the Parlement of Paris. By this procedure, the king hoped to satisfy both the principles of episcopal Gallicanism—by having the matter dealt with in France— and the principles of royal Gallicanism so jealously adhered to by the sovereign courts. Before his desire was fulfilled, however, Louis XIV's death in September 1715 created a new political situation. The reception of *Unigenitus* became a significant political issue in eighteenth-century France. Ironically, Gallicanist sentiments, which the king had hoped to overcome in order to destroy the Jansenist movement, became the means by which it survived.

VIII. *The Nature of Jansenism*

What was Jansenism? The most usual and obvious way to define
it is in terms of the five propositions condemned in the encyclical
Cum occasione. There was substantial disagreement among Jansenists, however, about the meaning of the propositions. Some had
doubts about whether the propositions were heretical, while others
believed that they were heretical but that they were not to be
found in the *Augustinus*. A definition of Jansenism in terms of
the distinction between *droit* and *fait* is complicated by the fact
that there were differences of opinion among Jansenists on this
issue as well. Some believed that an explicit reservation as to the
question of fact ought to accompany signature of Louis XIV's
formulary, others preferred a mental reservation, while still others
had doubts about having any reservation at all. Certainly all Jansenists adhered to the doctrine of contrition, believing that true
penitence proceeds from a love of God rather than from fear of
divine chastisement, but other Catholics who were not Jansenists
also repudiated attritionism. Jansenists were, for the most part,
Gallicanists, but so too were most Frenchmen in one way or
another before the Revolution. Although contritionism and Gallicanism formed significant elements within Jansenist belief, it
cannot be defined exclusively in these terms.[1]

Recent historians have rightly emphasized the differences of
opinion among Jansenists on religious and philosophical questions.
Saint-Cyran was less interested in contemporary philosophy than
was his protégé Antoine Arnauld. Le Maistre de Sacy was less
convinced of the beneficial effects of philosophy than was Pascal.
Angélique Arnauld's response to oppression was quite different
from that of the Abbé Le Roy of Hautefontaine, "where we do
not sign the formulary." The political opinions of Saint-Cyran
differed from those of his friend Arnauld d'Andilly in that the
abbé opposed war with Spain, whereas Arnauld d'Andilly sup-

ported the war and the Dutch alliance. Any definition of Jansenism must take into account these varying opinions and beliefs.

A precise definition of Jansenism is made more difficult by the fact that it shared common elements with other Catholic groups and with Protestant sects. Other Catholics were contritionists or Gallicanists, as has already been noted. The "Augustinian strain of piety" affected the followers of Cardinal Bérulle who became Jansenists as well as those who did not, and it was inherent in Protestantism in both Europe and America. A rigorous attitude toward penitential discipline was characteristic not only of Saint-Cyran and his followers but of such distinguished non-Jansenists as Armand de Rancé and Bishop Bossuet. "Conversion," or spiritual rebirth, was a crucial religious experience for Angélique Arnauld, Saint-Cyran, and Pascal, as it has always been for many Christians.

There can be no doubt that Jansenism was an offshoot of the Counter Reformation. Angélique Arnauld's successful efforts to reform the convent of Port Royal were part of a larger movement of monastic reform. The spirituality of Angélique and of Saint-Cyran was shared by many others who desired to revitalize the Church after the Council of Trent. The Catholic Reformation involved both personal and institutional reform. The individual was called upon to change his ways from satisfying his own ambitions to pleasing God. Saint Francois de Sales, Cardinal Bérulle, and the abbé de Saint-Cyran all shared the conviction that the reform of the individual involved an intensive effort that lasted the rest of his life. This involved long hours of mental anguish in solitude, for the purpose of stripping the sinner of his illusions and of acquiring a humble and a contrite heart. Saint-Cyran and his disciples also believed that true piety resulted from such intellectual activity as reading and writing on religious subjects and even familiarity with pagan literature in order to understand better the human condition. For the Jansenists, a reformed Christian was an informed Christian. Jansenists and other Catholics worked long and hard to improve the quality of the clergy. They insisted that membership in the priesthood or a religious order required a true vocation, and they denounced all who sought ecclesiastical benefices for selfish reasons. Proper instruction and a genuine vocation were necessary if a priest were to fulfill his responsibilities successfully. Thus, for example, the bishop of Alet spent many hours in conference with the priests of his diocese in order to help them learn more about the verities of the faith. Jansenists and other French Catholics believed that religious reforms could best be carried out within the Gallican framework.

As with other reform movements, the ideals of the Counter Reformation became somewhat tarnished by political and social realities. Vested interests in the Church discouraged changes that threatened them. Abbots and bishops frowned on the activities of monks and curés who were more enthusiastically committed to spiritual ideals than they, and vice versa. The crown was distrustful of efforts to limit its control over the Church—particularly its powers of appointment to benefices—and its use of the clergy for political purposes. Some devout Catholics—including Saint Vincent de Paul, Bishop Bossuet, Bourdaloue, and Cardinal Le Camus—learned to accept these realities, and they continued to sponsor what reforms they could without antagonizing the highest authorities of Church and state. Saint-Cyran and his disciples, on the other hand, were unable to accept these realities. Having undergone spiritual regeneration themselves, they soon discovered that they were surrounded by unreconstructed, hostile forces. Society as a whole, they realized, was unsympathetic to the strict penitential ethic of the Jansenists. Instead of working together with leading officials in the Church to further the purposes of the Counter Reformation, the Jansenists found that their own efforts were opposed by authorities in the Church whom they came to regard as worldly and incompetent. They soon discovered that the crown too was unfavorably disposed toward them. Instead of surrounding himself with wise and virtuous counselors who would help him improve the quality of religious life in France, the king preferred instead the advice of those who, in the estimation of the Jansenists, were sycophants. This profound and disturbing experience of finding oneself in an alien world was common to all Jansenists.

The antagonism between the Jansenists and the society in which they lived was aggravated by certain facets of their belief. The very intensity of their faith and their commitment to God were indications to Saint-Cyran and his followers that they were among the elect. Having suffered through the psychological agonies of introspection, they had come to feel God's grace stirring within them. The hardships imposed by a rigorous penitential discipline and the joy aroused by the inner movements of God's grace enabled the Jansenists to endure further suffering at the hands of hostile functionaries. Indeed, persecution at the hands of ignorant officials was a means by which God tested the faith of His elect. Thus Agnès Arnauld, old and sick, cast out of Port Royal by the angry archbishop of Paris in the summer of 1664, welcomed persecution as a test of her spiritual strength. Persecution at the hands of a hostile world reinforced that elitist attitude that François de Sales had criticized in Angélique Arnauld. To be one of God's chosen souls was a singular honor, because the number of God's redeemed was always very small. "Even among Christians," wrote Saint-Cyran, "only a very small number are saved after death."[2] Quesnel asserted that it was wrong to think that the road to Paradise was broad and well traveled. "Very few manage to find the road to heaven, fewer still enter it, fewer still remain on it, and even fewer persevere to the very end."[3] In a letter written from prison, Saint-Cyran seems to have anticipated the persecution that awaited the Jansenists. "God often turns kingdoms upside down in order to redeem one or two of his elect. All that is temporal is nothing, not even monasteries and temples. For God has only need of Himself in us where He has built His true temple. Just as in heaven, where there are many happy souls, there is no temple but God."[4] By worshiping at the temple within her while exiled to another convent, Angélique de Saint-Jean was able to withstand the terrible pressures brought to bear on her to submit to the authority of Archbishop Péréfixe.

Another aspect of their belief that further alienated Jansenists from the society in which they lived was their inclination to place the spiritual interests of the individual above the interests of society. The penitent Christian ought to prefer solitude to social action, and even when engaged in the world's business, he should remind himself of the blessings of solitude. When he decided to return to France from exile, Nicole declared that his own spiritual concerns were more important to him than those of his fellowmen. The primacy of the individual is apparent in a letter written by Barcos to Agnès Arnauld, advising her not to accept a particular woman as a postulant at Port Royal.

I do not speak of the harm done to your convent in admitting her because, even though the harm would be considerable, the needs of the convent should not take precedence over the spiritual needs of the individual, for whom religious orders were established, and not the other way round. I know full well that this order is usually reversed, and that people prefer the good of a convent to the good of a particular soul that, from this point of view, must yield to the common good. But this opinion is not to be found in the Gospels, nor was it held by Him who was willing to lose ninety-nine sheep for the sake of one. The well-being of a religious community is derived from the well-being of each member. . . . [5]

Because they believed that their own spiritual needs would best be served by not joining a particular religious order, the *solitaires* withdrew to the wilderness of Port-Royal-des-Champs in order to organize their religious lives on their own terms.

The Catholic Church found the elitism inherent in Jansenist belief objectionable because salvation appeared to be inaccessible to the ordinary mortal. The Church could hardly tolerate such discouraging religious convictions in an era when its missionary activities around the world were increasing and when it was trying to protect its members from the dangers of Protestantism and free thought. An elitist conception of the true Church of God's elect was unlikely to appeal to potential converts, who might think that they lacked the spiritual fortitude necessary for salvation. If redemption were placed beyond his reach, the ordinary mortal might be tempted to seek solace in some other belief. The Church disapproved not only of Jansenist elitism but also of the Jansenist emphasis on the individual. The Church had always discouraged religious beliefs that focused the attention of the individual on his own needs and that caused him to become indifferent to or even hostile toward the institution as a whole.

The Jansenists were not, of course, the only religious group alienated from the world around them in the seventeenth century. English Puritans were also contemptuous of their countrymen who refused to undertake a radical reform of the Church of England. Some decided to forsake their homeland in order to set up religious communities in the New World, while others became involved in an active rebellion against a corrupt church and a corrupt state. Both Jansenists and Puritans resisted authority, but the Puritans were, on the whole, more inclined toward activism than were the

Jansenists, some of them going so far as to attempt what has been described as a "revolution of the saints."[6] When they found themselves confronting the highest authorities of Church and state, the Jansenists resorted to passive resistance. Some, like Angélique Arnauld, Barcos, and Nicole, ultimately decided to remain silent not so much out of a willingness to submit but because of an attitude of indifference toward the world and its institutions. They resisted the world by withdrawing further from it and by becoming entirely preoccupied with their own lives. At the same time, they were willing to allow the authorities to believe that they had yielded, either by signing the formulary without reservation or by refusing to engage in further polemics. What the authorities saw as an act of obedience to them was regarded by Angélique, Barcos, and Nicole as an act of humility before God. Arnauld, Le Roy, Quesnel, and some of the nuns of Port Royal, on the other hand, while refusing to encourage active rebellion, continued to speak out in defense of their beliefs and in so doing were prepared to suffer the consequences of disobedience—exile and imprisonment.

Jansenism contained elements of Gallicanism and of *dévot* idealism as well as a measure of adherence to the theological opinions of Jansenius, which Jansenists took to be an accurate reflection of Saint Augustine's beliefs. But its essence consisted of a profound personal religious experience that altered the life of each person who came to be known as a Jansenist and, consequently, his or her attitude toward the world. The precise dimensions of this experience are, of course, impossible to measure, but its effects are readily apparent. As a result of "conversion," a Jansenist became more independent, and less likely to subject himself to "corrupting" influences. Thus Angélique Arnauld refused to bare her conscience to laxist confessors. She withdrew Port Royal from the Cistercian order and later from the direction of Sébastien Zamet because she did not think either to be a suitable influence on the convent. The abbé de Saint-Cyran declined offers of lucrative and prestigious benefices because acceptance of such would too much involve him in worldly affairs. Duguet resigned from the Oratory when he concluded that membership in the order no longer suited his spiritual needs. A sense of independence and of detachment from the world and its institutions, including the Church, characterized the attitudes of the *solitaires* as a result of their respective conversions, and it made them more self-sufficient. The way of life of the *solitaires* was summed up in a letter written by Singlin to a young man who wished to join them. At Port-Royal-des-Champs "we live completely independent of one another, being cordial and deferential to each other without anyone taking authority over us. There we discuss philosophy and read books. . . . In order to embrace this life without danger to oneself, one must be able to rely on oneself [*se soutenir soi-même*]."[7] Self-sufficiency prevented the Jansenists from submitting to demands that were unacceptable to them, and it strengthened their inclination toward passive resistance as they continued to experience persecution.

An outstanding characteristic of Jansenism was its emphasis on the individual—layman or cleric, nun or bishop. This individualism manifested itself not only in the particular religious experiences of those involved but also in the emphasis on conscience and reason. In the last analysis, the Jansenist was compelled to follow the dictates of his conscience as opposed to the demands of Church and state. Arnauld's defense of the *Augustinus* was based to a certain extent upon conscience; the nuns of Port Royal respectfully declined to sign the formulary without reservation because to do so would have offended their consciences; and Gabriel Gerberon proclaimed the enlightened conscience to be the ultimate authority in determining a proper course of action. In the Little Schools and in their pedagogical treatises, the Jansenists stressed the importance of training the judgment of the individual so that he might come to understand more clearly the verities of the faith and his religious responsibilities. By means of a properly trained judgment, the individual would learn to distinguish between the realm of faith and the realm of reason, and he would come to understand that in the realm of faith he must submit to divine authority, whereas in the realm of reason he was free to draw his own conclusions. An enlightened conscience, an informed judgment and right reasoning were attributes that helped the Jansenists to survive in an alien world.

Jansenist thought and belief were very much a part of the seventeenth-century intellectual crisis that consisted of a widespread assault on traditional Scholasticism, which had been the support for theological and philosophical assumptions since the Middle Ages. The crisis involved a quest for new principles by which to establish certain truths with respect to religion and natural phenomena. Catholic theologians including the abbé de Saint-Cyran were critical of Scholastic theology because it was too speculative and confusing. They preferred instead a more pragmatic theology that encouraged Catholics to perform their religious duties. The doctrine of efficacious grace stressed God's omnipotence and man's weakness, and in this respect it contributed to the reaction against Renaissance humanism and its emphasis on the human potential for good. If Jansenists reacted against certain aspects of humanism, they were themselves influenced by humanist learning. They believed strongly in the value of the classics as a means of understanding the nature of pagan culture and the roots of the Christian tradition. Thus Saint-Cyran, Quesnel, and Tillemont devoted many years to the study of patristic literature, the source of so many Jansenist ideas about penitential discipline and Church reform. In the humanist tradition, the Jansenists deplored the pseudo-Aristotelianism contained in the Scholastic synthesis, with its erroneous definitions and categories, and they advocated a more pragmatic logic and rhetoric that would help men understand more about the nature of things as well as enabling them to communicate more effectively with one another. Dissatisfaction with the synthesis caused some Jansenists to espouse a form of Pyrrhonism. They were led to believe that all conclusions arrived at by reason were to be doubted, because reason was corrupt and therefore subject to error. Jansenist Pyrrhonists disapproved of too great a reliance on reason in religious life because it encouraged pride rather than humility. Other Jansenists saw reason as a means of understanding and of defending religious truth as well as of acquiring further knowledge of the natural world. These Jansenists were attracted to Cartesian philosophy, which, they thought, clearly distinguished between the spiritual and the material worlds, between the supernatural and the natural. Furthermore, Cartesian philosophy, with its emphasis on clear and distinct ideas, was of great help in developing sound grammatical and logical rules that, in their opinion, greatly facilitated comprehension and communication.

Jansenist ideals were to a certain extent anachronistic. Jansenists advocated the revival of practices they associated with the primitive church. Christians were more virtuous in that era, they believed, and ecclesiastical institutions were stronger because penitential discipline was more demanding and because those in positions of authority responded to the needs of the Church as a whole instead of to the arbitrary and often un-Christian demands of pope and king. What Arnauld called the heresy of domination in the Church was, he thought, an ugly innovation in violation of the practices of the early Church, whose enlightened members were more respectful of one another. The ethical principles of the Jansenists and their ideas about Church reform were characteristic of earlier reform movements. The Jansenist appeal to conscience was reminiscent of earlier appeals made by reformers who refused to submit to higher authority. Luther had broken with the Church because his conscience would not let him do otherwise. When Arnauld and Gerberon insisted on the right to respect the demands of conscience, they were not asserting the modern ideal of freedom of conscience. Rather, like others before them, they were demanding respect for the enlightened conscience in possession of the truth. They did not advocate tolerance of differing religious beliefs. Wrong beliefs were as unacceptable to Jansenists as they were to most other Christians of the period. In fact, Jansenist writers attacked Huguenots and quietists as well as Jesuits for erring in the faith, and they approved of the revocation of the Edict of Nantes.

Though archaic and traditional in some respects, seventeenth-century Jansenism contained elements that appear to foreshadow the Enlightenment. As previously noted, Nicole's description of the beneficial effects of enlightened self-interest on social conduct anticipated the utilitarian ethic that was to come to full fruition in the eighteenth century. Duguet's critique of the mercantilist view that a sound economy depended on commerce and industry and his reassertion of the primacy of agriculture served as a link between traditional Christian agrarianism and eighteenth-century physiocracy.[8] But most important, the assertion of the autonomy of reason in the realm of nature that appears in the *Provincial Letters*, the *Pensées*, the *Port Royal Logic*, and Jansenist polemics relating to the *question de fait* may well have helped to cultivate that spirit of free inquiry that was so much a part of the Enlightenment. By making a clear distinction between the realms of nature and of grace, Jansenist writers were, in effect, suggesting a means of avoiding the great intellectual confrontation that took place in the following century between religious authority on the one hand and the intellectual rights of the individual on the other. Galileo had been condemned, according to Pascal and Arnauld, because the Church had sought to exercise its authority in an area outside its jurisdiction. A century later, d'Alembert, in the *Preliminary Discourse to the Encyclopedia*, deplored in terms strikingly similar to those used by Pascal and Arnauld, the "theological despotism or prejudice" that had attempted to silence Galileo. Also repudiating the authority of the Church in the realm of nature, d'Alembert wrote: "Although religion is intended uniquely to regulate our mode of life and our faith, [some theologians] believed it was to enlighten us also on the system of the world—in short, on matters which the All-Powerful has expressly left to our own disputations. They did not make the reflection that the sacred books and works of the Fathers, which were created to teach the common people as well as the philosophers the requirements of practice and belief, would have spoken only the language of the common people when it came to indifferent questions. However, theological despotism or prejudice won out."[9]

No study of Jansenism can be regarded as definitive until more is known about its sociology. Further investigation is badly needed in this area. Historians past and present have identified Jansenism with particular social groups, but their findings are inconclusive. Sainte-Beuve wrote that "Port Royal was the religious enterprise of the upper-middle class in France,"[10] that group better known as the *noblesse de robe*. More recently, Lucien Goldmann and his pupils have associated Jansenism with the magistracy. For Goldmann the tragic vision inherent in Jansenism reflected the declining fortunes of that group during the reigns of Louis XIII and Louis XIV.[11] The identification of Jansenism with the sovereign courts is based upon the fact that a number of prominent Jansenists came from robe families. Furthermore, the Parlement of Paris in particular appeared to defend Jansenism from time to time, as when it objected to *Ad sacram* in 1657 and when it strenuously objected to *Unigenitus*. Yet there were many magistrates who were unsympathetic and even hostile to Jansenism. The Parlement of Paris's opposition to the encyclicals was based, not on sympathy for the followers of Saint-Cyran, but on Gallican prejudices that caused suspicion of any command emanating from Rome.[12]

Other historians have attempted to establish a connection between Jansenist belief and the bourgeois ethic. Bernard Groethuysen has argued that Jansenism was diametrically opposed to the ideals and aspirations of the bourgeoisie. In his opinion, the ethical precepts of the Jesuits were more accommodating to middle class interests, in that Jesuit confessors were more favorably disposed toward capitalistic enterprise and their image of a reasonable God was more suitable to the bourgeois point of view.[13] There are historians, on the other hand, who have suggested that there were certain affinities between Jansenism and the bourgeois ethic. The individualism inherent in Jansenist thought, particularly with respect to reason and conscience, was likely to find favor within the middle class, as was the Jansenist emphasis on self-discipline and moral fortitude.[14]

The leading Jansenist spokesmen, to be sure, were of the *noblesse de robe* or from bourgeois social groups of one sort or another. Saint-Cyran's family, the Duvergiers of Bayonne, had played an important role in the affairs of that city throughout the sixteenth century and should be included in "the aristocracy of the middle class." The Arnauld family was of the robe, as were the Marions, the family of Catherine Arnauld. Pascal, Jean Domat, and Le Nain de Tillemont were all members of families with close ties to the magistracy. Nicole, Quesnel, and Duguet were of bourgeois origin. The fathers of Nicole and Duguet were lawyers, and the father of Quesnel was a bookseller. Yet the social background of these writers was not significantly different from that of most writers in the seventeenth century, for which reason it would be wrong to think of them as spokesmen for a broad social group. Certainly Jansenism appealed to those social groups, which were highly literate and were favorably disposed toward sound educational principles. Daughters of robe families were admitted to Port Royal, and their brothers to the Little Schools. The writings of Saint-Cyran and the *New Testament of Mons* were to be found in the libraries of merchants alongside the *Ordonnance du Commerce* and accounting manuals.[15] The Cartesian element within Jansenism—with its emphasis on the clear and distinct idea—as well as the Jansenist emphasis on the development of sound judgment may well have appealed to the bourgeois mentality. The sharp distinction between the realms of nature and of grace, each with a different set of operative principles, may have been attractive to those in search of greater precision of thought.

The fact that there were elements within Jansenism that may have appealed to pragmatists is a further indication that Jansenism was not entirely unconcerned with worldly affairs. Yet Jansenism understandably appealed to those for whom the world had little to offer. Among the friends of Port Royal were prominent nobles who had been involved in the Fronde. Were these notables attracted to the tragic vision contained in Jansenism because of the failure of their earthly aspirations? The question applies as well to the Jansenist bishop of Agde, Louis Foucquet, whose ambitions were thwarted when in 1661 Louis XIV arrested his brother Nicolas, *surintendant de finance*, for crimes against the state. Louis Foucquet was in Rome at the time, buying art treasures to embellish Nicolas's magnificent estate, Vaux-le-Vicomte.[16] Very likely these proud subjects of the king found spiritual solace in the Jansenist rejection of worldly interests in favor of total commitment to God. Paul Bénichou has argued that Jansenism was antithetical to the values of the nobility because it helped to undermine the heroic ideal of the *noblesse d'épée* by stressing the depravity of the human condition. Whereas French nobles pursued glory as a means of satisfying their honor, the Jansenists protested that such manifestations of pride were sinful in the extreme. The heroic ideals expressed in the drama of Corneille, a former pupil of the Jesuits, were diametrically opposed to the ideals of the Jansenists.[17] Yet a thoughtful analysis of Jansenism indicates that in fact the Jansenists substituted one kind of heroic ideal for another. For the quest for glory in this world, the Jansenists substituted a quest for glory in the next. Because the pursuit of divine glory involved suffering and persecution on earth, the Jansenists acted heroically in the eyes of many of their admirers then and since. The courage of the nobleman on the battlefield or in a duel was matched by the courage of the nuns of Port Royal as they resisted the commands of the archbishop. This inverted heroic ideal implicit in Jansenist action and belief may also explain its appeal to frustrated nobles. Furthermore, by ostentatiously associating with Port Royal, the antithesis of the king's court, great nobles like the duchesse de Longueville and the duc de Luynes were able to maintain a degree of detachment and independence that prevented them from becoming entirely absorbed in the king's entourage. Their *frondeur* spirit was sustained in a subtle way by virtue of their being friends of Port Royal.

The clergy was, of course, deeply affected by Jansenism. Only a handful of bishops and abbots were involved in it, because most of them lacked the commitment to religious reform or did not wish to challenge king and pope. It was among the lower clergy that Jansenism had a strong impact. Many curés in Paris and elsewhere resented the prestige and influence of the regular clergy, and especially that of the Jesuits. Many applauded the Jansenist assault on laxist ethics. The newly established seminaries improved the quality of parish priests, and some, like the one at Beauvais, exposed seminarians to Jansenist writings. Many priests appreciated the Jansenist exaltation of their office, as well as the insistence of some Jansenists, toward the end of the century, on a greater role for the lower clergy in the governance of the Church. The influence of Jansenism on the lower clergy continued into the eighteenth century and was a factor in the development of a revolutionary zeal by some priests resentful of their deteriorating economic condition and the widening gap between upper and lower clergy.[18]

Jansenism was a movement in opposition to authority of one sort or another throughout much of the seventeenth century. Its emphasis on the spiritual and intellectual integrity of the individual ran counter to the spirit of absolutism that prevailed in Church and state. In his *Lettre sur la constance et le courage*, the abbé Le Roy declared that the Christian who had overcome his worldly ambitions and placed himself entirely at God's disposal was capable of making kings tremble.[19] The *Frondeur* mentality that became fully developed among the Port-royalists during the 1650s is clearly reflected in this statement. Yet this elitist aspect of Jansenism made it virtually impossible for it to become a popular

religious movement in the seventeenth century. Its emphasis on
literacy prevented the vast majority of the king's subjects from
acquiring that enlightened spirituality that characterized the belief
of Saint-Cyran and his followers. Its austere ethic was unattractive
to many from all walks of life who believed that some accommodation was both possible and necessary between their religious
obligations and their worldly interests. Because Jansenism was
elitist and because it placed the interest of the individual above the
interests of society, it discouraged that missionary zeal that
enabled Calvinism to transform whole communities. For the Jansenists, the world was a place where God's elect should suffer
rather than a place that might be transformed into a community
of saints.

If Jansenism had been a movement that appealed only to
isolated individuals, it would very likely not have survived as long
as it did. There were, however, certain ideals and principles embodied in the movement that enabled it to become associated with
other movements and groups and that broadened its appeal. His
dévot ideals brought Saint-Cyran into contact with powerful
nobles and statemen who opposed Richelieu and his policies.
Although the cardinal-minister maintained the upper hand in his
struggle with the *dévots*, he was never able to destroy them. The
dévot opposition, with which the disciples of Saint-Cyran remained
affiliated, managed to survive and to flare up during the Fronde
and during the last tragic decades of Louis XIV's reign. The Jansenist exaltation of the role of the priest attracted significant
elements within the lower clergy, whose prerogatives were
threatened by the regular clergy, by bishops and popes, and by
the crown. The Richerist element within Jansenism sustained the
embattled lower clergy from the middle of the seventeenth century
to the Revolution of 1789. It was its Gallicanist sympathies more
than anything else that brought Jansenism into association with
powerful interests capable of protecting the movement at critical
times. The principles of episcopal Gallicanism caused Jansenists to
defend the rights of Cardinal de Retz, who in turn protected them
when he was at the height of his power. Episcopal intervention
prevented Louis XIV from suppressing defiant Port Royal in the
1660s and helped to bring about the Peace of the Church. Episco-

pal Gallicanism linked Cardinal Noailles and the Jansenists during the crisis over *Unigenitus* and contributed to the survival of the movement into the eighteenth century. Finally, because the Jansenists asserted fundamental principles of royal Gallicanism in opposition to the ultramontanist pretensions of the papacy, they eventually became associated with the parlements, traditional bastions of royal Gallicanism. The quarrel over the reception of *Unigenitus* became a significant political issue in the eighteenth century, because parlementary opposition became stronger and the crown weaker after the death of Louis XIV. The encyclical appeared to the sovereign courts as a threat to the integrity of the kingdom, and their resistance to it also contributed to the survival of Jansenism long after the destruction of Port Royal.

NOTES

BIBLIOGRAPHY

INDEX

Notes

Notes to Preface

1. Voltaire's attitude toward the Jansenists is expressed, among other places, in his *Siècle de Louis XIV* and in his *Lettres philosophiques*. Diderot's are to be found in his *Pensées philosophiques*.
2. For Joseph De Maistre's attitude toward the Jansenists, see *De l'église gallicane*, pp. 27-33, 95-102. Other expressions of conservative distaste for Jansenism include A. Fuzet, *Les jansénistes du XVIIe siècle: Leur histoire et leur dernier historien, M. Sainte-Beuve*; Pierre Varin, *La verité sur les Arnauld*; and Léon Séché, *Les derniers jansénistes depuis la ruine de Port-Royal jusqu'à nos jours*.
3. See, for example, Abbé Henri Grégoire, *Les ruines de Port-Royal*; Victor Cousin, *Jacqueline Pascal*; and Ernest Renan, *Nouvelles études d'histoire religieuse*, pp. 459-74.
4. From an unpublished draft of the preface to *Port-Royal*, quoted in Victor Giraud, *Port-Royal et Sainte-Beuve*, p. 56. Unless otherwise indicated, all English translations are mine.
5. C.-A. Sainte-Beuve, *Port-Royal*, 1:88, 746.
6. Ferdinand Brunetière, "Jansénistes et cartésiens," in *Etudes critiques sur l'histoire de la littérature française*, 4:111-78. For an interesting discussion of Brunetière's ideas about the origins of the Enlightenment, see Ira O. Wade, *The Intellectual Origins of the French Enlightenment*, pp. 32-36.
7. Similar opinions about Jansenism are to be found in two books by Henri de Lubac, *Surnatural* and *Augustinianism and Modern Theology*, as well as in Ronald Knox, *Enthusiasm*, pp. 176-230.
8. Another historian who views the Jansenists as innocent victims of the oppressive policies of the French crown is Paule Jansen. See her *Le Cardinal Mazarin et le mouvement janséniste française, 1653-1659*.
9. Lucien Goldmann, "Remarques sur le jansénisme: La vision tragique du monde et la noblesse de robe," and *Le dieu caché*.

Notes to Chapter I

1. Vicomte d'Avenel, "Le clergé et la liberté de la conscience," p. 314.
2. Robert Mandrou, "Spiritualité et pratiques catholiques au XVIIe siècle."
3. For the impact of the Counter Reformation on France, see Léopold Willaert, *Après le concile de Trente: La restauration catholique, 1563-1648*; Louis Prunel, *La renaissance catholique en France au XVIIe siècle*; and especially Jean Orcibal, *Jean Duvergier de Hauranne, Abbé de Saint-Cyran et son temps*. The most complete study thus far of religious life in the region around Paris in the seventeenth century is Jeanne Ferté, *La vie religieuse dans les campagnes parisiènnes, 1622-1695*.
4. René Pintard, *Le libertinage érudit dans la première moitié du XVIIe siècle*, 1:522; Richard H. Popkin, *The History of Skepticism from Erasmus to Descartes*, pp. 89-112.

5. Quoted in René Bady, *L'Homme et son "Institution" de Montaigne à Bérulle*, p. 326.

6. Ibid., pp. 297-327.

7. For extensive discussion of the "optimistic" view of human nature, see ibid.; Henri Brémond, *Histoire littéraire du sentiment religieux en France*, vol. 1; Antoine Adam, *Sur le problème religieux dans la première moitié du XVIIe siècle*; Louis Cognet, *Les origines de la spiritualité française au XVIIe siècle*; and Julien Eymard d'Angers, "Problèmes et difficultés de l'humanisme chrétienne (1600-1642)."

8. Letter written in 411 to Paulinus, bishop of Nola, quoted from Peter Brown, *Augustine of Hippo*, p. 355. A clear, succinct account of Augustine's quarrel with Pelagius is to be found in pp. 340-407 of this excellent biography.

9. Perry Miller describes "The Augustinian Strain of Piety" in *The New England Mind: The Seventeenth Century*, pp. 3-34.

10. Quoted in J. Dagens, *Bérulle et les origines de la restauration catholique*, p. 290.

11. For further discussion of the "pessimistic" view of human nature, see ibid.; Brémond, *Histoire littéraire du sentiment religieux*, vol. 2; Orcibal, *Saint-Cyran et son temps*; and Cognet, *Les origines de la spiritualité*.

12. For a comparison between the views of Saint Augustine and Saint Thomas Aquinas with respect to grace and free will, see Nigel Abercrombie, *The Origins of Jansenism*, pp. 113-86. Abercrombie's study constitutes the only major work on Jansenism in English. It is stronger on theological issues than on other aspects of the subject, and it is somewhat dated. For the medieval background to the question of justification by faith, see Heiko Oberman, ed., *Forerunners of the Reformation*, pp. 123-40.

13. For further discussion of the doctrinal controversies within the Catholic Church after the Council of Trent, see Abercrombie, *Origins of Jansenism*; Antoine Adam, *Du mysticisme à la révolte*; Louis Cognet, *Le jansénisme*; and Jan Miel, *Pascal and Theology*, pp. 1-63.

14. Popkin, *History of Skepticism*, p. 2.

15. Popkin's study, cited above, is valuable concerning seventeenth-century Pyrrhonism, as are Pintàrd, *Le libertinage érudit*, and J. S. Spink, *French Free Thought from Gassendi to Voltaire*.

16. Professor Roland Mousnier's brief description of the intellectual crisis is to be found in "Trevor-Roper's 'General Crisis' Symposium" in Trevor Aston, ed., *Crisis in Europe, 1560-1660*, pp. 103-4. For a more extensive discussion of the "crisis of the seventeenth century," see Theodore K. Rabb, *The Struggle for Stability in Early Modern Europe*.

17. For the reaction against the Scholastic tradition in French Protestant thought, see Brian G. Armstrong, *Calvinism and the Amyraut Heresy*.

18. Henri Gouhier, "La crise de la théologie au temps de Descartes."

19. For episcopal Gallicanism, see V. Martin, *Le gallicanisme politique et le clergé de France*, and Adam, *Du mysticisme à la révolte*, pp. 22-27.

20. For a description of Richerism, see E. Préclin, *Les jansénistes du XVIIIe siècle et la constitution civile du clergé*, pp. 2-4.

21. For the relationship between the crown and the assemblies of the clergy, see Pierre Blet, *Le clergé de France et la monarchie*.

22. For extensive discussion of the political ideals of the *dévots*, see Lionel Rothkrug, *Opposition to Louis XIV: The Political and Social Origins of the French Enlightenment*, pp. 3-131; Etiènne Thuau, *Raison d'état et pensée politique à l'époque de Richelieu*; especially William F. Church, *Richelieu and Reason of State*.

Notes to Chapter II

1. Quoted in Louis Cognet, *La réforme de Port-Royal, 1591-1618*, p. 74.

2. Ibid., pp. 116–17.

3. *Relation écrite par la Mère Angélique Arnauld sur Port-Royal*, ed. Louis Cognet, p. 114.

4. For the early history of Port Royal, see Sainte-Beuve, *Port-Royal*, vol. 1; Cognet, *La réforme de Port-Royal*; and *Relation écrite par la Mère Angélique*.

5. *Relation écrite par la Mère Angélique*.

6. Ibid., p. 100.

7. Ibid., p. 132.

8. Ibid., pp. 147–48.

9. Quoted in Orcibal, *Saint-Cyran et son temps*, p. 276.

10. Jean Orcibal, *Saint-Cyran et le jansénisme*, p. 6.

11. *Lettres inédites de Saint-Cyran*, ed. Annie Barnes, pp. 169–70.

12. Ibid., p. 57.

13. Orcibal, *Saint-Cyran et son temps*, p. 347.

14. Quoted in Sainte-Beuve, *Port-Royal*, 1:398.

15. Louis Cognet, "Le mépris du monde à Port-Royal et dans le jansénisme."

16. Jean Racine, *Abrégé de l'histoire de Port-Royal*, p. 31.

17. Quoted in G. Pagès, "Autour du 'Grand Orage': Richelieu et Marillac, deux politiques," p. 66.

18. Quoted from Church, *Richelieu and Reason of State*, pp. 203–4.

19. *Mars Gallicus* is summarized in ibid., pp. 385–90.

20. Orcibal, *Saint-Cyran et son temps*, p. 499n.

21. Saint-Cyran, *Oeuvres chrestiennes et spirituelles*, 2:210.

22. The "Vie d'Abraham" appears in *Lettres inédites de Saint-Cyran*, pp. 379–421.

23. Ibid., pp. 412, 389, 394–95, 411.

24. For Saint-Cyran's writings on contrition, see Jean Orcibal, *La spiritualité de Saint-Cyran avec ses écrits de piété inédits*, pp. 275–387. For the historical background of the contritionist controversy, see H. Dondaine, *L'Attrition suffisante*.

25. Richelieu, *Instruction du chrestien*, pp. 431–44.

26. Richelieu, *Traitté de la perfection du chrestien*, p. 83.

27. Other works in defense of the attritionist position include Antoine Sirmond, S.J., *La deffense de la vertu*, and Isaac Habert, *La deffense de la foy de l'église*, pp. 63–71.

28. V. Tapié, *La France de Richelieu et Louis XIII*, pp. 129–243.

29. René Rapin, *Histoire du jansénisme depuis ses origines jusqu'en 1644*, p. 377.

30. *Mémoires de Godefroi Hermant, Docteur de Sorbonne, sur l'histoire ecclésiastique du XVIIe siècle (1630–1663)*, ed. Augustin Gazier, 1:82.

31. Quoted in J. Laferrière, *Etude sur Jean Duvergier de Hauranne, Abbé de Saint-Cyran*, p. 169.

32. Jean Orcibal, *Port-Royal entre le miracle et l'obéissance*, pp. 13–32.

33. Saint-Cyran, *Oeuvres chrestiennes et spirituelles*, 4:6.

34. The human condition before and after Adam's fall is described in Saint-Cyran's essay "De la grace de Jésus-Christ, de la liberté chrétienne, et de la justification," in Orcibal, *La spiritualité de Saint-Cyran*, pp. 233–41.

35. Saint-Cyran, *Oeuvres chrestiennes et spirituelles*, 4:9–10.

36. For an informative discussion on this point, see Miel, *Pascal and Theology*, pp. 64–107.

37. Orcibal, *La spiritualité de Saint-Cyran*, pp. 88–89.

38. Quoted in Claude Lancelot, *Mémoires touchant la vie de M. de Saint-Cyran par M. Lancelot pour servir d'éclaircissement à l'histoire de Port-Royal*, 2:106–7.

39. *Lettres chrestiennes et spirituelles de Messire Jean Du Verger de Hauranne, Abbé de Saint-Cyran*, ed. Robert Arnauld d'Andilly, 2:646.

40. Orcibal, *La spiritualité de Saint-Cyran*, p. 282.

41. Quoted in Sainte-Beuve, *Port-Royal*, 3:495.

42. Pascal, *Pensées*, ed. and trans. A. J. Krailsheimer, p. 60.

43. Ibid., pp. 38, 169.

44. *Lettres de la Mère Angélique Arnauld, Abbèsse et Réformatrice de Port-Royal*, 1:97.

45. *Lettres chrestiennes et spirituelles de Saint-Cyran*, 1:189.

46. Quoted in *Recueil de plusieurs pièces pour servir à l'histoire de Port-Royal*, 2:206. Hereafter referred to as *Recueil*, Utrecht.

47. *Lettres chrestiennes et spirituelles de Saint-Cyran*, 2:189.

48. *Lettres inédites de Saint-Cyran*, p. 45.

49. Ibid., pp. 290–91.

50. *Traité de la comédie de Pierre Nicole*, ed. G. Couton, p. 72.

51. *Lettres chrestiennes et spirituelles de Saint-Cyran*, 2:459.

52. Ibid., 1:10.

53. Ibid., 1:40

54. Ibid., 2:249.

55. *Choix de lettres inédites de Louis-Isaac Le Maistre de Sacy (1650–1683)*, ed. Geneviève Delasseault, pp. 38–39.

56. Orcibal, *La spiritualité de Saint-Cyran*, pp. 445–46.

57. *Lettres inédites de Le Maistre de Sacy*, p. 20.

58. Singlin letter, n.d., ms. vol. 15, Bibliothèque des Amis de Port-Royal.

59. Richelieu, *Traitté de la perfection du chrestien*, pp. 357–58.

60. Quoted in Lanfranc de Panthou, *Richelieu et la direction des âmes*, p. 27.

61. *Lettres chrestiennes et spirituelles de M. de Saint-Cyran qui n'ont point été imprimées jusqu'à present*, 1:17. Hereafter referred to as *Lettres chrestiennes et spirituelles de Saint-Cyran* (1744).

62. Quoted in Sainte-Beuve, *Port-Royal*, 1:457.

63. *Lettres chrestiennes et spirituelles de Saint-Cyran* (1744), 1:58.

64. *Oeuvres chrestiennes et spirituelles de Saint-Cyran*, 1:180.

65. *Lettres chrestiennes et spirituelles de Saint-Cyran* (1744), 1:68, 191.

66. Orcibal, *La spiritualité de Saint-Cyran*, p. 202.

67. *Lettres chrestiennes et spirituelles de Saint-Cyran* (1744), 1:277.

68. Singlin to Angélique Arnauld, April 18, 1645, ms. vol. 15, Bibliothèque des Amis de Port-Royal.

69. *Lettres chrestiennes et spirituelles de Saint-Cyran* (1744), 1:711.

70. Ibid., 2:170–71.

71. *Lettres chrestiennes et spirituelles de Saint-Cyran*, 2:520.

72. Cécile Gazier, *Ces messieurs de Port-Royal*, pp. 199–204; Orcibal, *Saint-Cyran et le jansénisme*, pp. 39–46.

73. *Mémoires de Godefroi Hermant*, 1:189–90.

74. For details of Saint-Cyran's life see Lancelot, *Mémoires*; Jean Laporte, *Saint-Cyran*; and especially Orcibal, *Saint-Cyran et son temps* and *Saint-Cyran et le jansénisme*.

75. *The Political Testament of Cardinal Richelieu*, ed. and trans. Henry B. Hill, pp. 35–36, 69–70.

Notes to Chapter III

1. Lancelot, *Mémoires*, 2:106-7. For the relationship between Jansenius and Saint-Cyran, see *La Correspondance de Jansenius*, ed. Jean Orcibal; Orcibal, *Saint-Cyran et le jansénisme*, pp. 46-50; and Adam, *Du mysticisme*, pp. 69-79.

2. An excellent summary of the *Augustinus* is to be found in Abercrombie, *The Origins of Jansenism*.

3. *Lettres inédites de Saint-Cyran*, p. 127.

4. Antoine Arnauld, *De la fréquente communion*, p. v.

5. Ibid., p. iii.

6. Ibid., p. 136.

7. Ibid., p. 89.

8. Ibid., p. 353.

9. J. Gallerand, "Le jansénisme en Blésois: Le conflit entre le P. Brisacier et Jean Callaghan."

10. For a thorough analysis of the theological issues involved in the quarrels over the *Augustinus* and *De la fréquente communion*, see Cognet, *Le jansénisme*, pp. 51-54; *Mémoires de Godefroi Hermant*, vol. 1; and especially A. de Meyer, *Les premières controverses jansénistes en France, 1640-1649*.

11. "La Vie de Monsieur Pascal écrite par Madame Périer, sa soeur" in Pascal, *Oeuvres complètes*, ed. Jacques Chevalier, p. 27.

12. Racine, *Abrégé de l'histoire de Port-Royal*, pp. 91-92.

13. Ibid., p. 121.

14. Arnauld Family Papers, ms. 6549, Bibliothèque de l'Arsenal.

15. Arnauld Family Papers, ms. 6620, Bibliothèque de l'Arsenal.

16. "Avis à la reine," Arnauld Family Papers, ms. 6034, Bibliothèque de l'Arsenal.

17. "Mémoire pour un souverain," Arnauld Family Papers, ms. 6034, Bibliothèque de l'Arsenal.

18. *Choix de Mazarinades*, ed. C. Moreau (Paris, 1853) 2:434-35.

19. Tom T. Edwards, in a Ph.D. dissertation at Harvard University entitled "Jansenism in Church and State" (1960), attributes the authorship of *La vérité toute nue* to Arnauld d'Andilly because of the copy found among his papers with his handwriting. I examined this evidence at the Arsenal but was not entirely convinced that it definitely linked Arnauld d'Andilly to the pamphlet. I discussed the matter with René Pintard, who put me in touch with a student of his, Hubert Carrier, who was completing an exhaustive study of the *Mazarinades*. It was Carrier who discovered the copy of *La vérité toute nue* attributed to Arnauld d'Andilly in Leningrad, as well as the "Avis charitable au Sieur Dandilly" in the Cabinet des Manuscrits at the Bibliothèque Nationale. Carrier discusses the evidence in detail in a recent article, "Port-Royal et la Fronde: Deux Mazarinades inconnues d'Arnauld d'Andilly." In this article he concludes that both *La vérité toute nue* and *Avis d'état* were written by Arnauld d'Andilly. On the basis of his findings and of my own research into the political opinions of the Jansenists, I am inclined to agree with him. I believe that more scholarship needs to be applied to the connection between *dévot* idealism and the Fronde.

20. Arnauld d'Andilly's correspondence with the court is discussed in chapter 4.

21. Arnauld Family Papers, ms. 6034, Bibliothèque de l'Arsenal.

22. For the details of de Retz's life, see J. H. M. Salmon, *Cardinal de Retz*.

23. Richard M. Golden, "The Godly Rebellion: Parisian *Curés* and the Religious Fronde, 1652-1662," Ph.D. dissertation, the Johns Hopkins University (1974), pp. 256-323.

24. My discussion of the religious Fronde is based entirely on Golden's important study, cited above.

25. Ibid., p. 19.

26. Ibid., introduction. Salmon employs the term "ecclesiastical Fronde" in *Cardinal de Retz*.

27. Jansen, *Le Cardinal Mazarin*, p. 134.

28. Mazarin's policy toward the Jansenists is discussed in the work cited in note 27. I do not entirely agree with Jansen's thesis that Mazarin cynically and cold-bloodedly exploited the Jansenists in order to improve his relations with the papacy, despite the fact that he did not regard the Port-royalists as a threat. It is my contention that Mazarin regarded Port Royal as a threat because of traditional government suspicion of the Port Royal circle during times of political crisis and because, as Golden shows (in the work cited above), Mazarin was well aware of the connection between Port Royal and the religious Fronde in Paris.

29. The five propositions are to be found, among other places, in Cognet, *Le jansénisme*, pp. 50–51.

30. "Le petit catéchisme de M. de Saint-Cyran," in Orcibal, *La spiritualité de Saint-Cyran*, pp. 152-60.

31. Ibid., p. 236.

32. Antoine Arnauld, *Seconde apologie de M. Jansenius, evesque d'Ipres*, p. 290.

33. *Oeuvres de Messire Antoine Arnauld, docteur de la maison et société de Sorbonne*, 10:615–16.

34. Antoine Arnauld, *Apologie de M. Jansenius, evesque d'Ipres* (Paris, 1644), pp. 96–99.

35. Arnauld, *Oeuvres*, 17:718.

36. Pasquier Quesnel, *La foy et l'innocence du clergé de Hollande*, pp. 28–29.

37. Quoted in P. Jansen, *Le Cardinal Mazarin*, p. 41.

38. Ibid., pp. 80–100.

39. Léonard de Marandé, *Inconvéniens d'estat procedans du jansénisme*, p. 12.

40. Ibid., pp. 49, 58.

41. Ibid., p. 115.

42. The impact of the English Civil War on France is the subject of Philip A. Knachel, *England and the Fronde: The Impact of the English Civil War and Revolution on France*.

43. Arnauld Family Papers, ms. 6034, Bibliothèque de l'Arsenal.

44. Blet, *Le clergé de France et la monarchie*, 2:220.

45. For the role of the Parlement of Paris in the campaign against Jansenism during the 1650s, see Albert N. Hamscher's forthcoming article in the *Catholic Historical Review* entitled "Jansenism and the Parlement of Paris after the Fronde: An Evaluation of the Social Interpretation of Early French Jansenism." I am endebted to Professor Hamscher for allowing me to see a typescript of the article.

46. Quoted from ibid.

Notes to Chapter IV

1. Bernard Chedozeau, "Les années de jeunesse de Pierre Nicole et son entrée a Port-Royal."

2. Pascal, *Pensées*, trans. Krailsheimer, p. 309.

3. For details of Pascal's life, see Jean Mesnard, *Pascal*.

4. Paule Jansen, ed., *Arnauld d'Andilly, défenseur de Port-Royal, 1654–59: Sa correspondance inédite avec la cour conservée dans les archives du ministère des affaires etrangères*, pp. 11–31. In her introduction to this volume, Jansen reiterates some of the themes that she developed in her *Le Cardinal Mazarin et le mouvement janséniste française*, most particularly that the Port-royalists were innocent victims of the deceitful cardinal-minister. She fails to take into account their *Frondeur* mentality, which is described in this chapter.

5. Ibid., p. 56.

6. Ibid., p. 62.

7. Ibid., pp. 85, 810.

8. Pascal, *Provincial Letters*, ed. and trans. W. F. Trotter, p. 357.

9. Ibid., p. 362.

10. Ibid., p. 461.

11. François Annat, *Résponse aux lettres provinciales*, pp. 183, 193–94.

12. Pascal, *Oeuvres complètes*, pp. 915, 919.

13. Ibid., p. 924.

14. Richard Golden, "The Mentality of Opposition: The Jansenism of the Parisian *Curés*." I am grateful to Professor Golden for providing me with a typescript of this paper.

15. [Antoine Le Maistre], *Lettre d'un avocat au parlement à un de ses amis*, p. 2.

16. Ibid., p. 6.

17. Hamscher, "Jansenism and the Parlement of Paris."

18. Quoted in Lancelot, *Mémoires*, 1:39.

19. Quoted in Bruno Neveu, *Un historien à l'école de Port-Royal: Sébastien Le Nain de Tillemont, 1637–1698*, p. 247.

20. Pierre Nicole, *Essais de morale*, 2:302.

21. Ibid., 2:277.

22. Pierre Cousetel, *Les règles de l'éducation des enfants*, 2:73–104.

23. Ibid., 1:57, 33. There is no evidence that I know of that Locke read Coustel's work. He was, however, familiar with Nicole's work. For further details on life and study at the Little Schools, see H. C. Barnard, *The Little Schools of Port Royal*, and Louis Cognet, "Les petites écoles de Port-Royal."

24. *Lettres inédites de Saint-Cyran*, p. 57.

25. Jansenius, *De la réformation de l'homme intèrieur*, pp. 50–51.

26. Mesnard, *Pascal*, p. 31.

27. Pascal, *Pensées*, trans. Krailsheimer, p. 42.

28. Ibid., pp. 38–42.

29. Ibid., p. 40.

30. Jansenius, *De la réformation de l'homme intérieur*, pp. 49–50.

31. Pascal, *Pensées*, pp. 121–27. For an example of Sacy's proofs, see Geneviève Delasseault, *La pensée janséniste en dehors de Pascal*, pp. 43–48.

32. Pascal, *Pensées*, trans. Krailsheimer, p. 83.

33. Ibid., p. 83.

34. Ibid., p. 84.

35. Ibid., p. 83.

36. Nicolas Fontaine, *Mémoires pour servir à l'histoire de Port-Royal*, 2:53–54.

37. Fontaine's account is most likely based upon fragments of conversations between Pascal and Le Maistre de Sacy. See Geneviève Delasseault, *Le Maistre de Sacy et son temps*, pp. 61–79.

38. Pascal, *Oeuvres complètes*, p. 560. The entire text of Fontaine's account of the conversation is to be found in that edition of Pascal's works, pp. 560–72.

39. Ibid., pp. 563, 565, 572.

40. Pascal, *Pensées*, trans. Krailsheimer, p. 65.

41. See Fontaine, *Mémoires*, 2:53–56. See also Jean Orcibal, "Descartes et sa philosophie jugés à l'hôtel Liancourt;" and Geneviève Lewis, "Augustinisme et cartésianisme à Port-Royal."

42. Arnauld, *Oeuvres*, 38:37.

43. Quoted in ibid., 14:626. I have used the English translation of this passage by Elizabeth S. Haldane and G. R. T. Ross in Haldane and Ross, eds., *The Philosophical Works of Descartes* (New York, 1955), p. 253.

44. Arnauld, *Oeuvres*, 38:105–9.

45. Ibid., 38:113–16.

46. Ibid., 3:425.

47. Fontaine, *Mémoires*, 2:55.

48. Ibid., 2:53.

49. For Vaucel's critique of Descartes, see Lewis, "Augustinisme et cartésianisme à Port-Royal."

50. Pascal, *Pensées*, pp. 300, 355.

51. For an intelligent discussion of Descartes's influence on Pascal, see Mesnard, *Pascal*, pp. 171–73.

52. In discussing the *Port Royal Logic*, I have used a recently published American edition translated by James Dickoff and Patricia James. See Antoine Arnauld, *The Art of Thinking.*

53. Ibid., p. 7.

54. Ibid., p. 7.

55. Ibid., p. 26.

56. Ibid., p. 28.

57. Ibid., p. 340.

58. Ibid., p. 10; Pascal. *Pensées*, p. 83.

59. Antoine Arnauld, *The Art of Thinking*, pp. 12, 21, 29.

60. Ibid., p. 38.

61. Ibid., p. 66.

62. Ibid., p. 99.

63. Claude Lancelot and Antoine Arnauld, *Grammaire générale et raisonnée*, p. 4.

64. Arnauld, *The Art of Thinking*, p. 175.

65. Ibid., pp. 286–87.

66. Ibid., p. 288.

67. Ibid., p. 289.

68. Ibid., pp. 287, 290.

69. Ibid., p. 204.

70. Ibid., pp. 12–13.

71. Ibid., p. 147.

72. Ibid., pp. 150–51.

73. Arnauld, *Oeuvres*, 23:54.

74. Arnauld, *Apologie de M. Jansenius*, p. 359.

75. Pascal, *Oeuvres complètes*, p. 510.

76. *Lettres inédites de Saint-Cyran*, p. 192.

77. Nicole, *Essais de morale*, 6:3.

78. *Lettres chrestiennes et spirituelles de Saint-Cyran*, 1:193.

79. Orcibal, *La spiritualité de Saint-Cyran*, p. 493.
80. *Lettres de la Mère Angélique*, 1:214.
81. Arnauld, *Oeuvres*, 13:665.
82. Arnauld, *De la fréquente communion*, p. 5.
83. Pascal, *Oeuvres complètes*, p. 509.
84. Quoted in Neveu, *Un historien à l'école de Port-Royal*, p. 190.
85. *Lettres chrestiennes et spirituelles de Saint-Cyran* (1744), 1:504-5.
86. Ibid., 1:586.
87. *La correspondance de Martin de Barcos, Abbé de Saint-Cyran*, ed. Lucien Goldmann, pp. 71, 147.
88. Quoted in Racine, *Abrégé de l'histoire de Port-Royal*, p. 131.
89. Ms. vol. 6, pp. 11-12, Bibliothèque de la Société de Port-Royal.
90. Quesnel, *Réflexions morales*, 1:14.
91. *Lettres inédites de Saint-Cyran*, p. 256.

Notes to Chapter V

1. *Louis XIV: Mémoires for the Instruction of the Dauphin*, ed. and trans. Paul Sonnino, p. 25.
2. Ibid., p. 54.
3. The text of the formulary may be found in Marc Escholier, *Port-Royal*, p. 391.
4. Arnauld, *Oeuvres*, 10:705.
5. Ibid., 10:706-15.
6. Ibid., 19:6.
7. Arnauld, *Apologie de M. Jansenius*, p. 2.
8. *Seconde lettre de M. Arnauld, docteur de Sorbonne à un duc et pair de France*, pp. 139, 141-42.
9. Arnauld, *Oeuvres*, 1:124.
10. Ibid., 20:5-17.
11. Ibid., 21:49.
12. Ibid., 21:23.
13. Quoted in Charles Clemencet, *Histoire générale de Port-Royal*, 1:351.
14. Pascal, *Oeuvres complètes*, p. 899.
15. Golden, "The Mentality of Opposition: the Jansenism of the Parisian *Curés*."
16. These points of view have been identified by Lucien Goldmann in his book *Le dieu caché* and in his introduction to *La correspondance de Barcos*, pp. 1-62. Goldmann rightly relates the essence of Jansenism to the crisis over the signature, because it was by means of the crisis that the Jansenists were forced to assert their respective positions concerning authority.
17. *Lettres de la Mère Angélique*, 3:527-28.
18. Quoted in Racine, *Abrégé de l'histoire de Port-Royal*, pp. 132-33.
19. *La correspondance de Barcos*, pp. 180-212.
20. Ibid., p. 120.
21. Ibid., pp. 258, 326.
22. Ibid., p. 342.
23. Ibid., p. 566.
24. *Divers actes, lettres, et relations des religieuses de Port-Royal du Saint-Sacrement touchant au sujet de la signature du formulaire*, vol. 1. All references to this work are to volume number only, because it is not paginated.

25. Quoted in Mesnard, *Pascal*, p. 132.

26. Ibid., pp. 125–34.

27. Guillaume Le Roy, *Lettre sur la constance et le courage qu'on doit avoir pour la vérité*, pp. 1–33.

28. Quoted in G. Namer, *L'Abbé Le Roy et ses amis*, p. 127.

29. Ibid., pp. 127–33.

30. Arnauld, *Oeuvres*, 1:250.

31. Ibid., 1:405, 412.

32. Pierre Nicole, *De la foy humaine*, 2:1.

33. Hereafter referred to as *Relations*.

34. The confrontation between the nuns and the archbishop is the subject of a play by Henry de Montherlant entitled *Port-Royal*, first performed at the Comédie Française in 1954. I first became interested in Jansenism when I saw the play at that time.

35. Quoted in Orcibal, *Port-Royal entre le miracle et l'obéissance*, p. 56.

36. Orcibal's work, cited above, attempts to distinguish between the psychological attitudes of Flavie Passart and Angélique de Saint-Jean d'Andilly. It provides an interesting account of Flavie's transformation from resistance to obedience.

37. "Relation de la Soeur Marie-Angélique de Sainte-Therese Arnauld d'Andilly," *Relations*, vol. 1.

38. "Relation de la Soeur Madeleine de Sainte-Candide le Cerf," *Relations*, vol. 1.

39. Sainte-Beuve, *Port-Royal*, 2:742, 743.

40. "Relations de la Soeur Christine Madeleine," *Relations*, vol. 1.

41. Ibid.

42. Ibid.

43. "Relation de la captivité de la Mère Angélique de Saint-Jean d'Andilly," *Relations*, vol. 1, See also Sainte-Beuve, *Port-Royal*, 2:703–47.

44. Letter 7 from Angélique de Saint-Jean to Antoine Arnauld, *Relations*, vol. 1.

45. Ibid.

46. Arnauld, *Oeuvres*, 23:218. Arnauld also discusses the importance of properly assessing historical evidence in the *Port Royal Logic*.

47. Ibid., 23:384.

48. Ibid., 24:412, 412–14.

49. *Choix de lettres inédites de Le Maistre de Sacy*, p. 117.

50. Arnauld Family Papers, ms. 6024, Bibliothèque de l'Arsenal.

51. Quoted in Claude Cochin, *Henri Arnauld, Evêque d'Angers (1597–1692)*, p. 380.

52. Quoted in P. Brouton, *La réforme pastorale en France au XVIIe siècle*, p. 202.

53. Quoted in ibid., p. 407.

Notes to Chapter VI

1. For a description of the various editions of the *Pensées*, see Mesnard, *Pascal*, pp. 136–48.

2. Nicole, *Essais de morale*, 1:22, 18.

3. Ibid., 5:74–85.

4. Ibid., 2:24, 3–10.

5. Ibid., 2:54–63.

6. Ibid., 3:132.

7. Ibid., 2:159, 3:165.

8. Nicole, *Les visionnaires*, p. 295.

9. Nicole, *Essais de morale*, 3:104–42.

10. Ibid., 1:28.

11. Ibid., 1:439.

12. Ibid., 6:205.

13. Fonds français nouvelles acquisitions 43333, p. 99, Bibliothèque Nationale.

14. Pasquier Quesnel, *Abrégé de la morale de l'évangile*, pp. 533, 143, 409.

15. The quarrel over Quesnel's edition of St. Leo's works is set forth in J. A. G. Tans and H. Schmitz du Moulin, eds., *Pasquier Quesnel devant la congrégation de l'Index.* See the introduction, pp. vii–xlv, and pp. 21, 24, 68.

16. Arnauld, *Oeuvres*, 32:103.

17. Quoted in Bruno Neveu, *Sébastien Joseph du Cambout de Pontchâteau (1634-1690) et ses missions à Rome*, p. 489.

18. Arnauld Family Papers, ms. 6034, Bibliothèque de l'Arsenal.

19. Nicole, *Essais de morale*, 7:220.

20. Ibid., 7:204, 205.

21. Ibid., 7:206.

22. *Lettres du feu M. Nicole*, 2:258.

23. Letter included in ibid., 2:262, 267.

24. Ibid., 2:268–70.

25. Ibid., 2:277.

26. Arnauld Family Papers, ms. 6034, Bibliothèque de l'Arsenal.

27. Arnauld, *Oeuvres*, 2:725.

28. Ibid., 3:558.

29. Ibid., 38:96. In this work, Arnauld undertook to refute the ideas set forth in a pamphlet by A. le Moine, *Traité de l'essence du corps.*

30. Arnauld, *Oeuvres*, 38:95.

31. Ibid., 38:95–99.

32. Coustel, *Les règles de l'éducation des enfants*, 2:249–50.

33. Arnauld, *Oeuvres*, 38:98. The italics are Arnauld's.

34. Orcibal, *Saint-Cyran et son temps*, pp. 352–54.

35. *Mémoires de Godefroi Hermant*, 2:237–38.

36. Arnauld, *Oeuvres*, 37:10.

37. Ibid., 1:470–71.

38. Ibid., 11:366–68.

39. Ibid., 10:731.

40. Ibid., 37:682–91.

41. Orcibal, *Saint-Cyran et son temps*, pp. 353, 354–56.

42. Arnauld, *Oeuvres*, 30:178–81.

43. Pasquier Quesnel, *Nouveau testament en français avec des réflexions morales sur chaque verset*, 4:697, 605. Hereafter referred to as *Réflexions morales.*

44. Pasquier Quesnel, *Justification des droits des chapitres de l'église des Provinces-Unis*, p. 172.

45. Quesnel, *Réflexions morales*, 1:84.

46. Pasquier Quesnel, *La discipline de l'église tirée du Nouveau Testament*, pp. 16–17.

47. Ibid., p. 85.

48. Quesnel, *Réflexions morales*, 4:176.

49. Quesnel, *La discipline de l'église*, p. 17.

50. *Correspondance de Pasquier Quesnel*, ed. Madame Albert Le Roy, 2:301.

51. Quesnel, *La discipline de l'église*, p. 85.

52. Quesnel, *Réflexions morales*, 4:183.
53. The Edíct of 1695 on ecclesiastical jurisdiction is to be found in L. Mention, ed., *Documents relatifs aux rapports du clergé avec la royauté de 1682-1705*, pp. 112-34.
54. Quesnel, *Réflexions morales*, 2:291.
55. Arnauld, *Oeuvres*, 6:560-69.
56. Ibid., 8:290-94.
57. *La correspondance de Barcos*, p. 375.
58. Arnauld, *Oeuvres*, 8:630-31.
59. Ibid., 6:787, 8:678.
60. Ibid., 6:825.
61. Pascal, *Oeuvres complètes*, p. 1072.
62. Quesnel, *Réflexions morales*, 2:553.
63. Arnauld, *Oeuvres*, 8:378-80.
64. E. Préclin, *Les jansénistes du XVIIIe siècle*, pp. 25-28.
65. *Choix des lettres inédites de Le Maistre de Sacy*, p. 234.
66. Jean Hamon, *De l'excommunication*, pp. 454-55.
67. Ibid., p. 9.
68. Pierre Nicole, *Les imaginaires*, pp. 149-50. *Les imaginaires* consists of a series of public letters in the format established in the *Provincial Letters*. In the work, Nicole tries to show that the "Jansenist heresy" was imaginary and nonexistent, and he deals with such questions as *droit* and *fait*, papal infallibility, and excommunication.
69. Quesnel, *Réflexions morales*, 2:110.
70. Ibid., 2:186.

Notes to Chapter VII

1. Orcibal, *La Spiritualité de Saint-Cyran*, pp. 392, 393.
2. Arnauld, *Oeuvres*, 14:328.
3. Ibid., 13:33.
4. Jean Domat, *Les lois civiles dans leur ordre naturel*, preface.
5. Ibid., pp. x, i. For biographical details, see Henri Loubers, *Jean Domat: Philosophe et magistrat*. For an evaluation of Domat's place in the history of French legal thought, see William F. Church, "The Decline of the French Jurists as Political Theorists."
6. Pascal, *Pensées*, p. 36.
7. Ibid., pp. 51, 46-47.
8. Ibid., p. 52.
9. Pascal, *Oeuvres complètes*, pp. 620-21. The three *discours* are to be found in ibid., pp. 614-21.
10. Fonds français nouvelles acquisitions 4333. Bibliothèque Nationale.
11. Fonds français 19916, Bibliothèque Nationale.
12. Arnauld Family Papers, ms. 6626, Bibliothèque de l'Arsenal.
13. *Correspondance de Pasquier Quesnel*, 2:212.
14. Arnauld, *Oeuvres*, 22:220-24.
15. Ibid., 21:68.
16. *Pasquier Quesnel et les Pays-Bas*, ed. J. A. G. Tans, p. 244.
17. H. G. Judge, "Louis XIV and the Church" in John C. Rule, ed., *Louis XIV and the Craft of Kingship*, pp. 240-64.
18. Louis du Vaucel, *Traité général de la régale*, pp. 99, 106, 112.
19. Arnauld, *Oeuvres*, 3:384.

20. Ibid., 1:278.
21. Ibid., 2:342.
22. Ibid., 3:504-5.
23. Ibid., 3:320.
24. Ibid., 24:390-409.
25. Gabriel Gerberon, *La règle des moeurs contre les fausses maximes de la morale corrompue*, p. 6.
26. Ibid., p. 82.
27. Ibid., pp. 102-5.
28. Ibid., p. 173.
29. Herbert H. Rowen, "Arnauld de Pomponne, Louis XIV's Moderate Minister."
30. Rothkrug, *Opposition to Louis XIV*, p. 259.
31. Ibid., pp. 249-86.
32. Arnauld, *Oeuvres*, 2:143.
33. Ibid., 3:165-66.
34. Quoted in Sainte-Beuve, *Port-Royal*, 3:473.
35. Jacques-Joseph Duguet, *Institution d'un prince*, 1:168, 2:111.
36. Ibid., 2:152.
37. Ibid., 2:154.
38. Ibid., 2:251, 257.
39. Orcibal, *La spiritualité de Saint-Cyran*, p. 162.
40. Duguet, *Institution d'un prince*, 2:271-89.
41. Ibid., 2:289-320.
42. Ibid., 2:493-512.
43. Ibid., 2:586-652.
44. Ibid., 4:337-45.
45. Ibid., 4:240.
46. Rothkrug, *Opposition to Louis XIV*, pp. 249-86, describes the Christian agrarian opposition to Louis XIV's policies.
47. For the Jansenist crisis leading up to *Unigenitus*, see Adam, *Du mysticisme à la révolte*, pp. 295-336.
48. L. Ceyssens, "Les papiers de Quesnel saisis à Bruxelles et transportés à Paris en 1703 et 1704."
49. *Pasquier Quesnel et les Pays-Bas*, p. 464.
50. The text of *Unigenitus* may be found in Jacques-François Thomas, *La querelle de l'Unigenitus*, pp. 24-31. This work is useful for its discussion of the crisis arising out of *Unigenitus*.

Notes to Chapter VIII

1. An informative discussion of the problems involved in defining Jansenism may be found in Jean Orcibal, "Qu'est-ce que le jansénisme?"
2. *Lettres chrestiennes et spirituelles de Saint-Cyran* (1744), 2:504.
3. Quesnel, *Réflexions morales*, 1:74.
4. *Lettres inédites de Saint-Cyran*, p. 256.
5. *La Correspondance de Barcos*, p. 313.
6. Michael Walzer, *The Revolution of the Saints*.
7. Quoted in Neveu, *Sébastien de Pontchâteau*, p. 33.
8. For an extended discussion of the connection between Christian agrarianism and

physiocracy that does not include an analysis of Duguet's *Institution d'un prince*, see Rothkrug, *Opposition to Louis XIV*.

9. Jean le Rond d'Alembert, *Preliminary Discourse to the Encyclopedia of Diderot*, ed. and trans. Richard N. Schwab and Walter E. Rex (Indianapolis, 1963), p. 73.

10. Sainte-Beuve, *Port-Royal*, 1:99.

11. Goldmann, *Le dieu caché*, and "Rémarques sur le jansénisme: La vision tragique du monde et la noblesse de robe."

12. This is the point made by Hamscher in his forthcoming article, "Jansenism and the Parlement of Paris after the Fronde."

13. Bernard Groethuysen, *Origines de l'ésprit bourgeois en France*.

14. Paul Bénichou, *Morales du grand siècle*, pp. 114–15, and René Taveneaux, "Jansénisme et vie sociale en France au XVIIe siècle."

15. Pierre Goubert, *Louis XIV et vingt millions de français* (Paris, 1966), p. 114.

16. For the details of Foucquet's life, see Xavier Azéma, *Un prélat janséniste: Louis Foucquet, evêque et comte d'Agde (1656–1702)*.

17. Bénichou, *Morales du grand siècle*, pp. 15–18.

18. For the connection between Jansenism and the French Revolution, see Préclin, *Les jansénistes du XVIIIe siècle*. This subject requires further exploration by historians.

19. Le Roy, *Lettre sur la constance et le courage*, p. 22.

Bibliography

Vast amounts of source materials relating to Jansenism are scattered about archives throughout Europe and the United States. It would be impossible for one historian to examine every manuscript and pamphlet pertaining to the subject. Fortunately, the major works of the leading Jansenists as well as much of their correspondence have been published. The work of Jean Orcibal and Annie Barnes in publishing the letters and manuscripts of the abbé de Saint-Cyran, of Lucien Goldmann in publishing the correspondence of Martin de Barcos, and of Geneviève Delasseault in publishing some of the letters of Le Maistre de Sacy have greatly facilitated scholarly research.

The main collection of Jansenist materials are deposited in the Bibliothèque Nationale in Paris, in the Library of the Hague, the Netherlands (fonds d'Amerfoort), and in the Bibliothèque de la Société de Port-Royal in Paris. A useful introduction to this collection is to be found in Cécile Gazier, ed., *Histoire de la société et de la bibliothèque de Port-Royal* (Paris, 1966). The papers of the Arnauld family are to be found in the Bibliothèque de l'Arsenal (mss. 6024, 6034–6036, 6549, 6620, 6626) in Paris. Significant collections of published materials pertaining to the subject are to be found in this country in the Houghton and Widener Libraries of Harvard University, in the Newberry Library in Chicago, and in the Folger Library in Washington.

Bibliographies and other Reference Works

Ceyssens, L. *Sources relatives aux débuts du jansénisme et de anti-jansénisme.* Louvain, 1957.

Cioranescu, Alexandre, ed. *Bibliographie de la littérature française du XVIIe siècle.* 2 vols. Paris, 1968.

Colonia, R. P. de (S.J.). *Bibliothèque janséniste*. n.p., 1731.

Delumeau, Jean. *Le catholicisme entre Luther et Voltaire*. Paris, 1971.

Mandrou, Robert. *La France aux XVIIe et XVIIIe siècles*. Paris, 1967.

Patouillet, R. P. (S.J.). *Dictionnaire des livres jansénistes*. 4 vols. Antwerp, 1752.

Willaert, Léopold. *Bibliotheca jansenica belgica*. 3 vols. Paris, 1949–51.

Primary Sources

Annat, François. *Réponse aux lettres provinciales*. Paris, 1658.

Arnauld, Angélique. *Lettres de la Mère Angélique Arnauld, abbèsse et réformatrice de Port-Royal*. 3 vols. Utrecht, 1742.

———. *Relation écrite par la Mère Angélique Arnauld sur Port-Royal*. Edited by Louis Cognet. Paris, 1949.

Arnauld, Antoine. *Apologie de M. Jansenius, evesque d'Ipres*. Paris, 1644.

———. *The Art of Thinking*. Edited and translated by James Dickoff and Patricia James. Indianapolis, 1964.

———. *De la fréquente communion*. Paris, 1643.

———. *Impiété de la morale des calvinistes*. Paris, 1675.

———. *De la nécessité de la foy en Jésus-Christ*. Paris, 1701.

———. *Lettre d'un docteur de Sorbonne à une personne de condition*. Paris, 1655.

———. *Oeuvres de Messire Antoine Arnauld, docteur de la maison et société de Sorbonne*. 43 vols. Paris-Lausanne, 1755–83.

———. *Seconde apologie de M. Jansenius, evesque d'Ipres*. Paris, 1645.

———. *Seconde lettre de M. Arnauld, docteur de Sorbonne à un duc et pair de France*. Paris, 1655.

———. *La tradition de l'église sur le sujet de la discipline et la communion*. Paris, 1644.

Barcos, Martin de. *La correspondance de Martin de Barcos, Abbé de Saint-Cyran*. Edited by Lucien Goldmann. Paris, 1956.

Bauny, R. P. *Somme des pechez que se commetent en tous estats*. Paris, 1633.

Bouhours, Dominique de. *Sentiments des jesuites sur le péché philosophique.* Paris, 1694.

Catel, Maurice, ed. *Les écrivains de Port-Royal.* Paris, 1962.

Clark, Ruth, ed. *Lettres de G. Vuillart à L. de Préfontaine.* Paris, 1951.

Clémencet, Charles. *Histoire générale de Port-Royal.* 10 vols. Amsterdam, 1757.

Coustel, Pierre. *Les règles de l'éducation des enfants.* 2 vols. Paris, 1687.

Daniel, Gabriel. *Réponse aux lettres provinciales.* Rouen, 1696.

Delasseault, Geneviève, ed. *La pensée janséniste en dehors de Pascal.* Paris, 1963.

Divers actes, lettres, et relations des religieuses de Port-Royal du Saint-Sacrement touchant au sujet de la signature du formulaire. 3 vols. Utrecht, 1735.

Domat, Jean. *Les loix civiles dans leur ordre naturel.* 3 vols. Paris, 1694.

Duguet, Jacques-Joseph. *Institution d'un prince.* 4 vols. Leydon, 1739.

Faugère, M. P., ed. *Lettres de la Mère Agnès Arnauld, abbèsse de Port-Royal.* 2 vols. Paris, 1858.

Fontaine, Nicolas. *Mémoires pour servir à l'histoire de Port-Royal.* 2 vols. Utrecht, 1736.

Gale, Theophillus. *The True Idea of Jansenisme, Both Historick & Dogmatick.* London, 1669.

Gerberon, Gabriel. *Histoire générale du jansénisme.* 3 vols. Amsterdam, 1700.

——. *Le miroir de la piété.* Liège, 1677.

——. *La règle des moeurs contre les fausses maximes de la morale corrompue.* Cologne, 1688.

Habert, Isaac. *La deffense de la foy de l'église.* Paris, 1644.

Hamon, Jean. *De l'excommunication.* n.p., 1665.

Hermant, Godefroi. *Mémoires de Godefroi Hermant, docteur de Sorbonne sur l'histoire écclésiastique du XVIIe siècle (1630–1663).* Edited by Augustin Gazier. 6 vols. Paris, 1910.

Jansenius, Cornelius. *Correspondance de Jansenius.* Edited by Jean Orcibal. Paris, 1947.

——. *Mars françois,* n.p., 1637.

——. *De la réformation de l'homme intèrieur.* Paris, 1642.

Jansen, Paule, ed. *Arnauld d'Andilly, défenseur de Port-Royal, 1654–1659: Sa correspondance inédite avec la cour conservée dans les archives du ministère des affaires étrangères.* Paris, 1953.

Jourdain, C., ed. *Oeuvres philosophiques et morales d'Antoine Arnauld.* Paris, 1843.

——. *Oeuvres philosophiques et morales de Pierre Nicole.* Paris, 1845.

Lancelot, Claude. *Mémoires touchant la vie de M. de Saint-Cyran par M. Lancelot pour servir d'éclaircissement à l'histoire de Port-Royal.* 2 vols. Cologne, 1738.

——, and Arnauld, Antoine. *Grammaire générale et raisonnée.* Paris, 1660.

Le Febvre de Saint-Marc. *Supplement au necrologe de l'abbaye de N.D. de Port-Royal-des-Champs.* Amsterdam, 1760.

[Le Maistre, Antoine.] *Lettre d'un avocat au parlement à un de ses amis.* Paris, 1657.

Le Maistre de Sacy, Louis-Isaac. *Choix des lettres inédites de Louis-Isaac Le Maistre de Sacy (1650–1683).* Edited by Geneviève Delasseault. Paris, 1959.

Le Roy, Guillaume. *Lettre sur la constance et le courage qu'on doit avoir pour la vérité.* Paris, 1661.

Lewis, Geneviève, ed. *Descartes: Correspondance avec Arnauld et Moru.* Paris, 1953.

Marandé, Léonard de. *Inconvéniens d'estat procedans de jansénisme.* Paris, 1654.

Mention, L., ed. *Documents relatifs aux rapports du clergé avec la royauté de 1682–1705.* Paris, 1893.

Nécrologe de l'abbaye de Notre-Dame de Port-Royal-des-Champs. Amsterdam, 1723.

Nicole, Pierre. *Essais de morale.* 13 vols. Paris, 1730.

——. *De la foy humaine.* Paris, 1664.

——. *Les imaginaires.* Liège, 1667.

——. *Lettres du feu M. Nicole.* 2 vols. Lille, 1718.

——. *Oeuvres de controverse de M. Nicole.* 6 vols. Paris, 1755.

——. *Réfutation des principales erreurs des quiétistes.* Paris, 1695.

——. *Traité de la comédie.* Edited by G. Couton. Paris, 1961.

——. *Traité de l'oraison.* Lyon, 1687.

——. *Traité de l'usure.* Paris, 1720.

———. *Les visionnaires.* Liège, 1667.

Pascal, Blaise. *Oeuvres complètes.* Edited by Jacques Chevalier. Paris, 1954.

———. *Pensées.* Edited and translated by A. J. Krailsheimer. Baltimore, 1966.

———. *Provincial Letters.* Edited and translated by W. F. Trotter. New York, 1941.

Pinthèreau, F. *Le progrez du jansénisme decouvert.* Amiens, 1655.

Pirot, Georges. *Apologie pour les casuistes contre les calomnies des jansénistes.* Paris, 1657.

Quesnel, Pasquier. *Abrégé de la morale de l'évangile, ou, considérations chrétiennes sur le texte des quatres évangélistes.* Brussels, 1672.

———. *Correspondance de Pasquier Quesnel.* Edited by Madame Albert Le Roy. 2 vols. Paris, 1900.

———. *Défense de l'église romaine et des souverains pontifes.* Liège, 1697.

———. *La discipline de l'église tirée du nouveau testament.* Lyon, 1689.

———. *La foy et l'innocence du clergé de Hollande.* Delft, 1700.

———. *Justification des droits des chapitres de l'église des Provinces-Unis.* n.p., 1720.

———. *Nouveau testament en français avec des réflexions morales sur chaque verset.* 4 vols. Paris, 1693.

———. *La paix de Clement IX.* Chambéry, 1700.

———. *Pasquier Quesnel devant la congrégation de l'Index.* Edited by J. A. G. Tans and H. Schmitz du Moulin. The Hague, 1974.

———. *Pasquier Quesnel et les Pays-Bas.* Edited by J. A. G. Tans. Groningen, 1960.

Racine, Jean. *Abrégé de l'histoire de Port-Royal par Jean Racine.* Edited by Augustin Gazier. Paris, 1908.

Rapin, René. *Histoire du jansénisme depuis ses origines jusqu'en 1644.* Paris, 1861.

Recueil de plusieurs pièces pour servir à l'histoire de Port-Royal. Utrecht, 1740.

Richelieu, Armand du Plessis, Cardinal de. *Instruction du chrestien.* Poitiers, 1621.

———. *The Political Testament of Cardinal Richelieu.* Edited and translated by Henry B. Hill. Madison, Wis., 1965.

———. *Traitté de la perfection du chrestien.* Paris, 1646.

Saint-Cyran, Jean Duvergier de Hauranne, Abbé de. *Lettres chrestiennes et spirituelles de Messire Jean Du Verger de Hauranne, Abbé de Saint-Cyran.* Edited by Robert Arnauld d'Andilly. 2 vols. Paris, 1645, 1647.

———. *Lettres chrestiennes et spirituelles de M. de Saint-Cyran qui n'ont point été imprimées jusqu'à present.* 2 vols. n.p., 1744.

———. *Lettres inédites de Saint-Cyran.* Edited by Annie Barnes. Paris, 1962.

———. *Oeuvres chrestiennes et spirituelles.* 4 vols. Lyon, 1674–75.

———. *La somme des fautes et faussetez capitales contenues en la somme théologique de Père François Garasse.* 2 vols. Paris, 1626.

Simon, Jules. *Oeuvres philosophiques d'Antoine Arnauld.* Paris, 1843.

Sirmond, Antoine, S.J. *La deffense de la vertu.* Paris, 1641.

Sonnino, Paul, ed. and trans. *Louis XIV: Mémoires for the Instruction of the Dauphin.* New York, 1970.

Taveneaux, René, ed. *Jansénisme et politique.* Paris, 1965.

Thomas, Pierre. *Mémoires de Pierre Thomas, Sieur du Fossé.* 2 vols. Rouen, 1879.

Vaucel, Louis du. *Traité général de la régale.* Paris, 1681.

Secondary Sources

Abercrombie, Nigel. *The Origins of Jansenism.* Oxford, 1936.

Adam, Antoine. *Histoire de la littérature française au XVIIe siècle.* 5 vols. Paris, 1963.

———. *Du mysticisme à la révolte.* Paris, 1968.

———. *Sur le problème religieux dans la première moitié du XVIIe siècle.* Oxford, 1959.

Allier, Raoul. *La cabale des dévots.* Paris, 1902.

Angers, Julien Eymard d'. "Problèmes et difficultés de l'humanisme chrétienne (1600–1642)." *XVIIe Siècle* 62 (1964):4–29.

Armstrong, Brian G. *Calvinism and the Amyraut Heresy.* Madison, Wis., 1969.

Avenel, Georges, Vicomte de. "Le clergé et la liberté de la conscience." *Revue Historique* 32 (1886):313-49.

Azéma, Xavier. *Un prélat janséniste: Louis Foucquet, evêque et comte d'Agde (1656-1702).* Paris, 1962.

Bady, René. *L'Homme et son "institution" de Montaigne à Bérulle.* Paris, 1964.

Barnard, H. C. *The Little Schools of Port Royal.* Cambridge, 1913.

Bénichou, Paul. *Morales du grand siècle.* Paris, 1948.

Bera, M. -A., ed. *Blaise Pascal: L'Homme et l'oeuvre.* Paris, 1957.

Blet, Pierre. *Le clergé de France et la monarchie.* 2 vols. Rome, 1959.

Bourlon, J. *Les assemblées du clergé et le jansénisme.* Paris, 1909.

Brémond, Henri. *Histoire littéraire du sentiment religieux en France.* 12 vols. Paris, 1932.

Brouton, P. *La réforme pastorale en France au XVIIe siècle.* 2 vols. Paris, 1956.

Brown, Peter. *Augustine of Hippo.* Berkeley and Los Angeles, 1969.

Brunetière, Ferdinand. *Etudes critiques sur l'histoire de la littérature française,* vol. 4. Paris, 1911.

Busson, Henri. *La pensée religieuse française de Charron à Pascal.* Paris, 1933.

Carreyre, Jean. "Quesnel et le quesnellisme." *Dictionnaire de théologie catholique,* vol. 13 (cols. 1460-1535). Paris, 1923.

Carrier, Hubert. "Port-Royal et la Fronde: Deux mazarinades inconnues d'Arnauld d'Andilly." *Revue d'Histoire Littéraire de la France* 75 (1975):1-29.

Ceyssens, L. "Les papiers de Quesnel saisis à Bruxelles et transportés à Paris en 1703 et 1704." *Revue d'Histoire Ecclésiastique* 44 (1949):508-51.

Chaunu, Pierre. "Jansénisme et frontière de Catholicité." *Revue Historique* 227 (1962):115-38.

——. "Le XVIIe siècle religieux." *Annales: Economies, Sociétés, Civilisations* 22 (1967):279-302.

Chedozeau, Bernard. "Les années de jeunesse de Pierre Nicole et son entrée à Port-Royal." *XVIIe Siècle* 101 (1973):51-69.

Church, William F. "The Decline of the French Jurists as Political Theorists." *French Historical Studies* vol. 5, no. 1 (1967), pp. 1-40.

——. *Richelieu and Reason of State.* Princeton, 1972.

Cochin, Claude. *Henri Arnauld, Evêque d'Angers (1597–1692).* Paris, 1921.

Cognet, Louis. *Claude Lancelot: Solitaire de Port-Royal.* Paris, 1955.

——. "Etat présent des traveaux sur Port-Royal et le jansénisme." *L'Information Littérarie* 3 (1957):139–46.

——. *Le jansénisme.* Paris, 1960.

——. "Le mépris du monde à Port-Royal et dans le jansénisme." *Revue d'Ascétique et de Mystique* 41 (1965):387–402.

——. *Les origines de la spiritualité française au XVIIe siècle.* Paris, 1949.

——. "Les petites écoles de Port-Royal." *Cahiers de l'Association Internationale des Etudes Françaises* 3 (1955):19–55.

——. *La réforme de Port-Royal, 1591–1618.* Paris, 1950.

Cousin, Victor. *Jacqueline Pascal.* Paris, 1869.

Dagens, Jean. *Bérulle et les origines de la restauration catholique.* Paris, 1952.

——. *Entretiens sur Henri Brémond.* Paris, 1968.

Delasseault, Geneviève. *Le Maistre de Sacy et son temps.* Paris, 1957.

Dondaine, H. *L'Attrition suffisante.* Paris, 1943.

Edwards, Tom T. "Jansenism in Church and State." Ph.D. dissertation. Harvard University, 1960.

Escholier, Marc. *Port-Royal.* Paris, 1965.

Ferté, Jeanne. *La vie religieuse dans les campagnes parisiènnes, 1622–1695.* Paris, 1963.

Fuzet, A. *Les jansénistes du XVIIe siècle: Leur histoire et leur dernier historien M. Sainte-Beauve.* Paris, 1876.

Gallerand, J. "Le jansénisme en Blésois: Le conflit entre le P. Brisacier et Jean Callaghan." *Revue d'Histoire de l'Eglise de France* 55 (1969):2947.

Gazier, Augustin. *Histoire générale du mouvement janséniste.* 2 vols. Paris, 1923.

Gazier, Cécile. *Ces messieurs de Port-Royal.* Paris, 1932.

——. *Histoire du monastère de Port-Royal.* Paris, 1929.

Giraud, Victor. *Port-Royal et Sainte-Beuve.* Paris, 1953.

Golden, Richard. "The Godly Rebellion: Parisian *Curés* and the

Religious Fronde, 1652–1662." Ph.D. dissertation. The Johns Hopkins University, 1974.

——. "The Mentality of Opposition: The Jansenism of the Parisian *Curés*." A paper read at the annual meeting of the Catholic Historical Association, Boston, April 1975.

Goldmann, Lucien. *Le dieu caché*. Paris, 1957.

——. "Remarques sur le jansénisme: La vision tragique du monde et la noblesse de robe." *XVIIe Siècle* 19 (1956):177–95.

Gouhier, Henri. "La crise de la théologie au temps de Descartes." *Revue de Théologie et de Philosophie* 4 (1954):19–54.

——. *La pensée religieuse de Descartes*. Paris, 1924.

——. *La philosophie de Malebranche et son experience religieuse*. Paris, 1926.

Grégoire, Abbé Henri. *Les ruines de Port-Royal*. Paris, 1809.

Groethuysen, Bernard. *Origines de l'ésprit bourgeois en France*. Paris, 1956.

Guerard, Albert. *The Life and Death of an Ideal*. New York, 1928.

Hall, H. Gaston. "Racine, Desmarets de Saint-Sorlin, and the *Querelle des 'Imaginaires.'*" *Modern Language Review* 55 (1960):181–85.

Hamscher, Albert N. "The Parlement of Paris and Jansenism after the Fronde." *Catholic Historical Review*, forthcoming.

Honigsheim, Paul. *Die Staats-und-Soziallehren der Französischen Jansenisten im 17. Jahrhundert*. Heidelberg, 1914.

Ingold, Augustin. *L'Oratoire et le jansénisme*. Paris, 1887.

James, E. D. "The Political and Social Theory of Pierre Nicole." *French Studies* 14 (1960):117–28.

Jansen, Paule. *Le Cardinal de Mazarin et le mouvement janséniste français, 1653–1659*. Paris, 1967.

Keohane, Nannerl O. "Absolutism of Louis XIV: Nicole and Veiras." *Journal of the History of Ideas* 35 (1974):579–96.

Kirkenen, Heikki. *Les origines de la conception de l'homme-machine: Le problème de l'âme en France à la fin du XVIIe siècle*. Helsinki, 1960.

Knox, Ronald. *Enthusiasm*. New York, 1961.

Krailsheimer, A. J. *Armand-Jean de Rancé: Abbot of La Trappe*. Oxford, 1974.

——. *Studies in Self-Interest from Descartes to La Bruyère*. Oxford, 1962.

Labrousse, Elisabeth. *Pierre Bayle.* 2 vols. The Hague, 1963.

Laferrière, J. *Etude sur Jean Duvergier de Hauranne, Abbé de Saint-Cyran.* Louvain, 1912.

Lanfranc de Panthou, O. *Richelieu et la direction des âmes.* Evreux, 1896.

Laporte, Jean. *La doctrine de Port-Royal.* 2 vols. Paris, 1952.

——. *Saint-Cyran.* Paris, 1922.

Le Breton, Grandmaison. *Pierre Nicole, ou, la civilité chrétiènne.* Paris, 1945.

Lewis, Geneviève. "Augustinisme et cartésianisme à Port-Royal." Pp. 131–82 in *Descartes et le cartésianisme hollondaise.* Paris, 1951.

Loubers, Henri. *Jean Domat: Philosophe et magistrat.* Paris, 1873.

Lubac, Henri de. *Augustinianism and Modern Theology.* London, 1969.

——. *Surnaturel.* Paris, 1946.

Magendie, M. *La politesse mondaine et les théories de l'honnêteté en France au XVIIe siècle.* Paris, 1925.

Maistre, Joseph de. *De l'église gallicane.* Paris, 1820.

Mandrou, Robert. *Introduction à la France moderne, 1500–1640.* Paris, 1960.

——. "Spiritualité et pratiques catholiques au XVIIe siècle." *Annales: Economies, Sociétés, Civilisations* 25 (1970):136–46.

Marin, Louis. "Philippe de Champaigne et Port-Royal." *Annales: Economies, Sociétés, Civilisations* 25 (1970):1–29.

Martin, V. *Le gallicanisme politique et le clergé de France.* Paris, 1929.

Mesnard, Jean. *Pascal.* Paris, 1967.

——. *Pascal et les Roannez.* 2 vols. Paris, 1964.

Meyer, A. de. *Les premières controverses jansénistes en France, 1640–1649.* Louvain, 1917.

Miel, Jan. *Pascal and Theology.* Baltimore, 1969.

Miller, Perry. *The New England Mind: The Seventeenth Century.* Boston, 1961.

Montherlant, Henry de. *Port-Royal.* Paris, 1954.

Namer, G. *L'Abbé Le Roy et ses amis.* Paris, 1964.

Neveu, Bruno. *Sébastien Joseph du Cambout de Pontchâteau (1634–1690) et ses missions à Rome.* Paris, 1969.

———. *Un historien à l'école de Port-Royal: Sébastien Le Nain de Tillemont, 1637–1698.* The Hague, 1966.

Oberman, Heiko, ed. *Forerunners of the Reformation.* New York, 1966.

Orcibal, Jean. "Descartes et son philosophie jugés à l'hôtel Liancourt." Pp. 87–111 in *Descartes et le cartésianisme hollondaise.* Paris, 1951.

———. *Jean Duvergier de Hauranne, Abbé de Saint-Cyran et son temps.* 2 vols. Paris, 1948.

———. *Port-Royal entre le miracle et l'obéissance.* Paris, 1957.

———. "Qu'est-ce que le jansénisme?" *Cahiers de l'Association Internationale des Etudes Françaises* 3 (1953):39–53.

———. *La spiritualité de Saint-Cyran avec ses écrits de piété inédits.* Paris, 1962.

———. *Saint-Cyran et le jansénisme.* Paris, 1961.

Pagès, G. "Autour du 'Grand Orage': Richelieu et Marillac, deux politiques." *Revue Historique* 179 (1937):63–97.

Paquier, J. *Qu'est-ce que le jansénisme?* Paris, 1909.

Paradis, Edouard. *La pédagogie janséniste.* Lyon, 1910.

Pintard, René. *Le libertinage érudit dans la première moitié du XVIIe siècle.* 2 vols. Paris, 1943.

Popkin, Richard H. *The History of Skepticism from Erasmus to Descartes.* Assen, the Netherlands, 1964.

Préclin, E. "Les conséquences sociales du jansénisme." *Revue d'Histoire de l'Eglise de France* 21 (1935):167–88.

———. "L'influence du jansénisme français à l'étranger." *Revue Historique* 182 (1938):24–71.

———. *Les jansénistes du XVIIIe siècle et la constitution civile du clergé.* Paris, 1929.

Préclin, E., and Jarry, E. *Les luttes politiques et doctrinales aux XVIIe et XVIIIe siècles.* 2 vols. Paris, 1956.

Prunel, Louis. *La renaissance catholique en France au XVIIe siècle.* Paris, 1921.

Przyrembel, A. *La controverse théologique et morale entre Saint-Cyran et Père Garasse.* Paris, 1917.

Rabb, Theodore K. *The Struggle for Stability in Early Modern Europe.* New York, 1975.

Ranum, Orest. *Paris in the Age of Absolutism.* New York, 1968.

Raymond, Marcel. "Du jansénisme à la morale de l'intérêt." *Mercure de France* 330 (1959):238-55.

Remberg, Robert G. *Wisdom and Science at Port Royal and the Oratory.* Yellow Springs, Ohio, 1940.

Renan, Ernest. *Nouvelles études d'histoire religieuse.* Paris, 1863.

Rosenfield, L. C. *From Beast-Machine to Man-Machine.* New York, 1941.

Rothkrug, Lionel. *Opposition to Louis XIV: The Political and Social Origins of the French Enlightenment.* Princeton, 1965.

Rowen, Herbert H. "Arnauld de Pomponne, Louis XIV's Moderate Minister." *American Historical Review* 60 (1956):531-49.

Rule, John C., ed. *Louis XIV and the Craft of Kingship.* Columbus, Ohio, 1969.

Sainte-Beauve, C. -A. *Port-Royal.* Edited by Maxime Leroy. 3 vols. Paris, 1953.

Salmon, J. H. M. *Cardinal de Retz.* London, 1969.

Séché, Léon. *Les derniers jansénistes depuis la ruine de Port-Royal jusqu'à nos jours.* 3 vols. Paris, 1891.

Sée, Henri. *Idées politiques au XVIIe siècle.* Paris, 1923.

Snydors, Georges. *La pédagogie en France aux XVIIe et XVIIIe siècles.* Paris, 1965.

Spink, J. S. *French Free Thought from Gassendi to Voltaire.* London, 1960.

Steinmann, Jean. *Pascal.* Paris, 1962.

Strowski, Fortunat. *Pascal et son temps.* 3 vols. Paris, 1922.

Tans, J. A. G. "Les idées politiques des jansénistes." *Neophilologus* 11 (1956):1-18.

Tapié, V. *La France de Richelieu et Louis XIII.* Paris, 1967.

Taveneaux, René. *Le jansénisme en Lorraine, 1640-1788.* Paris, 1960.

———. "Jansénisme et vie sociale en France au XVIIe siècle." *Revue d'Histoire de l'Eglise de France* 54 (1968):27-46.

Thomas, Jacques-François. *Essai de morale de Port-Royal.* Paris, 1942.

———. *Le problème moral à Port-Royal.* Paris, n.d.

———. *La querelle de l'Unigenitus.* Paris, 1950.

Thouverez, Emile. *Pierre Nicole.* Paris, 1926.

Thuau, Etienne. *Raison d'état et pensée politique à l'époque de Richelieu.* Paris, 1966.

Varin, Pierre. *La verité sur les Arnauld.* 2 vols. Paris, 1847.

Vinot-Prefontaine, Jean. "Beauvais et le jansénisme dans le diocèse au XVIIe siècle." *Revue d'Histoire de l'Eglise de France* 19 (1933):347–71.

———. "La fondation du séminaire en Beauvais et le jansénisme dans le diocèse au XVIIe siècle." *Revue des Questions Historiques* 103 (1925):408–22.

Voltaire. *Lettres philosophiques.* Edited by R. Naves. Paris, 1964.

———. *Le siècle de Louis XIV.* Paris, 1872.

Wade, Ira O. *The Intellectual Origins of the French Enlightenment.* Princeton, 1971.

Walzer, Michael. *The Revolution of the Saints.* Cambridge, Mass., 1965.

Willaert, Léopold. *Après la concile de Trente: La restauration catholique, 1563–1648.* Paris, 1960.

Index